Color Schemes Take the Worry Out of Choosing Colors

Aqua	
Berry	
Black & Gray	
Black & White	
Bluebird	
Brown	
Burgundy	
Cavern	
Citrus	
Clay	
Cranberry	
Crocus	
Dark Blue	
Desert	
Eggplant	
Field	
Fjord	
Floral	
Garnet	
Glacier	
Green	
Grove	
Harbor	
Heather	
Iris	
Island	
Ivy	
Lagoon	
Lilac	

Purpose

The purpose of the *Design to Sell* Color Chronicles is to help you make the most of color in your publications

As shown at left, each Publisher Color Scheme consists of a professionally selected combination of colors that work well together as foreground and background colors.

Make your initial color choice on the basis of the emotional response it creates, and its appropriateness to your publication's message.

Working with Color Schemes

When formatting text and graphic elements (i.e., lines and fills), always choose from the Color Scheme options that initially appear, rather than choosing additional colors.

Suppose, for example, you have selected the Meadow Color Scheme, shown below.

Maroon	
Meadow	
Mist	

When formatting text and graphics, choose from of the Meadow options, below, that appear first, rather than one of the More Color options.

More Colors...

A Little Color, Carefully Used, Makes a Big Difference

Why color?

Because color adds life to your publications!

Color also helps to noticeably differentiate your message from those of your competitors.

We live in a color world. As a result, when we encounter a black and white publication, it inevitably looks dull and lifeless to us.

Even a few color highlights, such as subheads and borders, can breathe life into your publication. Color also adds impact to the photograph, the only four-color element on the page.

Saving money

One way to save money on color is to limit color to several key, unchanging areas of your publication, and preprint enough pages for the next several issues of your newsletter, as shown at left.

Even though you complete each issue by printing in black, the newsletter will still communicate in color .

Choosing an Appropriate Publisher Color Scheme

Restful	Restful
Corporate	**Corporate**
Restrained	**Restrained**
Toys	Toys
Upscale	Upscale
Outdoors	Outdoors
Discount	**Discount**

Choosing colors

Choose colors that project an image appropriate for your message and the way you want clients and prospects to view your firm.

In addition, choose colors that work well with the colors used in your firm's logo.

Wrong

Inappropriate choice of Publisher's Color Schemes results in publications that project an inappropriate image.

Right

Used differently, the same Color Schemes can reinforce your publication's intended image.

Four Common Problems When Working with Color

Decorative color

Avoid using color to embellish, or "brighten up," your pages. Decorative color can easily get in the way of your message.

Using Color Effectively

Color is one of Microsoft Office Publisher's most powerful, and, alas, least understood tools.

In the right hands, color can add impact to your pages, project a unique, distinctive identity, and provide selective emphasis.

In the wrong hands, however, color can weaken your pages, fail to differentiate your message from your competitors', and make it harder to read your words.

1. Avoid too much color

Emphasis and image are lost when color is over-used. Avoid newsletters printed entirely in colors other than black, especially if photographs are included!

3. Colored text

Avoid setting body text in color, such as serif typefaces set in 11 or 12 points. What may look good on-screen may be much harder to read than the same words set in black.

Foreground/background contrast

Color is one of Microsoft Office Publisher's most powerful, and, alas, least understood tools.

In the right hands, color can add impact to your pages, project a unique, distinctive identity, and provide selective emphasis.

In the wrong hands, however, color can weaken your pages, fail to differentiate your message from your competitors', and make it harder to read your words.

Foreground/background contrast

Color is one of Microsoft Office Publisher's most powerful, and, alas, least understood tools.

In the right hands, color can add impact to your pages, project a unique, distinctive identity, and provide selective emphasis.

In the wrong hands, however, color can weaken your pages, fail to differentiate your message from your competitors', and make it harder to read your words.

2. Light colored text

Bright colored text often looks better on-screen than it does when printed. This is because your monitor projects light, printed pages reflect light.

4. Foreground/background contrast

Exercise restraint when setting colored text against colored backgrounds. Sufficient foreground/background contrast is necessary if your words are to be easily read.

Four Examples of the Appropriate Use of Color

Using Color Effectively

Color is one of Microsoft Office Publisher's most powerful, and, alas, least understood tools.

In the right hands, color can add impact to your pages, project a unique, distinctive identity, and provide selective emphasis.

In the wrong hands, however, color can weaken your pages, fail to differentiate your message from your competitors', and make it harder to read your words.

Region	Q1	Q2	Q3	Q4
North	105	33	55	90
South	66	19	44	67
East	55	88	77	36
West	22	13	38	76
Misc.	16	27	43	12
Total	264	180	257	283

Color with a purpose

Use color purposefully, rather than decoratively. Color should enhance, rather than detract, from your message.

1. Restrict color to large, heavy type

Rather than adding color to body text, use it to add impact to headlines, subheads, and publication titles. Use dark colors which are easier to read.

3. Use color to organize content

Use lightly colored fills behind alternating rows in tables to help readers focus their attention on one row at a time.

Foreground/background contrast

Color is one of Microsoft Office Publisher's most powerful, and, alas, least understood tools.

In the right hands, color can add impact to your pages, project a unique, distinctive identity, and provide selective emphasis.

In the wrong hands, however, color can weaken your pages, fail to differentiate your message from your competitors', and make it harder to read your words.

Region	Q1	Q2	Q3	Q4
North	105	33	55	90
South	66	19	44	67
East	55	88	77	36
West	22	13	38	76
Misc.	16	27	43	12
Total	264	180	257	283

2. Restrict light colors to fills

Use light colored background colors, plus shades of them, to organize and emphasize short text elements like pull-quotes, a table of contents, or sidebars.

4. Use color for emphasis

Color works best when concentrated in one or two key areas of a page, such as fills behind publication titles, logos, or key border elements.

Exploring the Advantages of 2-Color Commercial Printing

To choose two-color printing for your publication, click Tools, Commercial Printing Tools, Color Printing.

When the Color Printing dialog box appears, click Spot Colors. Click the New Colors button, and choose the two colors that you want to include in your publication.

Why 2-color printing?

When taking your designs to a commercial printer, each additional color increases your printing costs.

Two-color printing, however, adds impact to your publication for much less than four-color printing.

In most cases, your colors will be black plus a second, accent, color chosen because its color is associated with your logo. Or, instead of black, you might choose a dark gray.

The next time you apply color to your publication, the first options that appear will be shades of the two colors you have chosen.

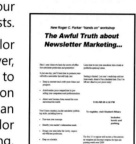

Black layer

Blue layer

2-color prepress

As shown above, when your commercial printer prepares your Publisher files for 2-color printing, they will create two "separations," one for each of the two ink colors.

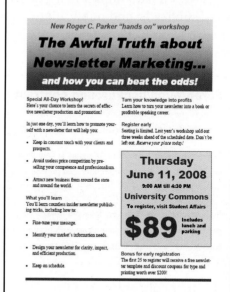

After printing...

The illustration above shows how the publication will look when printed.

Use 4-Color Printing for the Best Possible Quality

Four-color commercial printing is the best choice when you want the best possible price printing several thousand, or more, publications with the highest possible color quality.

Another indication that four-color printing is the right option is when your publication is going to include full color photographs.

Four-color printing gets its name from the fact that your commercial printer will prepare four separation layers. Each controls the placement of a different colored ink which—when added together—create all other colors.

4-color prepress

Later versions of Microsoft Office Publisher allow your commercial printer to create color separations during the prepress phase.

Compare the printed publication, left, with the individual color separations, below.

Cyan layer

Yellow layer

Magenta layer

Black layer

To confirm that your publication will produce the best possible quality, text, rules, or other elements that you've set to 100% black should appear only on the black layer.

Why 4-color printing?

Choose 4-color printing when:

–Your publication contains four-color photographs.

–You desire excellent color quality.

–Quantities are high (several thousand, or more).

–You want the best price.

Review Your Use of Color In Your Marketing

Get in the habit of reviewing your use of color in your publication every time you complete a project.

1. Resources

Before you began designing with color, did you check with your boss or client to confirm that the budget would allow for color printing?

2. Color model

Did you choose the right type of color for your publication, based on the quantity to be printed, the purpose of the color, and available resources?

3. Selection

Did you use Publisher's Color Schemes feature to select a combination of foreground and background colors guaranteed to work well together?

4. Consistency

Did you choose a Color Scheme compatible with the image you want to project and the colors in your firm's logo or existing marketing materials?

5. Purpose

Did you use color purposefully, to make your message clearer and more easily understood, or did you use color to "brighten" an otherwise dull publication?

6. Restraint

Did you use the minimum amount of color necessary to enhance your message?

7. Concentration

Instead of scattering color in small quantities around your pages--for example, in small text, on thin lines, or on small graphic accents--did you concentrate color in large type and a few key areas?

8. Readability

Can you easily read colored text in headlines, subheads and body copy?

9. Efficiency

Have you considered ways to reduce printing costs by pre-printing text and graphic elements that remain the same from project to project?

10. Proofs

Have you made arrangements with your commercial printer to receive proofs of your publication at several stages?

You can download a copy of the Color Review Worksheet at www.designtosellonline.com/color.html.

Free worksheet

Use the Color Review Worksheet, right, to double-check your use of color in your publications.

Advance Praise for *Design to Sell*

Design is everyone's business, and Roger C. Parker shows you how to do it right!
    —Daniel H. Pink, author, *A Whole New Mind*, www.danpink.com

What a needed book by Roger Parker, a dean of design! Today's multi-tasking generations will give your printed materials more than a split second's worth of attention with attractive design. Learn what you need to make this happen.
    —Paul and Sarah Edwards, authors of 16 books including a new edition of *Making Money with Your Computer at Home*, www.workingingfromhome.com

In Design to Sell, *the dependable Roger Parker has produced yet another of his insightful guides. As always, he is down-to-earth and practical in everything he recommends. Furthermore, he explains why he recommends it and why it will work, and the-the height of usefulness-shows how to apply it.*
    —Jan V. White, communication design consultant; author, *Editing by Design.*

Nobody does a better job of showing how to use design to build lasting customer relationships than Roger C. Parker.
    —Jay Conrad Levinson, author, *Guerrilla Marketing*, www.guerillamarketingassociation.com

Today, design is more than a pretty picture—it is business strategy. Learn from Roger how to design your own way to success!
    —Cliff Atkinson, author, *Beyond Bullet Points*, www.sociablemedia.com

Big firms, with bottomless pockets, can hire expensive designers to help them tap into the power of design. Until now, smaller firms have usually had to do without. Now, however, Design to Sell *provides the step-by-step guidance firms of all sizes need to use Microsoft Publisher to make design work for them-instead of against them.*
    —Doug Hall, author, *Jump Start Your Business Brain*, host, BrainBrew Radio, www.brainbrewradio.com

The key to our successful launch of the Island Institute 22 years ago was our annual Island Journal and a variety of other design-coordinated materials, and throughout, Roger Parker's consistently solid design and marketing counsel have kept us on the right heading. The success of our current campaign has only re-enforced the understanding that even the best "product" will benefit tremendously if it is clearly presented in a compelling and well designed manner. Roger Parker's sense of these qualities is unsurpassed!
    —Peter Ralston, Vice President and Co-Founder, Island Institute, Maine www.islandinstitute.org

I am a great fan of Roger C. Parker...the design genius of our generation who has taught desktop publishing excellence to hundreds of thousands.
    —Dr. Ralph Wilson, Internet Marketing Authority, www.wilsonweb.com

We all need a visual edge to be noticed, read, and remembered. Design to Sell *combines Roger's wisdom and experience as a writer and design expert with a user-friendly set of keys that permits you to unlock the full functionality of Microsoft Publisher.*
> —William Reed, Tokyo, author, *Mind Mapping for Memory and Creativity*, #1 best-seller, Amazon Japan, www.b-smart.net.

As always, Roger Parker is the pioneer in thinking and writing about design-treating design as an RIO-generating business tool and not a purely aesthetic function. With his clear, simple instructions, you will understand both the real purpose of design in business-to drive sales-as well as how to create materials that achieve that function using Microsoft Publisher.
> —Robert W. Bly, author, *The Copywriter's Handbook*, www.bly.com

The worksheets in this book, alone, are worth the investment. Design to Sell *not only showed me how to use Publisher to produce my own newsletter, but also showed me how to turn it from good to great! The details are amazing.*
> —Sean Greeley, www.wakeupmarketing.com
> Sean@WakeUpTraining.com

From creating your message to grabbing the attention of your audience, Roger's Design to Sell *has the steps you need to succeed in creating your own marketing pieces. I especially love the "ten tasks" that you will do over and over again. His action steps provide non-designers, like myself, the detailed help we need to market ourselves using one of the most popular software programs available.*
> —Romanus Wolter,
> Entrepreneur's magazine's Success Coach and author, *Kick Start Your Success,* *www.kickstartguy.com*

This is the book I recommend to our clients, large and small, who want to plan and create their own postcards as quickly and efficiently as possible. Design to Sell *is the perfect complement to today's advancing technology.*
> —Steven Willen
> President, AmazingMail.com

Roger C. Parker is a design evangelist who helps those who need design help the most: those who must produce their own marketing materials on a tight budget, even though they have had no previous design experience! Use this book to save time, money, and headaches.
> —Kathi Dunn, award-winning designer for best-selling authors, fast-track speakers and leading experts, www.dunn-design.com

Design to Sell *helped me learn how to give my printed material a visual edge without having to spend thousands of dollars or years of study. It should be compulsory reading in any marketing course aimed at small and medium businesses.*
> —Bryan O'Shannassy, Bryan O'Shannassy & Associates, Australia

Using the techniques Roger taught me, I was able to cut $10,000 from my advertising budget while attracting better-qualified prospects!
> —Gene Paltrineri, Certified Master Photographer, www.genepaltrineri.com

Microsoft

Design to Sell:
Use Microsoft® Publisher to Plan, Write and Design Great Marketing Pieces

Roger C. Parker

PUBLISHED BY
Microsoft Press
A Division of Microsoft Corporation
One Microsoft Way
Redmond, Washington 98052-6399

Library of Congress Control Number 2005939241

Printed and bound in the United States of America.

1 2 3 4 5 6 7 8 9   QWE   0 9 8 7 6

Distributed in Canada by H.B. Fenn and Company Ltd.

A CIP catalogue record for this book is available from the British Library.

Microsoft Press books are available through booksellers and distributors worldwide. For further information about international editions, contact your local Microsoft Corporation office or contact Microsoft Press International directly at fax (425) 936-7329. Visit our Web site at www.microsoft.com/mspress. Send comments to *mspinput@microsoft.com*.

Microsoft, Excel, Microsoft Press, the Office logo, OpenType, Outlook, PowerPoint, and Windows are either registered trademarks or trademarks of Microsoft Corporation in the United States and/or other countries.

The example companies, organizations, products, domain names, e-mail addresses, logos, people, places, and events depicted herein are fictitious. No association with any real company, organization, product, domain name, e-mail address, logo, person, place, or event is intended or should be inferred.

This book expresses the author's views and opinions. The information contained in this book is provided without any express, statutory, or implied warranties. Neither the authors, Microsoft Corporation, nor its resellers, or distributors will be held liable for any damages caused or alleged to be caused either directly or indirectly by this book.

Acquisitions Editor: Laura Sackerman
Project Editor: Sandra Haynes
Editorial and Production: Studioserv
Copy Editor: Jennifer Harris
Technical Editor: Steve Sagman

Body Part No. X11-97535

Contents at a Glance

Table of Contents

What do you think of this book? Microsoft is interested in hearing your feedback about this publication so we
We want to hear from you! can continually improve our books and learning resources for you. To participate in a brief online survey, please visit: *www.microsoft.com/learning/booksurvey/*

Master the eight principles of design success, and learn to identify the six building blocks of page architecture.

Learn the Three Truths of Marketing and the four tasks your messages must satisfy for your designs to succeed. Using list-based writing to get more done in less time.

Part Two   # Working with Publisher

Chapter Five   ## Getting Started with Microsoft Publisher 69

Familiarize yourself with Publisher's working environment and the tools needed to complete frequently used tasks. Customizing Publisher's working environment.

Chapter Six   ## Creating a Foundation for Design Success 85

Use a grid as the basis for placing text and graphics, adding text and graphics, linking text boxes; and the right way to choose colors.

Chapter Seven

Building Design Excellence into Every Page 103

Learn what you need to know about formatting headlines, subheads, and body copy text. Discover the importance of making your words as easy-to-read as possible, while working efficiently.

Chapter Eight

Taking Your Design Success to the Next Level 139

Use tools like baseline alignment and special characters to fine-tune the appearance of your pages. Use templates to maintain consistency among marketing messages.

Chapter Nine

Distributing Error-Free Messages in Print and Online 153

Preview your publication from the reader's point of view, and preparing files for error-free printing and distribution over the Internet

Part Three ## Publisher at Work

Chapter Ten

Promoting Your Business with Postcards 165

Learn why postcards work, use worksheets to plan your postcard marketing, create effective messages, and learn tips for building your client and prospect mailing lists.

Chapter Eleven

Using Newsletters and Tip Sheets to Promote Your Expertise

Discover the power of a platform. Identify the right newsletter format, size, and frequency. Learn copywriting and design tips, production tips, and profit from tip sheets.

Chapter Twelve

Profiting from Small Ads 217

Discover how to maximize the power of consistent small ads, and use them to promote your firm's benefits, newsletters, and tip sheets.

Part Four

Wrapping It Up

Chapter Thirteen

Reviewing the 10 Most Common Design Errors 231

Choose between makeovers and incremental improvements, learn what to look for when evaluating your designs and where to locate needed advice.

    Find out how to create a marketing plan that provides a calendar for keeping track of each month's marketing activities, plus a way to continually track the results of your marketing.

Acknowledgments

Design to Sell, proves, once again, that books are the result of partnerships and teams. It takes a supportive literary agent, like Matt Wagner, from Fresh-Books (www.fresh-books.com) and a forward-thinking acquisitions editor like Juliana Aldous, from Microsoft Learning, to breath life into the author's vision.

Then, it takes the efforts of hardworking individuals like Sandra Haynes, Developmental Editor, Microsoft Learning, to translate a detailed chapter outline into finished chapters. Next, even harder work begins, when a dedicated and skilled editorial team, like Jennifer Harris and Steve Sagman from Studioserv (www.studioserv.com) tactfully ask the right questions, helping the author to amplify, clarify, and simplify. These are just the most obvious contributors. My apologies to those at Microsoft Learning whose names should also be listed above.

I was fortunate to also enjoy a support team of clients, family, and friends who provided constant encouragement and feedback. My wife, Betsy, and Murphy (Golden Retriever), provided hours of companionship and support, and forgave occasional missed social engagements. Betsy's been by my side since the earliest days of *Looking Good in Print*; her comments, questions, and support have always been invaluable.

Numerous clients also deserve recognition for encouragement and providing permission to reproduce their projects. Thank you, Dr. Tony Fiore, (www.angercoach.com); Sean Greeley, (www.wakeupmarketing.com); Gene Paltrineri, Certified Master of Professional Photography, (www.genepaltrineri.com); David Salzman, (www.espressodave.com); Will Reed, Tokyo, (www.b-smart.net).

I also want to express my appreciation for the continuing support of authors and supporters like Jay Conrad Levinson, Jan V. White, Doug Hall, and numerous others, who took time from their busy schedules to read, and comment on, *Design to Sell* while I was writing it. The book benefited greatly from their encouragement and suggestions.

Finally, I want to thank my readers and newsletter subscribers for their comments and suggestions. E-mail for fast and easy comment and feedback from readers is definitely one of the benefits of living in the Internet age!

Roger C. Parker
roger@designtosellonline.com

Introduction

Design to Sell is for anyone who wants to use design to increase sales and profits through more effective and efficient marketing. It takes proven design and marketing principles and shows you how to achieve professional-level results using Microsoft Office Publisher, a robust and readily-available software program already found on hundreds of thousands of personal computers throughout the world.

I've long felt that Microsoft Publisher can make more of an immediate impact to the bottom line success of the vast majority of associations, businesses, and individuals, than any other software program. This book is a testament to that belief.

Who Should Buy This Book?

I wrote *Design to Sell* for readers who resemble the clients around the world whom I've had the good fortune to work with. These clients work in a variety of businesses, small to large, and share many characteristics.

Typically, they are self-starters, they have a mission to perform, and they want to do as much of the work themselves because they are not comfortable paying others to perform services they can neither comfortably afford nor fully understand.

They also take pride in mastering any new skills needed to promote their firm's mission, success, and profits, so they're willing to roll up their sleeves and do the work needed to help their venture succeed. They believe in investing in themselves. These individuals are typically found among the following categories of businesses:

- Self-employed professionals striving to establish a name for themselves. Because they're just starting out, these individuals have few, if any, additional resources at their disposal.

- Owners and marketing managers at start-ups and medium-sized businesses. These individuals want more hands-on involvement in their firm's marketing, because they need to save money and enjoy telling their firm's story.

- Department and product managers inside large firms. These individuals generally need to wring every penny out of their marketing budgets.

- Association, education, and non-profit executives. These individuals must keep their constituents and supporters informed and enthusiastic, and they generally don't have separate marketing budgets.

Why Design Matters

When asked why design is important, Jay Conrad Levinson—author of the best-selling *Guerrilla Marketing* series of books—responded:

> *Regardless of the brilliance of your words, your idea, and your offer, unless somebody actually looks at them, they are lost in that enormous vacuum of invisibility. How do you get people to look at them and begin to like them? One word answer: Design.*

As Dan Pink, author of *A Whole New Mind*, his study of the six most needed mental capabilities needed to survive in contemporary America, recently stated: *"Today, design is everyone's business!"*

My goal is to help you use design as a competitive tool, a tool that will help you profit from both the accumulated wisdom of graphic designers and visual communicators extending back hundreds of years, coupled with the technical virtuosity of Microsoft Publisher running on today's ubiquitous personal computers.

How Much Do You Need to Know About Design?

Design to Sell is based on a simple premise: you do not need to be a designer to profit from design!

You need to know enough about design to appreciate its power. You must understand the how's and the why's. And you must know how to apply previously-made design decisions while producing your ongoing marketing communications. But you don't need to spend all your time designing to put design to good use!

Why Publisher?

Microsoft Publisher is not the most expensive page layout software program available. Neither is it one of the two expensive and sophisticated software programs used by professional New York City and San Francisco design professionals to prepare fancy annual reports, advertisements, and glossy magazines.

But, at about a third of the price of its top echelon competitors, Microsoft Publisher can take a firm or individual with no platform—no tangible way of communicating their competence and expertise—and give them the ability to build and promote their brand and consistently keep in touch.

I know this is true, because I've been helping clients and friends do this for years. (As you read this book, you'll find several examples of Publisher-powered "obscurity to awareness" successes.)

Straight Talk About Capabilities

In a world where consumers obsess over product "specifications," few buyers actually ever approach the outer limits of their possession's performance capabilities.

Take automobiles, for example: "Which cars offer the best performance: BMW, Mercedes-Benz, or Porsche?" In nearly every case, the limiting factor is not the car, but the driver's ability to control it.

Likewise, it's as possible to create commonplace, hard-to-read marketing messages with more expensive programs, as it is to use Publisher to create an ongoing stream of attractive marketing materials that can take you, your firm, or your client's, to new levels of prosperity and profitability.

What You'll Learn in This book

Design to sell is divided into four parts, each part focused on the keys to marketing your message effectively.

Part One: Perspective on Marketing with Design   In Part One, you'll learn the basics of creating effective, reader-friendly marketing messages your clients and prospects will want to read. Part One provides a design and marketing context for the information that follows.

Part Two: Jumpstarting Your Page Layout Skills   The chapters found in Part Two cover how to use Microsoft Publisher to translate what you've just learned about design and marketing into effective marketing messages. You'll learn how to create a structure for design success and how to populate it with appropriately formatted text. You'll also learn how to enhance what you've created so far, and how to duplicate and distribute error-free marketing messages.

Part Three: Putting Publisher to Work   In this section, you'll learn how to apply what you've learned to specific categories of marketing messages: ads, brochures, newsletters, postcards, and other projects.

Part Four: Wrapping It Up   Finally, we look at several before-and-after versions of publications, each with important lessons to teach. The section concludes with a quick review of how you can use the lessons in this books to avoid common problems.

Companion Web Site   *Design to Sell* readers are invited to visit *www.designtosellonline.com*, where you'll find additional content to supplement the book. The content you'll find includes downloadable worksheets, tests to check yourself, and updated resources.

The Most Important Lesson

Ultimately, *Design to Sell* is based on a simple premise: Design once, produce often. This simple statement reflects everything I've learned about marketing during the last twenty-five years of helping firms and individuals create a presence for themselves in a crowded market.

There is often a fundamental difference to be observed between graphic designers and those who simply use design to become spectacularly successful in business.

- For designers, the challenge—and often the reward--is to constantly reinvent the wheel in new and better ways.

- For those who aspire to business success, however, the challenge is to use and reuse fundamentally strong designs in a way that permits constant contact with clients and prospects.

I dedicate *Design to Sell* to those who are attracted to the second alternative, and I thank my clients around the world whose real-world successes provided the ultimate foundation for this book.

Roger C. Parker
February, 2006
Dover, NH

Part One

Perspectives on Marketing Using Design

In this part

Chapter One

Using Design to Gain a Competitive Edge

What you'll find:

- ❑ Discover how to use design to gain a visual edge.
- ❑ Find out what design is—and what design isn't.
- ❑ Learn what design can do for you.
- ❑ Discover who can design.
- ❑ Learn the eight critical tasks that design must perform.
- ❑ Understand the importance of doing it yourself.
- ❑ Familiarize yourself with the tools of design.

Graphic design—the ability to create attractive, easy-to-read print communications—is more important today than ever before.

Today, to survive and prosper, you must be able to efficiently "market" words in ways that help them attract attention and appear as easy to read as possible. Whether you work for a boss, a client, or yourself, you need a *visual edge* if you want your words to convincingly inform, motivate, and persuade.

The reason is simple: messages today face intense competition for attention. Every day, thousands of marketing messages compete with your messages—whether these are messages you prepare for your boss or for clients. As a result, if the messages you provide don't attract attention or are hard to read, they'll be ignored! There are simply more than enough better-looking, easier-to-read messages for readers to turn to.

Design provides you with the visual edge you need to get messages noticed, read, and remembered. And best of all, you don't have to be a professional designer, with years of training and experience, plus access to thousands of dollars worth of professional software, to gain a visual edge.

Design provides you with the visual edge you need to get your messages noticed, read, and remembered.

Microsoft Office Publisher, a powerful yet accessible page layout program already installed on hundreds of thousands of computers, makes it easy to add a visual edge to all of your print communications—even if you have not had previous design training or experience!

Competing with a Visual Edge

Daniel Pink, in his recent best-selling book *A Whole New Mind: Moving from the Information Age to the Conceptual Age* (Riverhead, 2005), lists design as the first of the "Six Senses" he considers essential to economic and personal success in the twenty-first century.

Pink describes design as a "combination of utility and significance." He writes:

> *A graphic designer must whip up a brochure that is easy to read. That's utility. But at its most effective, her brochure must also transmit ideas or emotions that the words themselves cannot convey. That's significance.*

Your mastery of the ideas and techniques described in this book will open the doors of effective communications to you and—hopefully—your employer or clients. The power to design is the *power to earn* and the *power to sell*.

Master the ideas in this book, and you will have the power to earn more money as an employee or a freelance designer and the power to sell more if you are a self-employed professional.

What Design Is—and What It Isn't

Think of design as a lever, or a *multiplier*. Design takes everyday words and arranges them in a way that attracts attention, presells their importance, and makes them easy to understand.

Consider an unformatted page, as shown in Figure 1-1. Every word is set in the same typeface and type size. Every word necessary to communicate your message is present, yet few people are likely to read them. There's no starting point for the message, and there's nothing to help readers along.

Make design your marketing partner
Everyday documents deserve as much attention as fancy brochures and newsletters!
Your reputation is on the line every time you communicate with your market. Clients and prospects begin to
judge you and your message before they even start reading! Within a second, irreversible "accept" or "reject"
decisions are made solely on the basis of appearance.
If your designs don't *presell the importance of your message,* or if your design projects a *hard-to-read image,*
your message is likely to go unread.
Here are some tips to help you easily produce "everyday" publications that will simultaneously *sell the
importance of your words* and *presell your firm's competence.*
Headlines
Headlines play a major role in determining the success of your publication. If your headlines do not attract your
reader's attention, or are hard to read, the rest of your message is likely to be ignored...and the your effort
creating and distributing your message has been wasted!
Your competence is judged each time you send a message
Tried-and-proven headline tips include:
Typeface. Use a sans serif typeface like Arial, Helvetica, or Frutiger, or Gill Sans. When available, choose the
black or *heavy* options, which are considerably darker than the bold version.
Case. Avoid setting headlines entirely in upper case characters. Headlines set in uppercase take up more space
and are significantly harder to read than headlines set in a combination of upper and lowercase characters.
White space. Draw attention to headlines by framing them with white space.
Line breaks. Use line breaks (created by holding down the Shift key while pressing the Enter key) to equalize
line lengths and break lines at logical points.
Subheads
Use subheads to maintain reader momentum. Add a short, keyword, subhead each time a new topic is
introduced.
Avoid full sentences and two-line subheads. Limit subheads to short *keywords.* Format them using a smaller
version of the same typeface used for headlines.
Never underline subheads. Instead, emphasize them by adding extra space above them, or set them in a second
color.
Body copy
Use a serif typeface, like Times New Roman, Century, Minion, Stone Serif, or Palatino. The serifs guide your
reader's eyes from character to character.
Line length. Avoid long lines of type extending from margin to margin. Shorter lines are easier to read.
Line spacing. In general, default, (or automatic), line spacing is too narrow. Adding extra line spacing, or
leading, makes your lines much easier to read.
Widows and orphans. Avoid sentences, and sentence fragments, isolated at the top or bottom of columns or
pages. Paragraphs should contain at least two lines.
Watch out for *overset text.* When there are more words than can fit in the last text frame, the text is cut off.
Often, only a tiny icon indicates missing text!
Page numbers
Always number your pages. Page numbers help readers track their progress through your

Figure 1-1   Without the formatting power of graphic design, pages are boring
and hard to read.

Add graphic design, however, and the pages take on new utility and a new significance, as you can see in Figure 1-2. The same words, when formatted, now reach out to readers by "advertising" the importance of your message and making the words easier to use— that is, easier to read. Because they are easier to read, the words become easier to understand and easier to remember—and thus are more effective.

Figure 1-2 Graphic design creates pages that not only attract readership, but are also easier to read.

What Design Isn't

One of the best ways to understand the power of design is to consider what design *isn't*.

First, design is *not* entertainment or decoration. Design is not something you add to a page to make it "prettier" or "more fun." Design is not adding a holiday wreath to an annual report released in December, nor is design adding a picture of a hammock to an owner's manual published during the summer.

Decorative design, which does not support the purpose of your message (or your client's), is not only wasteful, it is also transparently obvious, and it devalues the importance of the words by projecting an amateurish image.

Second, design is never "passive." It either works for you (and your message), or it works against you (and your message). Design must be appropriate and relevant, or it undermines your message by appearing unprofessional or making your message hard to read.

Design Is Not a Cure-All

Design, as we have seen, adds utility and significance to your words. But design has limitations. Here are some of the limits on what design can accomplish:

Design cannot substitute for a lack of a meaningful message.   All the typographical and color pyrotechnics in the world cannot substitute for poorly written headlines, missing subheads, or long, disorganized paragraphs.

Design cannot force readers to take action.   Type, color, and layout cannot compensate for a lack of desire. If your message does not describe benefits that readers want to enjoy or is intended to persuade readers to take immoral, illegal, or expensive actions, all the typefaces and color in the world can't compel action.

Design cannot succeed without distribution.   Messages have to be printed and distributed to be effective. This is why production efficiency is so important. The more you pay for producing your designs, the less money you have left over for printing and postage to deliver them. That's one of the reasons it's so important to develop your own design capabilities.

Is This Effective Design?

If design is based on making appropriate decisions about the layout and formatting of your message, can we consider the message in this storefront an example of effective design?

Certainly it's not an example of subjectively "beautiful" design! But consider the goals:

Effectiveness   The sign clearly communicates the availability of the space for lease (but not for rent).

Efficiency   The message is communicated as inexpensively as possible.

Environment   Prospects in cars speeding by can immediately understand the message.

Image   A "do-it-yourself" image, in this case, is far more effective than a fancy or "art-directed" sign communicating the same message.

There are no absolutes in design. Effective design, rather, is based on appropriateness, on making correct decisions in the context of a particular message, market, and environment. Success depends not so much on what you like as on what works best for a particular situation.

What Can Design Do for You?

Design is the *purposeful*–rather than random–formatting and arrangement of the text and graphical elements that make up a page (or a publication). Design is based on making appropriate decisions about the layout and formatting of your message. *Layout* refers to the arrangement of parts–of text and graphical elements. *Formatting* refers to their colors, typeface choices, and spacing.

How Do You Measure Design Success?

Design should never be subjectively measured. The success or failure of a design should never be measured in terms of subjective impressions based on color, typeface, and layout.

Instead, it is relatively easy to measure the effectiveness of design. *Functionality* is the only meaningful way to measure design's success or failure:

- Design succeeds when it furthers the message by attracting and maintaining the reader's attention–for example, "utility," in Dan Pink's words (quoted earlier).

- Design succeeds when the layout and formatting of your message communicate more than what words alone can communicate–this is "significance," in Dan Pink's words.

- Design fails if it gets in the way of message. Visual pyrotechnics like bright colors and fancy visuals might attract attention, but they might attract so much attention that they make it hard for readers to concentrate on the adjacent text. This must never happen.

Who Can Design?

A "functional" view of design has many implications. One of the most important is that design is not so much a "creative" or "intuitive" ability as it is the result of mastering a set of tools and techniques and applying them in a careful and consistent manner.

As such, virtually anyone who wants to can learn how to create attractive, easy-to-read pages!

Design as a practical way to multiply the effectiveness of the written word has little in common with "creative," "artistic," or "self-expression" endeavors like oil painting, portraiture, or photography.

Design is the purposeful arrangement and formatting of the text and graphical elements used to communicate your message.

Design as a practical tool to multiply the effectiveness of written words has little in common with "creative," "artistic," or "self-expression" endeavors.

Creative design is *inwardly oriented*, intended to satisfy the artist's subjective desires. It succeeds when the result satisfies not only the creator, but also those who share the creator's interests and passions (and can afford to indulge that interest by purchasing the artwork).

The design of pages and publications, however, is *outwardly directed*. Design attempts to satisfy the following demanding constituencies:

Result-oriented clients   These are you, your client, or your boss, and (hopefully) they are more interested in making sales than in displaying favorite colors or typeface choices.

Intended readers   These people are not reading for pleasure, but are reading for information, and are always in a hurry.

Competitors   These are people or organizations whose messages are competing for the same readers. Your goal is to create publications that are obviously different from those of your competition.

Design is the process of acknowledging, understanding, and balancing the requirements of each of these groups.

Your goal is to create print communications that attract readers by promising an "easy read" and then to deliver on that promise by making the message as easy to read as possible.

Eight Tasks That Design Must Satisfy

If design is a *lever*, there are eight ways you can use design to multiply the impact of your message. Use the following sections as a guide to evaluating the success of your own designs, as well as the designs of others—including your competitors.

1. Design Must Attract Attention

Design takes ordinary words and makes them special by placing them on a page in unique and interesting ways. Headlines play a crucial role in determining the success or failure of your message, because if the headline isn't read, it's unlikely that the body copy will be read.

Consider the three steps involved in placing and formatting a typical headline:

1. Begin by placing the headline at the top of a page, surrounded by white space (*layout*, or *placement*).

2. Format the headline using a large, bold, easy-to-notice typeface that is hard to overlook (*formatting*).

3. Fine-tune the line and letter spacing and the break between the first and second lines to make the headline as easy to read as possible (*care* and *craftsmanship*).

2. Design Must Presell the Importance of Your Words

To succeed, design must project an image appropriate for your message and your market's expectations.

How would you feel if, after a 45-minute delay in the waiting room, you finally go in to meet the doctor and find her desk a mess, her hair unkempt, and her smock wrinkled and covered with mustard and coffee stains?

You'd probably think twice about taking her advice seriously! (And you might not even let her examine you!) Before she opened her mouth, the doctor's careless appearance communicated an uncaring, unprofessional attitude.

Covers *do* sell books. Design is the "cover" you put on your messages.

The same thing happens when your publications project an amateurish or a last-minute image! Covers *do* sell books. And design is the "cover" you put on all of your messages. In a bookstore, for example, have you ever noticed how some books immediately attract your attention, inviting you to pick them up and thumb through them, while you barely notice other books? That's design in action!

3. Design Must Differentiate

Design sets your message apart from those of your competition.

How would you feel if you were participating in a candidates debate for public office and you found yourself wearing the exact same outfit as your opponent? You'd probably be concerned that your words might be misinterpreted as coming from your opponent—and you'd be right!

Likewise, what do you think would happen if the *Boston Globe*, the *New York Times*, the *Wall Street Journal*, and *USA Today* all shared the same formatting—that is, the same page size, column layout, typefaces, and colors? The papers would lose their identity, and probably many of their readers.

Your messages *must* be clearly differentiated from those of your competition. You want to make sure that your words are associated with your identity in your market's eyes.

There's another aspect to this too. Effective design creates a *synergy*, or 1 + 1 = 3 effect, among your ads, brochures, business cards, letterheads, newsletters, and Web site. When your messages communicate a consistent identity, the power of each is multiplied.

4. Design Must Organize

Design provides a framework, or structure, for readers to use while navigating your message. At a glance, your readers should be able to instantly identify the key ideas on the page, allowing them to make intelligent "read" or "not read" decisions.

Ideally, each of
your marketing
materials—for
example, each
issue of your news-
letter—will present
a unique image
that "brands" it as
coming from you
and not your
competitors.

Well-designed pages, for example, contain a system of *reader cues* that indicate the relative importance of ideas and an outline of the way the ideas are organized on the page. At a glance:

Headlines   Clearly indicate the beginning of articles and their relative importance.

Subheads   Introduce new topics.

Pull-quotes   Summarize the important ideas on a page.

Sidebars   Highlight and separate information supporting the main ideas on a page, which can be read or ignored as desired.

In addition, subheads, or "mini-headlines," located within the columns of text perform an additional function. They "chunk" the content by breaking long passages into several, shorter, bite-size elements that promise an easier reading experience.

A page without subheads looks—and is—hard to read, as you can see in Figure 1-3. There's neither a starting point nor an obvious hierarchy of information. You have to read the whole page to make sense of its content, but reading the whole page looks like a big job! And, after you've finished, there's no easy way to review the information you just read.

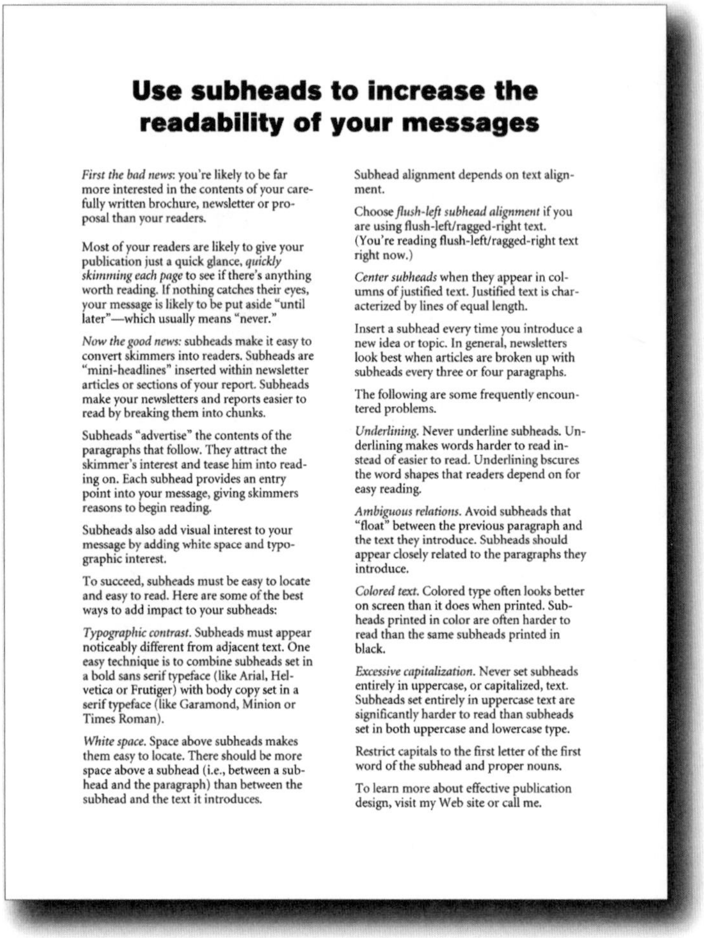

Use subheads to increase the readability of your messages

First the bad news: you're likely to be far more interested in the contents of your carefully written brochure, newsletter or proposal than your readers.

Most of your readers are likely to give your publication just a quick glance, *quickly skimming each page* to see if there's anything worth reading. If nothing catches their eyes, your message is likely to be put aside "until later"—which usually means "never."

Now the good news: subheads make it easy to convert skimmers into readers. Subheads are "mini-headlines" inserted within newsletter articles or sections of your report. Subheads make your newsletters and reports easier to read by breaking them into chunks.

Subheads "advertise" the contents of the paragraphs that follow. They attract the skimmer's interest and tease him into reading on. Each subhead provides an entry point into your message, giving skimmers reasons to begin reading.

Subheads also add visual interest to your message by adding white space and typographic interest.

To succeed, subheads must be easy to locate and easy to read. Here are some of the best ways to add impact to your subheads:

Typographic contrast. Subheads must appear noticeably different from adjacent text. One easy technique is to combine subheads set in a bold sans serif typeface (like Arial, Helvetica or Frutiger) with body copy set in a serif typeface (like Garamond, Minion or Times Roman).

White space. Space above subheads makes them easy to locate. There should be more space above a subhead (i.e., between a subhead and the paragraph) than between the subhead and the text it introduces.

Subhead alignment depends on text alignment.

Choose *flush-left subhead alignment* if you are using flush-left/ragged-right text. (You're reading flush-left/ragged-right text right now.)

Center subheads when they appear in columns of justified text. Justified text is characterized by lines of equal length.

Insert a subhead every time you introduce a new idea or topic. In general, newsletters look best when articles are broken up with subheads every three or four paragraphs.

The following are some frequently encountered problems.

Underlining. Never underline subheads. Underlining makes words harder to read instead of easier to read. Underlining bscures the word shapes that readers depend on for easy reading.

Ambiguous relations. Avoid subheads that "float" between the previous paragraph and the text they introduce. Subheads should appear closely related to the paragraphs they introduce.

Colored text. Colored type often looks better on screen than it does when printed. Subheads printed in color are often harder to read than the same subheads printed in black.

Excessive capitalization. Never set subheads entirely in uppercase, or capitalized, text. Subheads set entirely in uppercase text are significantly harder to read than subheads set in both uppercase and lowercase type.

Restrict capitals to the first letter of the first word of the subhead and proper nouns.

To learn more about effective publication design, visit my Web site or call me.

Figure 1-3 Pages without subheads provide no content clues for readers or incentive to begin reading.

Pages with subheads, however, provide numerous places to begin reading and also help you keep your place, as shown in Figure 1-4.

In addition, just as a large task becomes easier to complete when it is broken down into a series of individual steps, subheads make it easy for readers to navigate long messages as a series of short, easy-to-read topics.

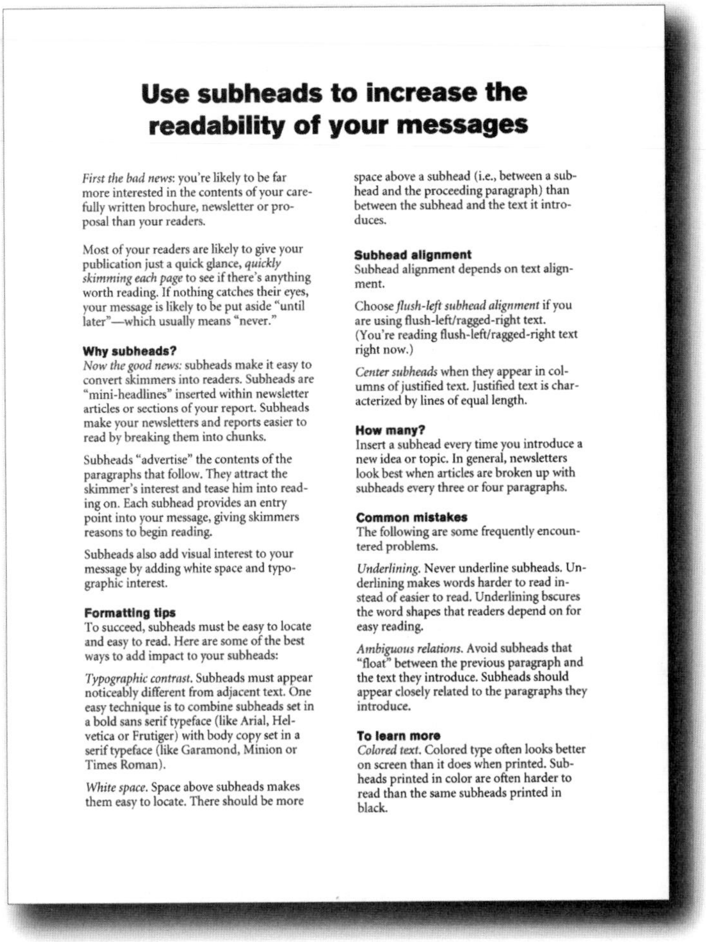

Use subheads to increase the readability of your messages

First the bad news: you're likely to be far more interested in the contents of your carefully written brochure, newsletter or proposal than your readers.

Most of your readers are likely to give your publication just a quick glance, *quickly skimming each page* to see if there's anything worth reading. If nothing catches their eyes, your message is likely to be put aside "until later"—which usually means "never."

Why subheads?
Now the good news: subheads make it easy to convert skimmers into readers. Subheads are "mini-headlines" inserted within newsletter articles or sections of your report. Subheads make your newsletters and reports easier to read by breaking them into chunks.

Subheads "advertise" the contents of the paragraphs that follow. They attract the skimmer's interest and tease him into reading on. Each subhead provides an entry point into your message, giving skimmers reasons to begin reading.

Subheads also add visual interest to your message by adding white space and typographic interest.

Formatting tips
To succeed, subheads must be easy to locate and easy to read. Here are some of the best ways to add impact to your subheads:

Typographic contrast. Subheads must appear noticeably different from adjacent text. One easy technique is to combine subheads set in a bold sans serif typeface (like Arial, Helvetica or Frutiger) with body copy set in a serif typeface (like Garamond, Minion or Times Roman).

White space. Space above subheads makes them easy to locate. There should be more space above a subhead (i.e., between a subhead and the proceeding paragraph) than between the subhead and the text it introduces.

Subhead alignment
Subhead alignment depends on text alignment.

Choose *flush-left subhead alignment* if you are using flush-left/ragged-right text. (You're reading flush-left/ragged-right text right now.)

Center subheads when they appear in columns of justified text. Justified text is characterized by lines of equal length.

How many?
Insert a subhead every time you introduce a new idea or topic. In general, newsletters look best when articles are broken up with subheads every three or four paragraphs.

Common mistakes
The following are some frequently encountered problems.

Underlining. Never underline subheads. Underlining makes words harder to read instead of easier to read. Underlining bscures the word shapes that readers depend on for easy reading.

Ambiguous relations. Avoid subheads that "float" between the previous paragraph and the text they introduce. Subheads should appear closely related to the paragraphs they introduce.

To learn more
Colored text. Colored type often looks better on screen than it does when printed. Subheads printed in color are often harder to read than the same subheads printed in black.

Figure 1-4 The same page, with subheads, offers numerous entry points and appears significantly easier to read.

5. Design Must Provide Selective Emphasis

All ideas are not of equal importance. Some ideas—and some words—are more important than others. The task of design is to help readers identify and focus on the important words, separating them from those of lesser importance.

When everything on a page is emphasized, nothing is emphasized, as you can see in Figure 1-5. Setting an entire paragraph in bold, for example, doesn't help readers pick out and appreciate the meaning of those words that are truly important.

> As when you are cooking with spices, "less is more" is a
> good rule to follow when adding emphasis to your ideas.
> ***Overemphasis leads to underemphasis, as the emphasized
> words become the "norm," reducing the visual contrast
> added to the important words,*** making it harder for readers
> to identify the truly important parts of your message.

Figure 1-5 When every word in a passage is emphasized, there is no emphasis.

Overemphasis
inevitably leads to
underemphasis, as
no single element
clearly indicates
that it is more
important than
the others.

Restraint when using the tools of emphasis—that is, color and bold type—is the key to helping your designs communicate as efficiently and effectively as possible, as shown in Figure 1-6.

> As when you are cooking with spices, "less is more" is a
> good rule to follow when adding emphasis to your ideas.
> ***Overemphasis leads to underemphasis***, as the emphasized
> words become the "norm," reducing the visual contrast
> added to the important words, making it harder for readers
> to identify the truly important parts of your message.

Figure 1-6 When too many words in a paragraph are emphasized, emphasis is lost!

6. Design Must Make Reading Easy

Effective design is based on an understanding of the ways humans read.

Although designers frequently talk about *readers*, the term is actually a misnomer. The correct term is *skimmers*. The mechanics of reading in most Western cultures is based on consistent left-to-right eye movements, each movement covering three or four words. Words are recognized by their shapes—and instantly translated into thoughts—rather than phonetically sounded out and silently spoken based on the letters that make up each word. Under ideal conditions, this "translation" takes place unconsciously and is characterized by high speed and high message retention.

Anything that interrupts the consistent eye movement and near-instantaneous translation of word shapes into ideas, however, seriously interferes with message comprehension. If the words are not easily recognized and attention has to be paid to individual letters, message comprehension drops like a brick and concentration weakens, making it harder for your customer or prospect to retain interest and keep reading.

In this book, you'll discover several ways to format your message to be as "recognizable" as possible by:

- Making the appropriate typeface and type size choices.
- Choosing the appropriate type case and style.
- Manipulating line and letter spacing.

Studies have shown that subtle differences in layout and typography can make huge differences in how your message is received. Make the right decisions, and your message will be read and remembered. Make the wrong choices, and your message doesn't stand a chance!

Readability is just one of the ways design leverages and multiplies your message.

7. Design Must Immediately Communicate

Design must make information obvious. Design involves understanding the meaning and purpose of data—words, numbers, and ideas—and presenting them concisely and as visually as possible.

Words alone do a poor job of communicating comparisons, hierarchy, and sequence. Consider this sentence: "East Coast sales are 20 percent lower than Midwest sales, which in turn are dwarfed by West Coast sales that are twice as large." Read as words, it's difficult to obtain a mental picture of the differing sales from each territory.

The same comparison takes on a new life when visually communicated using charts and graphs. A bar graph, for example, can communicate the same information far more effectively, as shown in Figure 1-7.

Words alone do a
poor job of
communicating
comparisons,
hierarchy, and
sequence.

8. Design Must Save Time and Money

Design isn't just for readers. Design is for you, your boss, and your clients. Design helps you communicate as efficiently as possible.

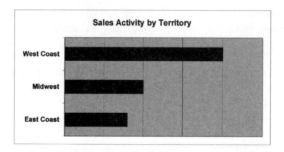

Figure 1-7 A bar chart does a better job of communicating a comparison of sales in three territories than words alone.

It's not enough to create an attractive, easy-to-read page if it takes you so much time to prepare that your message is obsolete before it is distributed. Design must speed your work. It does so when you use software features and techniques like these:

Keyboard shortcuts   Apply commands without removing your hands from the keys.

Text styles   Apply numerous formatting attributes with a single click. Text styles can also be set up so that one format automatically follows another. After formatting a subhead and pressing ENTER, for example, the Normal or Body Copy typeface can be set to automatically appear.

Templates   Give you a jump start on creating the various types of publications you prepare over and over again.

Shortcut menus (accessed by right-clicking)   Provide commands relevant to the selected text or graphics.

Built-in color schemes and font schemes   Make complicated choices easy by offering professionally designed combinations of colors and typefaces.

Efficiency also involves recognizing the differences between design and production. *Design* often refers to creating a basic publication framework from scratch–that is, setting up a column format; choosing colors; and assigning different typeface, type size, and line spacing options for each element of page architecture (headlines, subheads, body copy, captions, and so on). *Production*, however, refers to adding text and graphics to an existing framework, applying text formatting, and overseeing the printing and distribution of a project.

You don't have to be a designer to profit from design! It's reasonable to hire a professional designer to create a template for a unique and repeatable "look"—like a newsletter design—that you can complete monthly without incurring additional expense.

Why Do It Yourself?

Just about everyone in business—and nonprofit associations—can benefit from mastering the design basics and Microsoft Publisher skills described in this book. The ability to efficiently create attractive, easy-to-read pages can save you time and money, permitting you to communicate more effectively and more often with your clients, prospects, and supporters.

Save money.   Mastering design and Microsoft Publisher eliminates the need to pay others to do what you can do yourself. You'll not only save money for yourself, or your employer, but you'll also be able to make a seamless transition between writing and formatting.

Eliminate delays.   When you work with freelance designers, days can go by between the time you prepare something and the time you get a proof back from your designer. If you format, duplicate, and distribute your message yourself, however, you can save significant amounts of time.

Achieve better quality.   By doing the work yourself, you can also end up with a more effective message. Working with freelancers often resembles the game of "telephone"—messages get scrambled, or the person formatting your project doesn't quite understand your ideas. This doesn't happen when you can both write and format your message yourself.

Put your knowledge to work!   You know more about your message and its goals than anyone, because you know your product or your service better than anyone else. You know your market's needs better than anyone else. You know your competition better than anyone else. You'll also probably work more carefully on your project than anyone else, because you are personally invested in it.

When Is Design Appropriate?

Many feel that only "formal" and expensively printed documents warrant design.

Nothing can be further from the truth. You should get in the habit of paying attention to design whenever you're preparing a print communication that you want read and positively acted on. In addition to projects like ads, brochures, catalogs, and newsletters, you should also take care to design for attention and easy reading when you prepare less formal publications such as:

■   Letters, faxes, and memos

- Proposals

- Postcards

- Résumés

- E-books

In each of these cases, you're using design—the purposeful arrangement and formatting of text and graphical elements—to sell the value of your words. In every case, you want the reader to pay attention to your words—and read every word you've written!

These publications in particular might be more deserving of design excellence because they're distributed to qualified recipients at or close to the moment of sale:

Résumés and cover letters   Are sent to those who are looking to hire.

Proposals   Go to prospects who have asked for more details.

E-books   Go to buyers who must be satisfied (or they will ask for a refund) or to prospects who are using your e-book to see how informed and professional you are.

If your words are important, it's imperative that they be as attractive and easy to read as possible. And only design can help you achieve those goals.

How Much Do You Need to Know About Design?

To build equity in your career, you don't have to take a few years off to earn a master's of fine arts degree. You can learn as much, or as little, about graphic design and Microsoft Publisher as you need.

If you can use a
word processing
program, you're
well on your way to
success with
Publisher.

Best of all, you can learn as you go. You don't have to know everything all at once—you can begin with simple formatting and then step up to increased responsibilities as your abilities grow and you become more confident.

You'll find it easy getting started with Microsoft Publisher. If you can use a word processing program such as Microsoft Office Word, you're well on your way to success. Many of the same commands and techniques are used in both programs.

Building Your Personal Equity

When you invest time and money mastering design and Microsoft Publisher, you're adding value to your career, building equity that you not only can use now, but that you also can take with you wherever you want to go in the future.

The ability to effectively communicate in print is an asset that can take you in directions you might not even imagine:

- If you're an employee, your ability to help your employer communicate more effectively—and efficiently—in print will make you more valuable and, hence, can result in higher pay and more job security. A mastery of the basics of design and an ability to implement them using Microsoft Publisher gives you a significant advantage over your coworkers.

- If you're an entrepreneur, a mastery of design and Microsoft Publisher can help you do a more effective job of promoting yourself, or you can become a valuable resource for your clients who—without you—cannot communicate as effectively.

- If you're looking for new challenges, you will find numerous opportunities at firms and associations of all sizes that need assistance communicating their message to their clients and supporters.

The ability to effectively communicate in print can take you in directions you might not even imagine.

The Tools of Design

Design involves placing and formatting four key elements: color, layout, type, and graphics. Everything you work on, from the simplest business card to complex catalogs and newsletters, is formatted by manipulating the four building blocks of design.

Color

Color is the most immediately noticeable design element. Your initial impression of a message, and the way you approach it, is based on the color of the paper it is printed on and the colors used for text and graphics. Color communicates emotions like urgency, attraction, or rejection. In general, the following associations are true:

Red Instantly communicates danger.

Blue Communicates tranquility.

Green Communicates optimism and the outdoors.

Gray Communicates conservativeness.

Yellow Communicates cheapness.

There are exceptions, of course, and color associations are often culturally biased. But it is vitally important that the dominant colors you choose for your messages are appropriate for the image you want to project.

The colors you select for your designs not only influence the emotional state with which your readers approach your message, colors can also communicate associations, such as different historical eras or different seasons of the year.

Layout

Layout, or the way text and graphics are placed on a page, is the second major way that your formatting decisions influence the utility and significance of your message.

Controlling the amount and placement of white space—the absence of text and graphics—is one of the most important ways layout impacts the effectiveness of your message. Publications with a lot of white space project a more attractive, easier-to-read image.

A comparison of two publications, one with narrow margins and the other with generous margins, illustrates the difference. One invites readership; the other looks uncomfortably cluttered and cramped.

ROGER C. PARKER'S
DESIGN to SELL
Using design as a strategic marketing tool

Make design your marketing partner

Everyday documents deserve as much attention as fancy ads, brochures, and newsletters

Your reputation is on the line every time you communicate with your market. Clients and prospects begin to judge you and your message before they even start reading! Within a second, irreversible "accept" or "reject" decisions are made solely on the basis of appearance.

If your designs don't *pre-sell the importance of your message,* or if your design projects a *hard-to-read image,* your message is likely to go unread.

Here are some tips to help you easily produce "everyday" publications that will simultaneously *sell the importance of your words* and *pre-sell your firm's competence.*

Headlines
Headlines play a major role in determining the success of your publication. If your headlines do not attract your reader's attention, or are hard to read, the rest of your message is likely to be ignored…and the your effort creating and distributing your message has been wasted!

Tips
• *Typeface.* Use a sans serif typeface like Arial, Helvetica, or Frutiger, or Gill Sans. When available, choose the *black* or *heavy* options, which are considerably darker than the bold version.

• *Case.* Avoid setting headlines entirely in upper case characters. Headlines set in upper-are harder to read than headlines set in both upper and lower case.

• *White space.* Draw attention to headlines by framing them with white space.

• *Line breaks.* Use line breaks (created by holding down the Shift key while pressing the Enter key) to equalize line lengths and break lines at logical points.

Subheads
Use subheads to maintain reader momentum. Add a short, keyword, subhead each time a new topic is introduced.

Avoid full sentences and two-line subheads. Limit subheads to short *keywords.* Format them using a smaller version of the same typeface used for headlines.

Never underline subheads. Instead, emphasize them by adding extra space above them, or set them in a second color.

Body copy
Use a serif typeface, like Times New Roman, Century, Minion, Stone Serif, or Palatino. The serifs guide your reader's eyes from character to character.

Line length. Avoid long lines of type extending from margin to margin. Shorter lines are easier to read.

Line spacing. In general, default, (or automatic), line spacing is too narrow. Adding extra line spacing, or *leading,* makes your lines much easier to read.

Make design your marketing partner

Everyday documents deserve as much attention as fancy ads, brochures, and newsletters

Prospects judge your competence by your marketing

Your reputation is on the line every time you communicate with your market. Clients and prospects begin to judge you and your message before they even start reading! Within a second, irreversible "accept" or "reject" decisions are made solely on the basis of appearance.

If your designs don't *pre-sell the importance of your message,* or if your design projects a *hard-to-read image,* your message is likely to go unread.

Here are some tips to help you easily produce "everyday" publications that will simultaneously *sell the importance of your words* and *pre-sell your firm's competence.*

Headlines
Headlines play a major role in determining the success of your publication. If your headlines do not attract your reader's attention, or are hard to read, the rest of your message is likely to be ignored...and the

your effort creating and distributing your message has been wasted!

Tips
• *Typeface.* Use a sans serif typeface like Arial, Helvetica, or Frutiger, or Gill Sans. When available, choose the *black* or *heavy* options, which are considerably darker than the bold version.

• *Case.* Avoid setting headlines entirely in upper case characters. Headlines set in upper-are harder to read than headlines set in both upper and lower case.

• *White space.* Draw attention to headlines by framing them with white space.

• *Line breaks.* Use line breaks (created by holding down the Shift key while pressing the Enter key) to equalize line lengths and break lines at logical points.

Subheads
Use subheads to maintain reader momentum. Add a short, keyword, subhead each time a new topic is introduced.

Avoid full sentences and two-line subheads. Limit subheads to short *keywords.* Format them using a smaller version of the same typeface used for headlines.

News, tips, and resources to increase sales while saving time and money
Issue 36

ROGER C. PARKER'S
DESIGN *to* SELL
Using design as a strategic marketing tool

© 2005
Roger C. Parker
Author, designer,
coach, consultant
www.designtosell.com
rcpcom@aol.com

In addition, the number and placement of text columns on the page influence line length. Long lines of type are hard to read. Long lines of type also make it easy for readers to get lost as they make the transition from the end of one line to the beginning of the next. Line length is reduced when two or more columns are placed on the page, aiding readership.

White space aids readability and projects an inviting, easy-to-read image.

Type

Chances are, a large percentage of your design time will involve typography—choosing the right typefaces and formatting the type as appropriately as possible.

Like color, type is immediately noticed and instantly communicates an image to readers that determines how they will approach your message. Type, like design in general, is never passive—it is always either with you or against you.

Your message's credibility drops when the formatting of your message is inconsistent with its content.

At best, inappropriate typeface choices add an element of ambiguity that causes your readers to approach your message with uncertainty. At worst, typeface choices immediately undermine your credibility and the impact of your words. Take a look at the difference between these two ads.

Choosing an appropriate typeface empowers your message.

As you become more comfortable working with type, you will be able to create text styles that can be shared between categories of publications—ads, brochures, newsletters, and so on. This saves you time and contributes to the creation of a unique visual image that differentiates your messages from those of your competitors.

Inappropriate text formatting makes paragraphs difficult to read.

Type formatting greatly influences the readability of your publications. Formatting decisions involving case, style, and line spacing, for example, can transform an unreadable paragraph into one that can be quickly and easily understood, as the following examples illustrate.

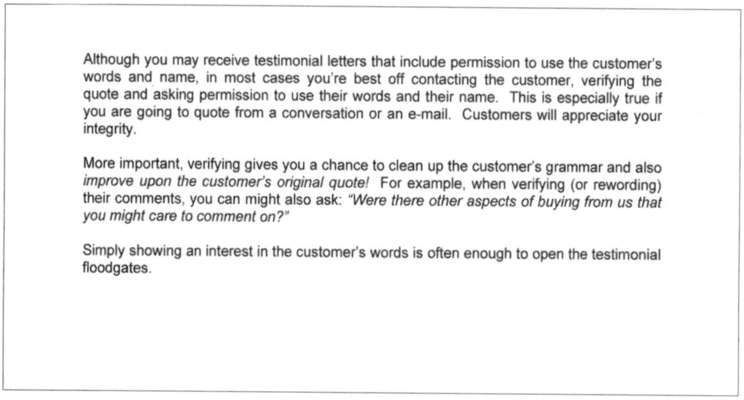

Although you may receive testimonial letters that include permission to use the customer's words and name, in most cases you're best off contacting the customer, verifying the quote and asking permission to use their words and their name. This is especially true if you are going to quote from a conversation or an e-mail. Customers will appreciate your integrity.

More important, verifying gives you a chance to clean up the customer's grammar and also *improve upon the customer's original quote!* For example, when verifying (or rewording) their comments, you can might also ask: *"Were there other aspects of buying from us that you might care to comment on?"*

Simply showing an interest in the customer's words is often enough to open the testimonial floodgates.

Figure 1-8   Text prior to proper type formatting is harder to read.

Although you may receive testimonial letters that include permission to use the customer's words and name, in most cases you're best off contacting the customer, verifying the quote and asking permission to use their words and their name. This is especially true if you are going to quote from a conversation or an e-mail. Customers will appreciate your integrity.

More important, verifying gives you a chance to clean up the customer's grammar and also *improve upon the customer's original quote!* For example, when verifying (or rewording) their comments, you can might also ask: *"Were there other aspects of buying from us that you might care to comment on?"*

Simply showing an interest in the customer's words is often enough to open the testimonial floodgates.

Figure 1-9 Text that has had type formatting properly applied becomes quickly and easily understood.

Graphics

Graphics refers to everything on a page *except* type. Examples of graphics include:

- Photographs
- Illustrations
- Cartoons
- Business graphics—for example, charts and graphs
- Tables—with information displayed in cells that are arranged in rows and columns
- Borders
- Backgrounds
- Rules—a graphics term for horizontal or vertical lines

All of these elements must be placed and resized on the page in a way that complements, rather than distracts from, the text of your message, which is usually set in paragraphs.

The size and position of your graphics must reflect their importance. Important photographs that communicate at a glance—setting a mood or reinforcing your words—should be larger and more noticeable than photographs that merely provide additional atmosphere or support.

Choosing a more appropriate typeface, adjusting line spacing and paragraph formatting, turning on hyphenation, and adding italics for emphasis makes the same words easier to read and understand without occupying more space.

Text wraps
interrupt message
comprehension by
forcing readers to
accommodate
changing line
lengths.

One of the big challenges you will face will be adding graphics to a page in a way that does not create text wraps. *Text wraps* occur when a graphic interrupts an adjacent text column, reducing line length. Text wraps force readers to readjust the number and speed of their left-to-right eye movements. This slows reading and prevents readers from focusing their entire attention on understanding and remembering your message. Figure 1-8 illustrates how a text wrap can interfere with the message in the adjacent columns.

Figure 1-10   A poorly conceived text wrap can interfere with the message in the surrounding text.

Summary

Today, it's not enough to be simply a competent writer. If you want your words to be easily read, remembered, and acted on, you have to be able to format them, creating attractive, easy-to-read pages.

Your messages must stand out among the thousands of marketing messages your readers encounter each day. Your words must attract your reader's attention and be as easy to read as possible. Otherwise, your words will probably go unread—as if you didn't write them at all!

In the following chapters, you'll look at the steps you can take to improve the communicating power of everything you create with Microsoft Publisher—and you'll probably discover many ideas that you can apply to Microsoft Word documents too!

In the next chapter, we'll look at how to plan your documents so that they'll be easier to create and more effective. From there, we review a number of surprisingly simple design concepts that you'll never outgrow; in subsequent chapters, you'll learn how to use Microsoft Publisher to apply these design concepts.

You're already well on your way to designing your future!

Test Yourself

Before beginning the next chapter, take a break and review the important ideas communicated so far.

Go to page for this chapter on the companion Web site for the book (www.designtosellonline.com/01chap.html). There you'll find:

- A self-scoring assessment. You'll download and print a sample newsletter and worksheet, and then identify as many mistakes as you can. This example is also a great makeover project that you can show prospective clients and potential employers.

Additional bonus materials and Web features will be frequently added to the Web site.

Chapter Two

Planning Your Way to Design Success

What you'll find:

❏ Learn the importance of planning.

❏ Discover the six criteria of effective design.

❏ Learn how good design balances creativity and achieving objectives.

❏ Learn how to work with Project Planning Worksheets.

❏ Find out how printing options influence design decisions.

Planning is a necessity for effective and efficient design. Planning involves making decisions to achieve desired outcomes, based on available resources. A commitment to planning is, ultimately, more important than any preexisting "talent" or "creativity" you might—or might not—possess.

Planning eliminates subjectivity as a design criterion and replaces it with marketing effectiveness. Design success is not based on color, paper, or typeface choices decided in isolation as much as it's evaluated on the basis of results. The question used to evaluate design is always: "Does the design attract my market's attention, reinforce my message, and differentiate me from my competition—all at the most appropriate cost?"

> Does the design attract my market's attention, reinforce my message, and differentiate me from my competition—at the appropriate cost?

In this respect, design is not different from any other human activity. Take a look at anyone who has achieved great success in business, politics, or personal development, and you'll discover that planning is the common thread. As Pablo Picasso, one of the forefathers of modern art in the twentieth century, wrote:

> *Our goals can only be reached through a vehicle of a plan, in which we must fervently believe, and upon which we must vigorously act. There is no other route to success.*
>
> — *Pablo Picasso, quoted in J. Pincott, Success: Advice for Achieving Your Goals from Remarkably Accomplished People (Random House Reference, 2005)*

Luck often seems to play a role by presenting a critical opportunity, but if you look closely, you'll find that those who routinely take advantage of the opportunities that luck presents have generally prepared for luck in advance—by planning!

The Six Criteria of Effective Design

Effective design always aims to satisfy six criteria. Basing your design on these criteria helps you replace subjectivity and uncertainty with appropriateness backed up by confidence. By carefully analyzing each of your projects before you begin working, you gain a laser-like focus that will unerringly guide you through the decision-making process that constitutes graphic design and production.

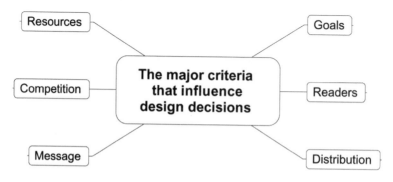

1. Goals

Six criteria guide every design decision you make.

Start by identifying the goals of each project. This can begin with a simple question like, "What is the purpose of the project you are working on?" Involve your coworkers and your boss or client in answering this question. The more time you spend addressing this question, the more details you're likely to uncover.

The following are some other goal-oriented questions, along with their design implications:

What is the desired action you want your client or prospect to take?   Be as specific as possible in your answer. This answer will help you come up with, and emphasize, the appropriate call to action.

The more time you spend addressing project goals, the more details you're likely to uncover.

How can readers—that is, your customers and prospects—take the action you want them to take?   If the action is ordering something by mail, you should include a large, easy-to-fill-out order form. If you want readers to call you or visit your Web site, you should emphasize the Web address. If you want readers to visit a specific location, you should include a map, directions, and hours.

What obstacles stand in the way of achieving your goal?   What are the reasons your market has not yet taken the action you want it to take? If you're introducing a new product, you'll want to emphasize new features and benefits. If you're describing benefits, you might want to include before-and-after illustrations or graphics.

2. Readership

Planning for your readers begins by identifying them, their expectations, their objectives, and their likely objections. Planning also involves recognizing that readers are always in a hurry, and are never as interested in your message as you are.

Key Reader Questions

Here are some of the key questions you should ask, and the implications of the answers:

What are your reader's image expectations?   The overall image of your publication should be consistent with reader expectations. Are your readers more likely to respond to something that looks cheap or expensive, traditional or contemporary, friendly or professional? Once you know your readers' image expectations, you can create an appropriate image using color, layout, type, and graphics.

How interested are readers likely to be in your message?   You need to know this, because the lower the readers' interest, the harder your publication has to work to attract their attention and retain their interest.

How old are your readers?   Eyesight declines with age. If you're writing for an older audience, you'll probably want to use a larger type size than if you're designing for younger readers.

> Readers are never as interested in your message as you are!

3. Message

Next consider your message. It's important to analyze your message in terms of content and hierarchy. The starting point is to inventory the text and graphical elements that make up your message.

Message Elements

Message elements include:

Word count   What is the length of the word-processed copy?

Reader clues   Are there many headlines and subheads to be accommodated?

Text elements   How long are most sentences and paragraphs?

Visuals   What types of visuals must be accommodated—photographs, illustrations, cut-away drawings, charts and graphs, tables, lists, business graphics (timelines, organization charts, flow charts, and so on)?

Message Goals

The importance of an idea should be reflected in the way the words or graphics communicating it appear in your publication. Important ideas should be significantly more noticeable than lesser ideas. This requires analyzing message goals and the arguments used to support them. Here are some of the questions you should ask and their design implications:

What is the "big idea" you want to communicate? Knowing the big idea behind your message will help you identify what to emphasize using text and graphics.

What points are of key importance, and which simply provide supporting information?   Selective emphasis is impossible unless you can identify the key points—or arguments—in favor of the action you want readers to take. Critical text and graphical elements must be larger and more prominent than elements of lesser importance.

Designing with a Yellow Highlighter

One of the best aids to design is a yellow highlighter. Use the highlighter to mark up a printed version of the text that makes up your message as follows:

Draw a line between paragraphs when one topic ends and another begins.   This helps you identify where to insert subheads.

Highlight key words and phrases the first time they appear.   This helps you identify which words should be inserted as subheads.

Highlight key sentences.   These can become pull-quotes that summarize important ideas on each page.

Draw a box around ideas that go into detail on specific topics.   This helps identify where you should format text as sidebars so that the information doesn't detract from the overall momentum of your message.

4. Competition

Your message must be visually distinct from the messages of your competitors. This means that one of the first things you should do is simultaneously take an inventory of design elements used by your firm as well as your competitors.

One technique that usually works well is to hang samples of your firm's marketing materials, as well as examples of your competitors' marketing materials, on the walls of your conference room or in the hallways of your firm. Organize the examples into categories so that you can compare ads to ads, brochures to brochures, and newsletters to newsletters. This is called a *design assessment*. This exercise helps you focus on the trends of your marketing rather than specific projects.

Focus on the
trends of your
marketing, rather
than specific
projects.

Invite your coworkers, boss, and clients to comment on what they see. To stimulate communication, ask questions like:

What are the strongest and weakest points of our marketing designs? Helps you identify strong areas that can remain the same and also identify weak areas needing immediate attention.

What are the key design characteristics of our designs? Identifies the key color, layout, text, and graphical elements that make your designs unique. If you can't identify any key elements that set your designs apart, chances are your market can't either!

How consistent are we in working with these characteristics? Determines the consistency of your designs. If six of your marketing messages reflect six different sets of design elements, chances are your marketing materials are not projecting a distinct and memorable image.

What are the strongest characteristics of our competitors' marketing designs? Identifies key elements of your competitors' designs and answers the questions "What are they doing right?" and "What are they doing wrong?" This will help you identify the specific design characteristics you must change to project a more effective image.

5. Distribution

The design of your message will be influenced by its distribution. Two key distribution questions must be answered as early as possible:

How are you going to distribute your marketing messages? Will your marketing messages appear in other publications (like magazines or newspapers) or will they be handed out, displayed in brochure racks, mailed through the postal service, or distributed electronically from your Web site or as e-mail attachments? If you're going to mail your message, will your message be a self-mailer or inserted in an envelope?

How many copies are you going to distribute? The quantity to be printed might play a major role in determining the appropriate project quality level. If resources are tight, for example, you might have to adjust your design so that you can afford to print the required number of copies. You might also have to make changes in paper choice, publication size, and the number of colors to be used.

The many issues involved in printing your message—a key element in its distribution—are so important that they are considered separately, in the section "Planning, Quantities, and Printing," later in this chapter.

6. Resources

Few designers—even those who work for Fortune 500 firms—enjoy unlimited budget and time resources. Firms large and small around the world are under increasing owner and stockholder pressure to "do more with less." Marketing managers at firms of all sizes must justify every dime of printing and distribution costs.

Using heavy, reflective paper stocks, fancy shapes and folds, and extensive custom photography must all be justified in the name of increased marketing effectiveness, or you must choose less-expensive alternatives.

Time too is usually a scarce resource. Faster product introductions and shorter life cycles mean that marketing messages have to be created on a production-line basis—just as you create the products themselves.

Additional concerns you should routinely address before beginning work on your publication include the following:

What is the anticipated budget for this project?   As a designer, it's important to begin with an understanding of the size of the budget resources available. It doesn't make sense to come up with a "champagne" design if your boss or client is limited to a "beer" budget.

What is the street date of the project?   The *street date* refers to the date clients and prospects will encounter the message, in their mailbox or elsewhere. It's important to know how much time is available for a project so that you don't include time-consuming design elements (like custom photography and extra printing steps, such as die-cuts or varnish) that cannot be comfortably accommodated.

Design as Balance

As the preceding overview of the six criteria illustrates, effective design is often more a result of balance than creative self-expression or design excess.

Your designs will improve to the extent that they are based on goals, readership, message, competition, distribution, and resources. A failure to address these issues leads to subjective, "creative" design unrelated to the tasks that the marketing message must achieve. Likewise, placing too much emphasis on some while failing to fully acknowledge others also leads to designs that fail to achieve their goals.

The primacy of *planning* and *balance* should come as good news to those who have always considered design as purely a creative or an intuitive task. Design, in terms of creating marketing materials that achieve their goals, is within reach of all who are willing to plan and master the appropriate techniques and tools.

The Role of Creativity

This is not to say that creativity does not have a place in design. Creativity does play a major role in design, one that you will probably take great pleasure and satisfaction in utilizing.

The appropriate place for creativity is in trying out different arrangements of text and graphics, to come up with an arrangement that satisfies—in a balanced way—the six criteria.

Creativity and Design

Design is a series of compromises and tradeoffs. As a designer, you constantly manipulate text and graphics to strike a balance, or achieve a harmony, between:

- Type size and the number of words on a page.
- The number and size of graphics images and the number of words on a page.
- Using color in printing and the number of copies you can print.

Creative breakthroughs will occur to the extent that you're willing to try out different ways to satisfy your own, your boss's, or your client's marketing goals.

You'll also need to develop creative ways to convince bosses and clients that your decisions are sound ones—even if they don't fully understand the rationale behind your decisions. You'll need to develop the ability to defend your layout, color, typeface, and graphics choices to those who make statements like, "All typefaces look the same."

Obtaining Agreement on Project Goals

One of the best ways to garner support for your design decisions is to involve coworkers, bosses, and clients in the planning process. The easiest way to do this is to fill out a Project Planning Worksheet in their presence. By including clients and coworkers in the planning process, you're ensuring their "buy-in," which will eliminate potential problems later.

Distribute copies of the Project Planning Worksheet shown in Figure 2-1. (You can download copies for distribution from the Design to Sell Web site, at www.designtosellonline.com/02chap.html.)

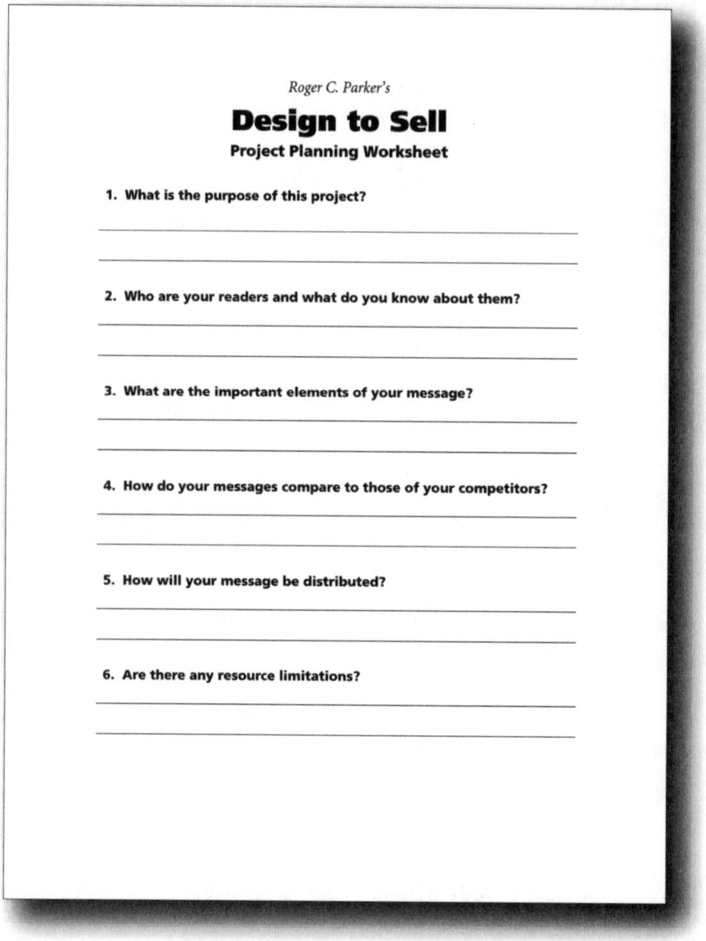

Roger C. Parker's
Design to Sell
Project Planning Worksheet

1. What is the purpose of this project?

_____

_____

2. Who are your readers and what do you know about them?

_____

_____

3. What are the important elements of your message?

_____

_____

4. How do your messages compare to those of your competitors?

_____

_____

5. How will your message be distributed?

_____

_____

6. Are there any resource limitations?

_____

_____

Figure 2-1   Encourage coworkers, bosses, and clients to help you fill out a
Project Planning Worksheet before you begin work on any project.

You can go a step further and encourage coworkers, bosses, and clients to initial the
completed Project Planner Worksheet, signifying their agreement on project goals.

Planning, Quantities, and Printing

Many of the projects you will be working on are intended for quantity distribution.
Because printing costs often represent the largest expense in a marketing project, it is
important to fully understand the advantages, disadvantages, and costs of the different
printing options available.

Printing options can be categorized in terms of the quantities that can be efficiently produced, the speed of production, the quality of the printed pieces, and the number of options available.

Small-Quantity Printing

One of the most exciting trends in the past decade has been the proliferation of color desktop printers for home and office use. Color ink-jet and color laser printers are no longer luxuries; they are available at surprisingly low "commodity" prices.

Advantages

These low prices are associated with quality output. In many cases, sub-$100 printers can do a very credible job of printing color flyers and newsletters. And often, two-sided printing is possible—either by reinserting the paper or by using the printer's duplexing feature.

Concerns

The key to taking advantage of desktop printers is to understand their two biggest limitations: printing time and supply costs.

Time   Even with printer spooling software, which manages print jobs and frees your computer to do other things, printing multiple copies of your marketing materials might tie up your computer and printer for longer than you would like. In addition, you might have to stay relatively close to the printer so that you can keep the paper tray filled and clear an occasional paper jam.

Costs   If your marketing materials contain large, detailed graphics such as four-color photographs, you might find that you have to frequently replace the ink cartridges or toner and that per-page printing costs are much higher than you would like. Many printers are sold at a loss, with the profits coming from sales of supplies.

Durability is another issue to consider. Marketing materials printed with ink-jet printers are very vulnerable to water. They should not be mailed without an envelope. Moisture from damp hands can damage papers printed by some printers.

Avoid large areas of color, like colored backgrounds. These can really increase your printing costs. Reverses—white text against a colored background—can also cause quality problems, as the text might not be as sharp as desired for easy reading. In addition, some printers might not be able to print *bleeds*—text and graphical elements that extend to the edges of a page.

Suggested Applications

If you are distributing the bulk of your newsletters or flyers electronically, as e-mail attachments or Web site downloads, it makes sense to use your desktop printer to produce copies for mailing to key clients or handing to key prospects when you meet them or submit a proposal.

When quantities grow beyond 25 copies, or the page count of individual projects increases, you might want to explore other options.

Print on Demand for Moderate-Quantity Distribution

Digital print on demand is a relatively new technology offered by copy centers, office supply stores, and progressive commercial printers (in addition to their traditional ink-based printing). In some ways an outgrowth of the merger of personal computers and office photocopiers, print on demand suppliers use digital printing to efficiently produce high-quality black-and-white or color copies in moderate quantities.

Advantages

Digital print on demand makes color affordable in quantities greater than what you can efficiently create on your desktop printer but smaller than can be efficiently printed by commercial ink—or offset—printers. Advantages include:

No minimum quantities   If you need just eight color copies, you can get just eight copies, without paying a premium.

Durable   Digital print on demand materials are less susceptible to moisture damage than items created using ink-jet printing, which are often more prone to smearing.

Fast and easy   Files can be submitted to a print on demand supplier through the Internet, and same-day or next-day delivery is usually available in major cities.

Quality   Color saturation and text sharpness is usually better than all but the best desktop printers.

Binding   A variety of binding options are usually available.

Concerns

Although digital print on demand is a breakthrough technology, there are some limitations you should be aware of:

No discount for quantity.   Unlike conventional offset printing, where the cost-per-unit declines as the number printed increases, digital print on demand pricing is uniform. The first and the fiftieth copy you print will probably cost the same.

Don't be misled by low per-copy prices.   Be sure to inquire about project setup fees.

No changes.   Unlike commercial printers, who can optimize files on the press to achieve the best quality, digital print on demand suppliers rarely make changes to your files.

Limitations.   Bleeds—where colors extend to the edge of the paper—are not possible. Die-cuts and special folds are usually not appropriate.

Suggested Applications

Digital print on demand is ideal for quantities of several hundred copies. Beyond that, offset printing might make more sense.

Because there are no minimums or quantity discounts, you can print only as many copies as needed, and if necessary, you can print more copies later.

An example of the proper use of digital print on demand is printing 50 or 100 copies of a monthly newsletter that is primarily distributed electronically over the Internet. Even if most of the copies are downloaded from your Web site or sent as e-mail attachments, you should always have enough copies on hand to take to networking events; send to key clients, business editors, and writers; and include with new business proposals.

Digital print on demand is also appropriate for corporate marketing and sales managers who want to distribute promotional information and educational materials for their sales staffs.

Offset Printing for Quality and Quantity

Commercial printing has traditionally been ink-based. Instead of spraying tiny droplets of ink on a page, like color desktop printers, commercial printers use an offset process involving two cylinders. One cylinder holds a *plate*—or negative—of the text and graphics images to be applied to the paper. Ink adheres to the exposed portion of this plate, is passed on to the second cylinder, and is then transferred to the paper.

Offset printing offers significant quality advantages, in terms of both color sharpness and saturation, as well as the ability to print on a broader range of paper stocks. Offset printing makes most sense for quantities beyond 1,000 copies, making this the best option for point-of-sale brochures and marketing materials distributed at conventions and trade shows.

Advantages

Unlike the relatively fixed prices of digital print on demand, the cost per copy for offset printing drops as the quantity printed goes up. Prices per copy drop at quantities such as 2,500 copies or 5,000 copies, and continue to fall at each additional 1,000 copies.

During the *prepress* stage, when files are prepared, offset printers can make major quality improvements. They can selectively lighten or darken images, control ink coverage, and adjust points where different color inks touch or overlap. (Where two inks meet, a slight overlap is necessary to avoid the possibility of a gap appearing between the two inks. Yet the inks should not overlap too much, or they will mix and create a distracting third color.)

There is basically no limitation to the printing quality possible. Offset printers usually have access to a far broader range of paper stocks and can easily accommodate options like varnishing (to emphasize photographs or headlines) or special die-cuts and folds.

Offset printing can include one, two, three, or four—or even more—ink colors. Two-color printing can be very effective while saving significant amounts of money. *Tints*—solid colors printed at less than full saturation—can create lighter shades of black or any other color, adding considerable design flexibility.

With four-color printing, your publication can include color photographs as well as all the colors in the rainbow. You can also add a fifth color, to precisely match a color used as a critical part of your firm's corporate identity, such as a logo or trademark.

Concerns

Offset printers differ in capabilities and specialties. Some specialize in offering the lowest possible prices, others take the high road and focus on quality and customer satisfaction. It's important that you shop around and locate a printer that wants your business and is used to dealing with clients like you.

Be sure to check out the "Standard Printers Terms" in your area. These differ from place to place. They usually allow printers to print—and charge for—more than the agreed-upon quantity. In some cases, the final quantity delivered can differ by 10 or 15 percent from the original order. If the delivered quantity is less than the desired quantity, the invoice will be smaller than the estimate. But if the delivered quantity is greater than anticipated, the printer can charge for the extra copies. The final quantity delivered often depends on the amount of paper wasted during press setup and during printing.

Always get all costs in writing, including file preparation and delivery charges.

When dealing with offset printers, it's important to provide all of the files necessary to print your project, including the graphics files (that is, photographs and illustrations) and the fonts used in your publication.

Prices differ greatly from printer to printer, even within a short time period, depending on how busy the printers are. Make sure that you can complete your project so that it can be printed when scheduled, or you might end up paying more if your project falls into a busier time.

Additional Considerations

Some design decisions can increase offset printing costs. Areas of heavy ink coverage, such as a large colored background, for example, can increase costs, as more ink is used and more care has to be taken to ensure smooth ink coverage.

Bleeds also can increase printing costs, because they often require the use of oversize sheets of paper that must be trimmed to final size after printing. Other techniques include using a varnish finish to add shine to a photograph or a matte finish to add depth and texture to a background.

Other choices include special cover stocks, special binding, die-cuts (where part of one page is cut out to allow you to see the next page, for example), and folds. These options are in addition to the ability to utilize a virtually endless selection of paper sizes, textures, thickness, opacity (which refers to the ability to see what's printed on the other side of a sheet of paper), and reflectivity.

Summary

Design is not a subjective activity. Design success can be objectively measured by how effectively it balances project goals, reader needs, message, competition, distribution, and resources.

Designers must identify priorities and achieve a workable balance that results in printing the necessary number of copies at the highest possible quality level, on time, and at the lowest possible cost.

To achieve this, tradeoffs are necessary—for example, three-color printing might need to be cut back to two-color printing to add pages required by the use of a larger type size or wider margins.

Creativity comes from the designer's willingness to come up with a project plan that identifies the important criteria, the design choices, and production tasks described throughout this book.

In the next chapter, we'll examine the secrets of design "magic," as well as the building blocks of attractive, easy-to-read marketing messages.

Test Yourself

Before moving on to Chapter 3, take a few moments to review the important ideas in this chapter.

Visit this book's companion Web site, www.designtosellonline.com/02chap.html, and locate the Chapter 2 bonus materials. Here you can:

- Download printable copies of the Project Planning Worksheet.
- Use a self-scoring assessment to find out how comfortable you are with the six criteria, and the pros and cons of the various printing alternatives.
- Test your memory by defining the key words introduced in this chapter.

Chapter Three
Principles of Design Success

What you'll find:

❑ The eight principles of effective design.

❑ The building blocks of page architecture.

❑ The origins of design success.

Microsoft Office Publisher provides you with a cost-effective and efficient way to create inviting, easy-to-read marketing messages. Even if you have not had previous desktop publishing or design experience, you'll find that Publisher makes it easy for you to manipulate layout, color, text, and graphics in ways that increase the effectiveness of your message.

Later on, in Part Two, you'll learn how to use Publisher to support your design and marketing goals. But before you can move on, you must identify the design goals—or results—that you want to achieve. You have to understand the elements of successful design before you can create successful designs! In this chapter, you'll gain the design background you need for success.

The Eight Principles of Effective Design

It is, of course, impossible to reduce effective design to a series of strict rules or equations such as "If you're working with 12-point type, use 14 points of line spacing." However, it is possible to identify eight principles that characterize attractive, reader-friendly design. Familiarity with the following principles won't guarantee the success of your designs, but understanding them will definitely help you make better-informed decisions as you use Microsoft Publisher to multiply the effectiveness of your marketing messages.

> You have to understand the elements of successful design before you can create successful designs!

Note It is not necessary for you to memorize the information on the following pages. Simply reading through these principles will provide you with a framework of design ideas that will be fleshed out in greater detail as we analyze Publisher capabilities and look at specific projects.

---

1. Readership Is Never Guaranteed

Incorporating these eight principles into a design strategy doesn't guarantee that your designs will succeed, but ignoring them is almost certain to result in easily ignored marketing materials!

Never assume that your message will be read just because you designed it, printed it, addressed it, and mailed it. Readership is a reward, not an entitlement. You have to struggle to attract readers, and you have to struggle to keep them. Readers are always in a hurry, and alternatives to your message are all around them.

There are several guidelines you can use to attract and maintain your readers' attention:

Start with headlines and titles that "sell" the message that follows. For headlines to sell, they must be easily noticed and easily read. In longer documents, headlines must be consistently formatted so that readers can identify them at a glance.

Just because you designed, printed, addressed, and mailed your message doesn't mean that clients and prospects are going to read it!

Text must be formatted for easy recognition. Reading is based on *serial pattern recognition* (SRP). Readers do not decipher and "sound out" the characters that make up each word. Instead, they scan groups of several words and translate the word shapes into concepts and meaning, as shown in Figure 3-1, which is adapted from "The Magic of Reading," by Bill Hill, Microsoft Corporation. Anything you can do to make the word shapes of your message easier to recognize will reward you with increased readership.

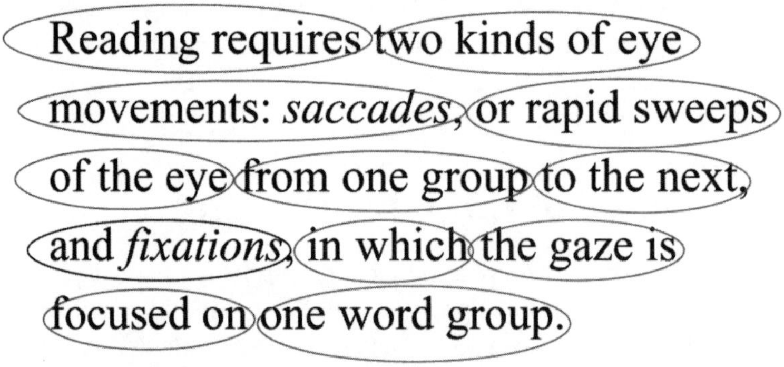
Reading requires two kinds of eye
movements: saccades, or rapid sweeps
of the eye from one group to the next,
and fixations, in which the gaze is
focused on one word group.

Figure 3-1 Western readers don't stare at individual words. Instead, their eyes continuously move from left to right, scanning several words at a time.

Readers are always in a hurry, and alternatives to your message are all around them.

Serial pattern recognition has numerous implications. Among these are the importance of avoiding setting headlines entirely in uppercase type and the importance of choosing the appropriate typefaces and line spacing.

2. Slice and Dice for Success

One of the best ways to increase readership is to "chunk" your content. This involves breaking long messages into a series of easier-to-read, bite-size elements.

Subheads ("mini-headlines" that introduce new topics) and *sidebars* (short text elements that elaborate on specific aspects of longer adjacent messages) help add visual interest to your pages as well as make long messages easier to read.

An unbroken string of twelve paragraphs presents readers with a daunting challenge. The same content appears much easier to read when it is broken into three 4-paragraph segments, each introduced by a subhead that summarizes the topic or importance of the paragraphs that follow.

3. Less Is Always More

Simplicity is one of the most important design tools available to you. Simplicity reveals; clutter confuses and hides. There are many causes of clutter, including:

Excessive text formatting   This can take the form of too many typefaces, too many changes in type size, too many type style variations (for example, overuse of bold and italics), and inconsistent line spacing.

Too many graphical accents   Appropriately used, borders and backgrounds can enhance parts of your message by drawing your reader's eyes to them and separating them from their surroundings. But overuse of graphical accents simply adds clutter.

Overuse of color   The overuse of color—too many colors or large areas of bright color—can distract from, rather than enhance, your message. A few carefully chosen colors, applied with restraint, can do far more to clarify your message and project a distinct image, or "look."

Too many text and graphical elements   Clutter can also result from trying to shoehorn too many text and graphical elements on a page. Reducing the number of page elements, as shown in Figure 3-2, allows those that remain to attract more attention.

Simplicity reveals; clutter confuses.

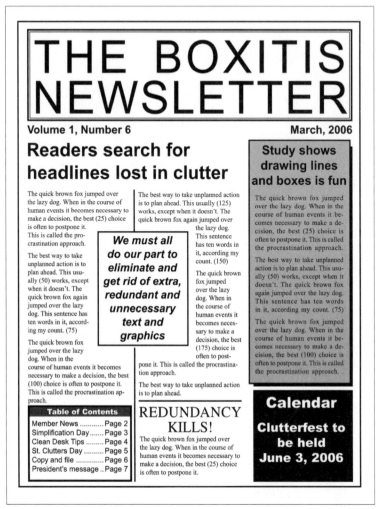

Figure 3-2 A recipe for disaster: too many typefaces, too many fills, too many borders, too many lines—and not enough editing of unnecessary words.

4. Consistency Builds Comfort

Changes in page structure from one page to the next usually result in lost readers. Because reading is based on the reader's unconscious, rhythmic, left-to-right eye movements, change interrupts continued reading.

The primary implication of this is that the structure of your pages should remain consistent throughout your document. If the first few pages of your message use a two-column structure, don't change to a three-column layout for page 4 and then switch to a one-column layout for page 5. The number of columns on a page influences line length, so each change requires readers to readjust their eye movements as they scan from left to right.

Consistency is also important because it creates a repeating background against which contrast can be used to provide selective emphasis. One large photograph, bled to the edges of a page and following a series of pages with relatively small photographs, instantly communicates "important!" But if large photographs are used on every page, size alone fails to communicate.

Finally, consistency creates familiarity, which presells the success of future messages from you. If prospects have enjoyed and learned from your previous messages, when they recognize something new from you, they are likely to immediately begin reading it. Figure 3-3 shows an example of a series of newsletters that reflect a strong family resemblance to each other.

Consistency creates familiarity, which presells the importance of your future messages.

Figure 3-3   The use of consistent layout, colors, type, and visuals over a period of several years immediately communicates that each issue of the newsletter is part of a welcome series.

5. Change Must Be Significant

Change, in terms of formatting or size, must be significant enough to appear purposeful rather than accidental. The implications for this include:

Typeface choices   Avoid using two serif typefaces or two sans serif typefaces in a single project. Readers are likely to notice that "something is different," even if they can't pinpoint the exact change, but because differences within typeface categories are usually subtle, they'll suspect a formatting error rather than an attempt to add clarity through contrast.

Alignment   Your reader's eyes are surprisingly sensitive to tiny changes in alignment. When text and graphical elements are improperly aligned with each other, they project a haphazard image that undermines the effectiveness of your message. The best results are usually achieved by aligning text and graphical elements with the underlining grid structure.

6. Visuals Illuminate Content

Words in paragraphs are often not enough to help readers make sense of details or appreciate comparison, hierarchy, or sequence. That's where tables, charts and graphs, triads, and timelines come in. They emphasize meaning by converting textual and numeric information to easily understood visuals, as shown in Figure 3-4.

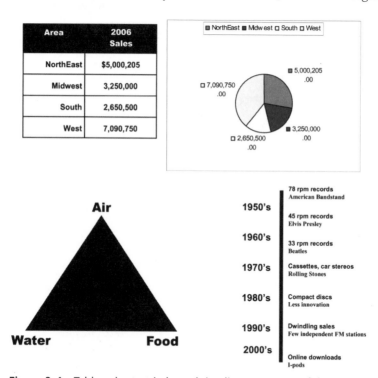

Figure 3-4   Tables, charts, triads, and timelines are some of the ways you can translate numbers into easily understood comparisons.

Tables   Make it easy for readers to analyze and compare detailed information.

Pie charts   Facilitate comparisons.

Triads   Emphasize three elements of equal importance.

Timelines   Place events in the correct sequence, in the context of other current events.

Whenever possible, try to replace textual information with visuals communicating the information.

7. Details Count

Your readers are constantly searching for clues that will either enhance or detract from your message.

If your words are accompanied by amateurish design, readers will discount the importance of those words. But if your designs project pride and professionalism, readers will approach your words presold on their value. Professionalism can be communicated by techniques as simple as striving for consistent spacing between text and graphical elements and eliminating unwanted spacing within paragraphs.

Always make sure that headlines and subheads are consistently spaced away from adjacent text elements. Likewise, make sure that captions appear a consistent distance from photographs and adjacent text.

If you, or someone you're designing for, unconsciously adds two spaces after each period—a holdover from the typewriter era—your columns will contain awkward gaps between sentences. Eliminating these gaps ensures consistent spacing and prevents gaps between sentences from unintentionally aligning, creating distracting "rivers" of white space.

8. Contrast Clarifies Content

Selective emphasis is one of the most powerful design tools available to you. Selective emphasis is the result of making some words, sentences, or graphical images more noticeable than others by setting them in a different typeface, a larger typeface, or a bolder typeface or by using color to set them apart from other words,

The information hierarchy of your publication should guide your design. If a text or graphical element communicates something important, that element should be large and more easily noticed than others. If the element merely provides supporting arguments or details, it should be smaller.

Examining the Contrast Tools

The following sections describe the contrast tools that you can use to communicate selective emphasis. Figure 3-5 shows the contrast tools at work.

Contrast at Work

Typeface

Size

CASE, CASE

style, *style, style*

Weight, weight

Background **Background**

Color

Position

♦ **Graphic accents**

Figure 3-5   The contrast tools at work.

Typeface   Using shape is one of the easiest ways to put contrast to work. You can put shape to work by combining sans serif headlines and subheads with a serif body copy. The distinct differences between serif and sans serif type visually signifies "something different" to your readers. Notice that the tiny strokes at the edges of each serif character are not present in the sans serif characters. Another difference is that while the strokes that make up each sans serif typeface character are of equal thickness, the width of the strokes making up each serif typeface character typically change from thick to thin.

Size   Text size should be consistent with importance. Headlines should be larger than subheads, and subheads should be larger than body copy. Likewise, important photographs should be larger than unimportant photographs. At a glance, readers should be able to immediately identify what's important.

Case   The judicious use of uppercase type can add emphasis. Uppercase type must be used with discretion, as discussed in "Formatting Headlines," in Chapter 7.

The use of small caps is another way to add selective emphasis. Small caps are uppercase characters scaled to a smaller size. Small caps take up less space than words set entirely in uppercase. They also permit you to clarify meaning by capitalizing the first letter of a sentence, as well as the first letter of proper nouns, which is not possible when heads and subheads are set entirely in uppercase type. The advantage of small caps is that the *descenders*, or parts of a character that extend below the line of type, are omitted. This permits tighter line spacing, which is useful in headlines, logos, and publication titles.

Style   Use text style options, like bold, italics, and bold-italics, to provide contrast within sentences, helping readers quickly identify important words, phrases, and titles.

If a text or graphical element communicates something important, it should be large and easily noticed.

Never use underlining to provide text emphasis. Underlining makes words harder to read, instead of easier to notice! Readers can also confuse underlined words with text links.

Weight   Many sans serif typefaces contain alternative versions. Heavier weights, as well as lighter weights, are often available. These weight variations permit you to "voice" your headlines and titles with precisely the right amount of emphasis.

Background   One of the most powerful ways to add selective emphasis to a page is to enhance the contrast between text and its background. There are two ways to modify foreground/background contrast:

Fills   Place backgrounds behind important text and graphical elements. Fills can be used to emphasize and separate instructions, warnings, or sidebars.

Reverses   Place white text against a black background; an extreme use of fills. *Screens* and *tints* are created when text is placed against background shades of gray.

Color   Color is a powerful way to add selective emphasis to important text and graphical elements. Headlines and subheads set in a contrasting color help readers immediately identify these important visual clues. Setting text hyperlinks in an alternative color also helps them stand out from the other words.

Position   Varying margins and alignment is another way to create selective emphasis in headlines, subheads, and quotations. One of the best ways to emphasize headlines, for example, is to place them in a deep *sink*, or area of white space, above the text columns.

Hanging headlines and subheads draw attention because they begin to the left of the text column. Block quotations, on the other hand, are often indented on both the right and the left.

Photographs are usually aligned with the text columns. However, when you have an important photograph that you want to emphasize, have it extend beyond the text columns, all the way to the edge of the page. This is called a *bleed*.

Graphical Accents   Graphical accents include rules and special characters:

Rules   A fancy name for "lines." Can be used to add borders around important text elements and separate topics from each other. In multicolumn publications, *intercolumn rules* prevent readers from jumping from the end of a line in the first column to the beginning of the line in the next column.

Special characters   Include bullets and symbols used to indicate the end of an article.

Spacing   Spacing is an extreme form of contrast that converts characters from words to symbols, like logos or product packaging intended to be recognized more than "scanned and read." Many logos and titles on book covers illustrate the power of exaggerated or reduced letter spacing. Extra spacing can also be used to draw attention to sections or headings used to organize the contents of a long document.

Using Multiple Forms of Contrast

The various forms of contrast are often used together, although you have to exercise restraint and avoid "contrast overkill." Your goal is to add just enough selective emphasis, without creating visual clutter. And you want to be sure to apply the same contrast tools throughout your projects so that readers will instantly recognize and understand the degree of emphasis you want to apply.

Lists, for example, combine position and graphical accent contrast, often enhanced by the use of style to emphasize the keywords in the list.

Contrast, of course, adds more than selective emphasis. The appropriate use of these contrast tools adds visual interest to your pages, helping them attract more readers and maintaining readers' interest as they encounter each new page.

Test Your Ability to Identify Contrast at Work

How many forms of contrast are used in Figure 3-6? List them on a sheet of paper.

Figure 3-6   How many forms of contrast can you identify in this example? What are they?

To find the answers, visit www.designtosellonline.com/03chap.htm.

Building Blocks of Page Architecture

Design involves consistently formatting the building blocks of your marketing messages. The following sections describe the key building blocks that you'll be working with in later chapters.

White Space

White space—that is, the absence of text and graphics—is important. White space at the margins of your pages frames your message and isolates it from competing messages. White space also provides room for your readers' fingers to hold your publication.

A great deal of your design success working with headlines involves eliminating unwanted white space from *inside* the headlines—primarily line and character spacing— and replacing it with white space *around* the headlines. Often a smaller headline, with adequate white space around it, will be far easier to notice and read than a larger headline without a "halo" of white space to emphasize it.

Likewise, visuals such as photographs benefit from appropriate white space.

Headlines, Titles, and Logos

Headlines and titles are crucial to the success of your marketing materials. Each has its own formatting requirements—based on different readability needs:

Headlines succeed or fail on the basis of readability as well as "noticeability."   Headlines must be prominent enough to attract attention, but they must be also be recognizable and readable at a glance.

Titles are a bit less critical.   Once read, it's enough for most titles to be simply recognized. This gives you more flexibility for using highly stylized typefaces for book and newsletter titles. Each month, your readers will glance at the title and then move on to spend more time with the headlines.

Logos can be even more stylized.   Logos, such as the way the name of your business appears as a graphic, are an extreme case of text that is recognized more than "read." Letter spacing and character distortions that would torpedo a headline's effectiveness are acceptable in logos.

Subheads

Subheads are critical design elements that provide busy readers with a way to quickly scan the contents of a page and—perhaps—begin reading in the middle when something attracts their interest and then return to the top of the page to pay more attention.

Subheads need contrast with the adjacent body copy to be noticed but, for consistency, should use a typeface similar to that used for headlines.

Body Copy

The bulk of your message is likely to appear in columns of paragraphs. The design of these paragraphs must be as "transparent" and easy-to-read as possible. Anything that interrupts or distracts your reader's rhythmic left-to-right eye movements can cause the loss of your reader's attention—and the failure of your message.

Typeface and type size are only the beginning of the formatting tools that you can use to present an attractive, easy-to-read image to your busy readers.

Headers and Footers

Headers refer to information—such as titles, chapters, authors, and dates—repeated at the top of each page. *Footers* refer to additional information—such as page numbers or copyright information—repeated at the bottom of each page. Headers and footers must be consistently spaced and noticeable enough to be seen, but not so noticeable that they compete with adjacent body copy.

Visuals, Captions, and Pull-Quotes

Visuals refer to charts, graphs, illustrations, photographs, and tables used to communicate at a glance. Visuals can also consist of text elements, such as oversize chapter numbers or pull-quotes. Visuals also include *drop caps*, which refer to using an oversize character to emphasize the start of a new article or topic. Initial caps provide a transition between the headline and the first word in a paragraph.

Initial caps are referred to by designers as *raised caps* when they are taller than the words they introduce. They're called *drop caps* when they extend down to the second, third, or fourth line in the paragraph.

Pull-quotes consist of a key phrase or sentence that is repeated at large size on the page where the words originally appeared. Pull-quotes are often read both before and after the other text on the page, reinforcing their message.

Becoming an Artisan

An artisan is someone who takes pride in the work he or she produces. Artisans are craftspeople who have carefully mastered the techniques of their craft and who consistently take the time to do things right.

Production accuracy and consistency are as important as creativity. It's not enough to come up with a design that attracts attention and is easy to read. As a designer, you also have to shepherd the design through to completion—and then check your work over and over again for the details.

A single spelling mistake, a subhead or paragraph set in the wrong typeface, or a visual that obscures part of the adjacent text is enough to brand you an amateur—and your message not very important. Likewise, your message loses a great deal of credibility if the last few lines are inadvertently cut off.

An occasional home run gets the fans cheering, but consistency wins games.

Summary

The goal of this chapter has been to demystify design by reducing it to eight simple, easily remembered principles that apply to everything you're likely to work on: advertisements, books, e-books, brochures, business cards, newsletters, and postcards.

Throughout the rest of this book, you'll learn the specific commands to apply in Microsoft Publisher to incorporate these eight principles into your marketing messages.

In the next chapter, we'll explore the message itself—the "meat and potatoes" of your marketing materials. As you saw in Chapter 1, "Using Design to Gain a Competitive Edge," graphic design cannot substitute for a lack of a meaningful message.

Test Yourself

Before moving on, visit www.designtosellonline.com/03chap.html, where you'll find a variety of bonus materials to test and expand your understanding of the concepts and terms introduced in this chapter. In the Chapter 3 bonus materials, you can:

- Print out color versions of several of the illustrations shown in this chapter.

- Use a self-scoring assessment that will help you identify the contrast tools at work.

- Review and test your understanding of the new terms introduced in this chapter.

- Download new ideas and resources relating to the contents of this chapter.

Chapter Four

Crafting Messages That Clients and Prospects Will Want to Read

What you'll find:

- ❑ Discover the three truths of effective marketing.
- ❑ Learn the tasks that your messages must accomplish.
- ❑ Learn the basics of list-based writing.

This chapter is intended for entrepreneurs, self-employed professionals, and designers who want to gain a stronger understanding of what goes into creating the messages that their designs will communicate.

Remember from Chapter 1, "Using Design to Gain a Competitive Edge," design cannot compensate for a lack of message. No matter how attractive the formatting and layout of your message, your message cannot succeed without meaningful and well-organized content—compelling content that your clients and prospects will want to read.

A full discussion of marketing and copywriting strategies is obviously beyond the scope of this book. But before we turn our focus to Microsoft Office Publisher in Part Two, it's important to review some of the basic beliefs that will guide the way we use design and Publisher.

The Three Truths of Effective Marketing

Although advances in technology, such as fax machines and the Internet, have changed the way marketing messages are communicated, the basics remain the same. Success comes from close adherence to the three truths of marketing, which guide the success of firms of all sizes around the world.

The following truths form the foundation of successful marketing programs for firms of all sizes.

1. Target Your Market

Target marketing works. It pays to spend your money on those most likely to buy from you.

Many firms have underachieved—or even gone out of business—because they believed in marketing to "everyone." There's an entire industry out there waiting to take your money in exchange for advertisements in media such as billboards, community and local newspapers, and radio and television. Their message is "exposure," and they promote their ability to "reach" a lot of people.

But are the people you are reaching your people? Or are you paying for a lot of waste circulation? It's not the number of people you reach that's important, it's the number of *qualified* people likely to buy!

It's not the number
of people you reach
that's important, it's
the number of
qualified people
likely to buy!

Most businesses don't need to reach a lot of people. Instead, they need efficiency and qualified buyers—*efficiency* to spend the least amount of money, and *qualified buyers* to reach those who have expressed an interest in the firm's product categories; they've contacted the firm previously or made a prior purchase.

In many cases, the firm's invoices and prospect lists are enough to seed new growth and profitability!

Customer Retention vs. Customer Acquisition

Customer retention is more profitable than customer acquisition. It costs 7 to 10 times more to acquire a new customer than to retain (and resell to) a previous customer.

Acquisition costs—in the form of advertising and marketing—are usually high, plus new customers often require price concessions to cause them to leave their current vendor. In addition, sales cycles are longer for new customers than for previous customers because of a lack of familiarity and trust.

Often firms that run into trouble following aggressive customer acquisition programs turn to their previous customers when it's time to regroup and work more efficiently. Low-cost marketing tools like newsletters and postcards, prepared using Microsoft Publisher and sent to your customers and prospects, can provide the tools you need for increased sales and profits.

2. Educate Your Market

Education leads to higher profits by building market loyalty. Today, no business is free from competition—in particular, price competition. Globalization and the Internet have removed the protections that previously shielded firms from price competition. There is always someone, somewhere, who can sell a product or service cheaper, and—thanks to the Internet—these competitors are only a click away.

Educational marketing provides an alternative to competing solely on the basis of price. Educational marketing involves gaining your market's trust by providing information that will help clients and prospects make better-informed buying decisions and better-informed usage decisions. By becoming a resource to your clients and prospects, you can build strong loyalties that will result in continuing sales and word-of-mouth referrals.

Thanks to the Internet, there is always someone, somewhere, who can sell a product or perform a service cheaper—and they're only a click away.

David Ogilvy, in his *Confessions of an Advertising Man* (Southbank Publishing, 2004), said it best: "The more you tell, the more you sell." Knowledge trumps price when you present the right arguments. And best of all, you don't need to be "creative"—you just need to know how to translate the knowledge you already possess into the benefits your market is searching for, which you'll learn to do later in this chapter.

3. Keep in Touch with Your Market

Keeping in constant touch with your clients, customers, and prospects is the third crucial marketing truth. You must keep in contact with your market because it's impossible to predict when they will want to buy.

Educational marketing gains your market's trust by helping clients and prospects make better-informed buying decisions and better-informed usage decisions.

If you're invisible when your client's budget is approved—or on the day a customer or prospect receives a bonus, severance package, inheritance, or lottery winnings—you'll lose the sale. To succeed, you must be constantly visible.

Think of the oscilloscope on television programs set in hospital emergency rooms or intensive care units. Each time the patient's heart beats, the oscilloscope trace pings and hits the top of the screen. If the pings stop, we know the patient is in trouble.

Similarly, infrequent advertising can quickly spell trouble to firms that fail to keep in touch with their market. The more time that goes by between marketing messages, the more likely your firm will be forgotten. Successful marketing is based more on quantity—that is, consistent messages—than on the number of words communicated. Monthly one-page newsletters, for example, are far more effective than bimonthly four-page newsletters or quarterly eight-page newsletters.

In addition to building and maintaining customer loyalty, frequent market contact also builds familiarity and comfort among prospects who haven't yet purchased from you. Each additional contact establishes a comfort factor that eliminates the uncertainty and distrust that prevents many buyers from switching suppliers.

Perhaps the greatest contribution that using Microsoft Publisher can provide is to make it possible for you to create a cost-effective and easily implemented ongoing marketing program that will consistently send educational marketing messages to those most likely to buy from you.

Tasks That Your Messages Must Accomplish

Because design cannot succeed without a relevant message, it's important to understand the major tasks that your message must accomplish. Without compelling messages at the core of your design, the only things you can create with Microsoft Publisher are pretty pictures.

Compelling messages satisfy the following requirements.

Engage the Reader's Interest

Your message must immediately engage your readers' interest. Readers are in a hurry, and so they are extremely selective (and selfish) about what they read. Their number-one concern is: "What's in it for me?" You have just a few seconds to attract their attention and provide them with a reason to pay attention to your message.

Tip   If you'd like to explore copywriting in greater depth, numerous copywriting books are available. (Many of these copywriting resources are listed on this book's companion Web site, at www.designtosellonline.com/04chap.html)

You have just two tools to engage your readers: one is your *headline*, and the other is the *appearance* of your marketing message.

Headline

Your headline must appeal to your readers' need to solve a pressing problem or achieve a desired goal. This headline—which might be the only words in the advertisement or on the page that your readers will pay attention to—has to describe a problem and a solution or a goal and how you can help clients and prospects achieve it.

Headlines must also be brief. The shorter the headline, the more likely that readers will read it. In addition—and this point traditionally has not been emphasized enough—the shorter the headline, the larger the type size you can use when it appears in your message. This boosts the headline's impact by making it easier to notice and easier to read.

If your firm is targeting a specific market, you can increase the engagement power of your headline by identifying the target market—or market niche—in your headline.

Appearance

There are two ways you can use the appearance of your marketing message to increase its effectiveness: you can use graphics to translate your message into a visual message, and you can use white space and careful text formatting to present an image that is as easy to read as possible.

Graphics   If you have the budget, the most effective solution might be to include a custom photograph that visually communicates the problem or frustration your market might be experiencing. You can also use a photograph to communicate the solution you are offering. Or you can use a chart or graphs to demonstrate the "before" and "after" results of employing your solution.

Appearance   Ads and publications with significant amounts of white space always project a more appealing image. Likewise, you can insert frequent subheads and fine-tune type size and line spacing to project an easy-to-read image.

In any case, it's important that your readers become immediately involved in your message—because if that doesn't happen immediately, it probably never will!

Provide Proof

Having stated your offer, you have to include proof. Your market is skeptical. They are bombarded with hundreds of offers, claims, and promises every day. To stand out, you have to do a better job of proving what you say is true than your competition does. There are three ways you can substantiate your messages: specificity, story, and testimonials.

Specificity

You must quantify and specify the benefits that you are offering. You have to prove superiority. The very fact that you translate a benefit into a specific adds power to your headlines and messages. Compare:

- Save Time and Money!
- Save 8 Minutes Per Transaction!
- Save $3.50 or More Each Time You Order!

Which offer is the strongest, and which is the weakest? Which helps you visualize the benefits as concretely as possible?

Notice how much strength the phrase *Each Time You Order* adds to the last example. In contrast, *Per Transaction* in the second example is not nearly as specific and fails to create as powerful an image.

Visuals can also be used to reinforce your point. *Save 8 Minutes* could be visually communicated with a photograph of a clock, or a series of clocks, to emphasize the cumulative effects of adding up 8-minute savings throughout a day, week, month, or year!

Likewise, a photograph of a mound of cash representing a year's worth of $3.50 savings, or a check plainly marked "Return on Investment," could add power to a specific claim.

Stories

Stories are one of humankind's oldest and most effective ways to communicate information. Messages that readers wouldn't pay any attention to become irresistible when the messages are communicated in a story format. The story format helps readers better identify with the problems and solutions your story is based on.

One of the best ways to utilize the power of the story is to present case studies showing how your products or services solved a client's problems. Your case studies can be "composites" of several stories, or—even better—you can base the stories on a specific client's experiences.

Be sure to obtain permission first, of course, and offer the client some form of thanks or recognition. Or disguise the client's identity, but offer to make it available on request.

Testimonials

A final way to add proof to your message is to insert brief (one or two sentences) testimonials from clients.

One of the main advantages of this approach is that the testimonials can be sprinkled through your message, adding visual interest while reinforcing your offer, as shown in Figure 4-1. Format the testimonials similarly to the way you format pull-quotes, setting them in a typeface that forms a strong contrast with the adjacent text. Use a contrasting typeface to provide the source of the quote.

Readers might overlook three testimonials that appear next to each other, but they're more likely to read three separate testimonials placed in the margins of your document. Testimonials can come from experts in your field or—better yet—from previous clients that your market can identify with.

Maintain the Reader's Interest

The struggle for readers never ends. After engaging your clients' and prospects' interest, you have to struggle to keep them reading. The tools of momentum include subheads. Each subhead adds white space and typographic contrast, as well as an additional opportunity for clients and prospects to begin reading your message.

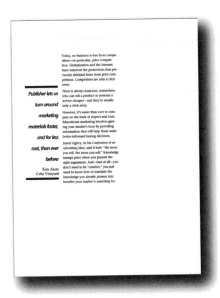

Today, no business is free from competition—in particular, price competition. Globalization and the Internet have removed the protections that previously shielded firms from price competition. Competitors are only a click away.

Publisher lets us turn around marketing materials faster, and for less cost, than ever before.
Kim Akers
Coho Vineyard

There is always someone, somewhere, who can sell a product or perform a service cheaper—and they're usually only a click away.

However, it's easier than ever to compete on the basis of respect and trust. Educational marketing involves gaining your market's trust by providing information that will help them make better-informed buying decisions.

David Ogilvy, in his *Confessions of an Advertising Man*, said it best: "the more you tell, the more you sell." Knowledge trumps price when you present the right arguments. And—best of all—you don't need to be "creative," you just need to know how to translate the knowledge you already possess into benefits your market is searching for.

Figure 4-1 Testimonials not only can provide proof, but they can also add visual interest to your marketing messages.

Characteristics of a reader-friendly writing style include short, active, sentences and short paragraphs, lists, pull-quotes, and appropriate text formatting.

Short sentences and paragraphs   Short sentences are the result of careful editing. Eliminate duplicate, redundant, or unnecessary words. Make every word count. Avoid run-on sentences—that is, sentences that convey two or more thoughts. Avoid passive verbs; active constructions are easier to read and require fewer words. For example, compare "Charles turned the light off" (active) with "The light was turned off by Charles" (passive).

Lists   Words in lists stand out more, and the lists themselves add white space to your message. (Too many lists, of course, can undermine the flow of your message.)

Pull-quotes   Repeat important words found in paragraphs, and highlight them at large size in the margins of a page.

Text formatting   Most of all, choose the right type size and line spacing for the width of the columns in your message. Type that is set too large or too small for the column width significantly undermines your message's readability. Adding line spacing makes the text easier to read.

After engaging your clients' and prospects' interest, you have to make it easier for them to read your whole message, instead of stopping in the middle.

Offer a Call to Action

The final element of your message should be a call to action. You have to tell your readers:

- *What* action you want them to take.
- *How* to perform the desired action.
- *Why* they should act.

Here are some of the ways you can not only educate your market, but also convert interest to sales.

Specify a Next Step

What is the immediate step you want your prospects to take? Start by identifying the various actions you want readers to take: visit a Web site, visit your office or store, sign up for a free trial, register for a free newsletter, or recommend a friend as a potential customer.

By listing as many options as possible, you can identify—and emphasize—the most efficient way for prospects to advance to the next step of the sales cycle. Notice that, often, when dealing with expensive products, the desired step isn't to buy something, but simply to order a "no obligation" information package, Web site download, or video.

After the hook has been baited, a different call to action will be used.

Provide Detailed Instructions

Next explain "how" prospects should complete this step—for example:

- Provide a coupon or registration form.
- Provide directions, and perhaps include a map, to a physical location.
- Offer a special phone number, or "hot line," for orders or reservations.
- Provide downloadable coupons on your Web site.

The Big Tease

One of the best ways to encourage readers to stick with your message is to promise a provocative statement—but then save the statement for the end of your message.

For example, "This Dishwasher Is Great for All but a Few" tantalizes readers with the question: "Who *isn't* it good for?" If you continue to refer to the dishwasher's "limitation," readers will want to continue reading to find out what the limitation is.

Of course, when you finally reveal the fatal flaw, it can be something as innocuous as "Not enough capacity for the White House kitchen" or "Not big enough for households of more than 50 individuals." If you have the budget to include a photograph showing an evening meal in a firehouse, you could use a headline like "Not good for firehouses!"

As always, whenever possible, your directions should be both verbal and visual—that is, you should use graphics—to visually represent the various alternatives.

Add Immediacy

The last step is to summarize your offer and its benefits, repeat your instructions, and then provide a reason to act right now! Time-tested ways to add immediacy include:

- Warnings of scarcity, such as "Limited quantities."

- Appeals for involvement, such as "Bring a toy for charity to qualify."

- Offers of bonuses, such as free delivery, free shipping, and so on.

These "call to action" approaches might not be 100-percent appropriate for your market, but just thinking in terms of these proven marketing techniques will help you prepare effective marketing messages.

Using Lists to Create Content

Are you at a loss for words? If you like the idea of educational marketing and engagement but don't know where to start, this section provides a dozen topic ideas that your market—or any market—will want to read. Each of the following ideas can be adopted for any category of product or service.

What these ideas have in common is that they make it easy for you to craft messages that will promote your competence by addressing issues of interest to your clients and prospects that will help them make better decisions.

Putting List-Based Writing to Work

You'll find list-based writing, based on topics like those that follow, surprisingly easy. After you select an appropriate list topic, the remainder of the message virtually writes itself. After you choose a topic and create a headline, such as "How to Avoid the Biggest Mistakes When Buying a DVD Player (or Prepaid Legal Services)," all that remains is to:

You'll never go wrong by helping your market avoid making an expensive mistake.

- Identify the 6, 8, or 10 points that you want to make. This generally takes just a few minutes, and you can enlist your coworkers to help.

- Develop each point with a few sentences or a few paragraphs, depending on how much space is available. It doesn't take many words to complete an advertisement or prepare an issue of your newsletter.

List-based writing involves creating a structure to write about what you already know. It replaces the stress of staring at an empty screen with the simpler tasks of filling in blanks in a "paint by number" format. Once you identify the keywords used to provide the information promised in the headline, it becomes relatively easy to complete your message.

Topic Ideas

Use the following ideas to jump-start your message crafting skills.

Start your topic and headline writing by choosing one of the following lead-in phrases:

Once you identify the keywords used to provide the information promised in the headline, it becomes relatively easy to complete your message.

- How to profit from...

- How to avoid....

- How to take advantage of...

- How to learn from...

- What to watch out for...

Complete your topic or headline by combining your starting phrase with one of the following options:

- Biggest mistakes that first-time buyers (or categories such as homeowners) make.

- Trends affecting your readers' business, relationships, health, or income.

- Checklists for buyers, users, renters, and travelers.

- Recommended procedures, or steps, to complete a task.

- Questions to ask. (The advantage of this option is that your readers' answers can emphasize your firm's strengths.)

- Terms—a glossary of important words that readers should know about.

- Shortcuts, tips, or techniques. (This option attracts the interest of current users who might have bought elsewhere.)

- Symptoms, signs, or indications.

- Bibliographies and resources—for example, "Ten Books All Gardeners Should Know About."

- Qualifications—what to look for when selecting a service provider.

- Recommended accessories and upgrades. (This option helps current owners justify moving up.)

- Maintenance strategies for long life. (This option too appeals to current owners.)

With a little bit of practice, you'll find that your copywriting skills will improve as quickly as your design skills!

Summary

You're now equipped with some fundamental tools for crafting your message. Now that we've surveyed the necessity of design, the basics of design, the three truths of marketing, and the techniques that you can use to craft a message, we can turn to learning how to use Microsoft Publisher to put it all together and start creating attractive, effective marketing materials for yourself, your clients, or your boss.

In the next chapter, we'll take a look at the Microsoft Publisher window to get an idea of what commands are located where. You'll like working with Microsoft Publisher. If you're comfortable working with a word processing application such as Microsoft Office Word, you'll easily make the transition to a dedicated page layout program.

Test Yourself

Before moving on, take a few minutes to visit www.designtosellonline.com/04chap.html and explore the Chapter 4 bonus materials. Here you'll find:

- "Power terms" to help you promote your competence to your market.

- A self-scoring assessment to help you test your comprehension of the ideas and new terms introduced in this chapter.

- Updated copywriting resources, including blogs, books, and Web sites.

Part Two

Working with Publisher

In this part

Chapter Five

Getting Started with Microsoft Publisher

What you'll find:

❑ Become familiar with the Microsoft Office Publisher working environment.

❑ Discover the power of text boxes and master pages.

❑ Learn how to navigate from word to word, page to page.

❑ Master keyboard shortcuts.

❑ Customize Publisher to your working habits.

This chapter is for you if you are new to Microsoft Publisher. It's also for you if you already know a little about Publisher and want to create a stronger foundation for mastering Publisher's full power.

In general, if you are familiar with word processing programs such as Microsoft Office Word, you'll probably find the transition to Microsoft Publisher an easy journey. This chapter emphasizes the most important commands that you'll be using over and over again and the primary areas where Publisher differs from software programs you might have already used.

Fundamentals of Microsoft Publisher

Rather than repeat information that appears in the online Help, this chapter and the next provide an impressionistic look at the key features of Microsoft Publisher as they apply to creating attractive, easy-to-read marketing materials from scratch.

Starting Your Work in Microsoft Publisher

Whenever you start Publisher, the New Publication task pane that's displayed invites you to begin work immediately. One option in the task pane is to open and continue working on an existing publication, but if you're starting a new project, you'll want to choose one of the following approaches:

■ Work with one of Publisher's design wizards, selecting a design and type of publication from the options provided.

- Create a new publication from scratch.

- Create a new publication based on an existing publication.

After you've created some custom templates, you can create a new publication based on one of them. Publisher displays all of your available templates, as shown in Figure 5-1.

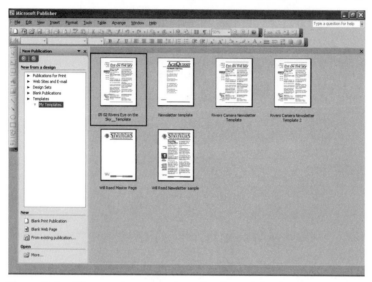

Figure 5-1 After you have templates for the publications you create most often, you can start new publications from your existing templates.

Because templates are such powerful tools, saving time and ensuring accuracy and consistency, you'll probably frequently start new publications from templates.

A Word About Templates

Templates are read-only files that contain the framework for publications that you use over and over again. Templates are frequently used for advertisements, newsletters, and postcards.

Why reinvent the wheel every time a new employee joins? Just add a new name and e-mail address to an existing business card rather than create the whole business card from scratch.

Likewise, the basic layout and formatting of your newsletters should remain consistent from issue to issue. Major changes each month will confuse your readers and project amateurism

One of Publisher's most useful template features is the ability to categorize your templates. You can categorize templates by *document type*—for example, business card templates or postcard templates. If you have several clients, you can create a folder for each client.

In Chapter 6, "Creating a Structure for Design Success," you'll learn how to create your own customized templates that you can use over and over for years to come.

The Publisher Window

Publisher's menu and toolbars will be familiar to you if you already work with Microsoft Word or Microsoft Excel.

Worthy of notice, because you'll be using these tools frequently, are the Select Objects tool and the Text Box tool. You'll use the Select Objects tool, on the Objects toolbar at the left side of the window, to select an object for formatting, moving, or resizing. Below it is the Text Box tool, which you'll use to create new text boxes. A little below that is the Picture Frame tool, which you'll use to add photographs to your publication.

As you work with Publisher, you'll frequently need to change screen magnification using the Zoom percent box and the Zoom Out and Zoom In tools on the Standard toolbar. For some tasks, you'll want to zoom out to view the entire page or two-page spread. For other tasks, you'll want to zoom in to magnify just part of a page. Figure 5-2 shows the Objects toolbar and the Zoom tools on the Standard toolbar.

Figure 5-2   You will frequently access the tools on the Objects toolbar and change screen magnification by using the Zoom tools.

Working with Text Boxes and Picture Frames

If you're familiar with Microsoft Word, you know that in Word, you can immediately begin typing on a new page. Publisher is different. Just about anything you want to add to a Publisher document has to be placed in a *container*. The two most important containers are *text boxes* and *picture frames*.

Creating Text Boxes

To create a text box, click the Text Box tool, and then click the upper-left corner of the location in your document where you want to add text. Hold down the left mouse button and drag to the right and downward until you have created a text box of the desired size. Release the mouse button, and your text box is ready for you to begin adding text.

Notice the blinking insertion point. This indicates that you can begin typing to add text.

Resizing, Formatting, and Moving Text Boxes

Notice the eight selection handles located on the sides and corners of the text box. By clicking and dragging these handles, you can resize the text box. Notice that as you move the mouse pointer near the border of the box, it changes to a small four-headed arrow, indicating that you can move the entire box.

Note that you don't have to use the mouse to drag a text box you've selected to a new location. You can "nudge" the text box into position by using the RIGHT, LEFT, UP, and DOWN ARROW keys. Each key press nudges the text box 0.03 inches in the desired direction. Holding down the SHIFT key as you nudge causes each key press to move the text box a greater distance.

After you select a text box by clicking it, you can format the box by adding borders or backgrounds. To add a colored background behind the text, click the Fill Color tool on the Formatting toolbar. To add a border around the text box, choose a border by using the Line/Border Style tool located on the Formatting toolbar. Specify a desired color by using the Line Color tool on the Formatting toolbar.

A final text box formatting option adds a transparency effect to a text box, allowing background elements to be visible through the box. To make text boxes transparent, click the Fill Color drop-down arrow on the Formatting toolbar, click More Fill Colors in the drop-down list, drag the Transparency slider in the Colors dialog box, and then click OK.

Adjusting Text Box Margin Spacing

Here's how to adjust the "padding," or the amount of white space between the text in a box and the text box borders. Right-click the text box, and then click Format Text Box on the shortcut menu. In the Format Text Box dialog box, click the Text Box tab, as shown in Figure 5-3.

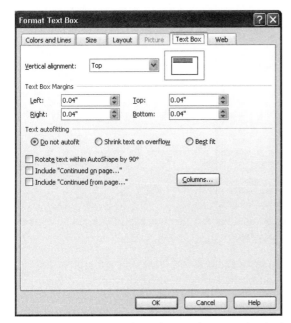

Figure 5-3 You can adjust the text box margins in the Format Text Box dialog box.

Notice that, by default, Publisher adds 0.04 inches of white space between the borders of the text box and text that you add to the text box. This default was originally intended to prevent lines of text in adjacent boxes from bumping into each other. Because you're unlikely to run into that problem, and because the subtle indents are enough to noticeably indent the text, it's a good idea to change the default 0.04-inch margins to no margins. To do so, simply type **0** in all four Text Box Margins boxes.

Next click the Colors And Lines tab, and then select the Apply Settings To New Text Boxes check box, as shown in Figure 5-4. All of the formatting changes you made in the Format Text Box dialog box will now appear in any new text boxes you add to the document.

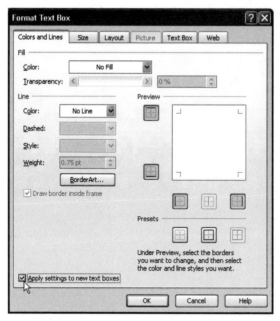

Figure 5-4 Any formatting changes made in the Format Text Box dialog box can be applied to new text boxes added to the current document.

There will be times, however, when you want to increase the text box margins. This typically occurs when you are setting text against a black, shaded, or colored background, as shown in Figure 5-5.

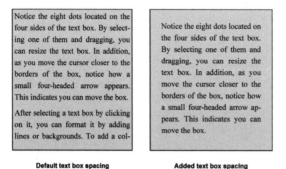

Default text box spacing   Added text box spacing

Figure 5-5 Increasing text box margins will indent the text, allowing the background fill and text box border to properly frame text placed against a dark background.

Linking Text Boxes

When a Text In Overflow icon appears at the bottom of a text box, there is too much text to fit in the text box, as shown in Figure 5-6. One of the most important text box options permits you to link text boxes to each other. Linking permits text to flow, or "snake," through multiple text boxes.

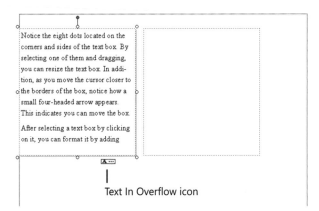

Text In Overflow icon

Figure 5-6   The presence of the Text In Overflow icon indicates that there is too much text to fit in the text box.

To link a text box with overflowing text to another text box, select the first box, and then click the Create Text Box Link tool on the Connect Text Boxes toolbar.

The mouse pointer turns into a coffee pot when positioned over an empty text box, as shown in Figure 5-7.

Note   Text links can be added only to empty text boxes.

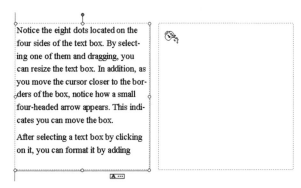

Figure 5-7   Note the coffee pot, indicating text that is ready to be "poured" into the next text box.

Notice what happens when the text link has been added. The Text In Overflow icon at the bottom of text box on the left disappears, and a Go To Previous Text Box icon appears at the top of the text box on the right, as shown in Figure 5-8, indicating that the text is a continuation of text from another text box.

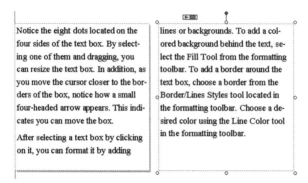

Notice the eight dots located on the four sides of the text box. By selecting one of them and dragging, you can resize the text box. In addition, as you move the cursor closer to the borders of the box, notice how a small four-headed arrow appears. This indicates you can move the box.

After selecting a text box by clicking on it, you can format it by adding

lines or backgrounds. To add a colored background behind the text, select the Fill Tool from the formatting toolbar. To add a border around the text box, choose a border from the Border/Lines Styles tool located in the formatting toolbar. Choose a desired color using the Line Color tool in the formatting toolbar.

Figure 5-8   The Text In Overflow icon below the text box on the left disappears after the text flows into the linked text box on the right.

Creating Picture Frames

Publisher's picture frames behave like text boxes. To create a picture frame, click the Picture Frame tool on the Objects toolbar, and then specify how you want the picture frame filled. You can choose from the following options:

Clip Art   Choose this option to select from photographs and illustrations included in Publisher that are intended to communicate broad concepts or themes, such as "vacation" or "big-city life."

Picture From A File   Choose this option when you want to include digital files created from previously scanned photographs or downloaded files from a digital camera.

Empty Picture Frame   This option produces a placeholder that you will fill later. It allows you to indicate how big an illustration or photograph will appear, even if you have not yet obtained the image.

Picture From A Scanner Or Camera   Choose this option when you have a camera or image scanner hooked up to your computer.

After you choose an option and then place the picture frame on the page the same way you do a text box, the picture frame can be moved, resized, or formatted like a text box.

Working with Master Pages

One of the major ways that Publisher differs from other programs you might have worked with is the concept of master pages.

Master pages enable you to add text and graphical elements—such as logos, borders, and page numbers—to a background *layer* that is automatically applied to every page. Master pages ensure consistency throughout a document. More importantly, master pages save time because any changes you make are automatically applied to every page based on the master pages. In addition, the advantage of placing repeating elements on master pages is that there is less likelihood that the elements will be inadvertently deleted, moved, or omitted. By using master pages, repeating elements will always appear in the correct location.

For example, consider a typical newsletter, shown in Figure 5-9. The front page of every newsletter usually contains the *nameplate*, or the newsletter's title, set as a formatted graphical element. Accompanying the nameplate will be the newsletter's mission statement, a testimonial, and (perhaps) the editor's photograph, and there will likely be borders at the top and bottom of the page.

Figure 5-9   The front page of this newsletter consists of a combination of foreground elements that change with each issue, plus background elements that remain unchanged from issue to issue.

To view the master page behind the page, shown in Figure 5-10, click View, Master Page or press CTRL+M.

Figure 5-10 The master page contains the newsletter elements that remain the same from issue to issue.

When you click View, Master Page, the Edit Master Pages task pane appears, as shown in Figure 5-11. This task pane contains commands that enable you to create, edit, rename, and delete master pages.

Creating Multiple Master Pages

Publisher also enables you to create multiple master pages with specialized content and layouts for different pages of your publication.

For example, you might prepare the following master pages for even a simple newsletter:

- Front page (with nameplate)
- Back page (with space for addressing)

- Left inside page
- Right inside page
- Left calendar page
- Right calendar page
- Left survey form

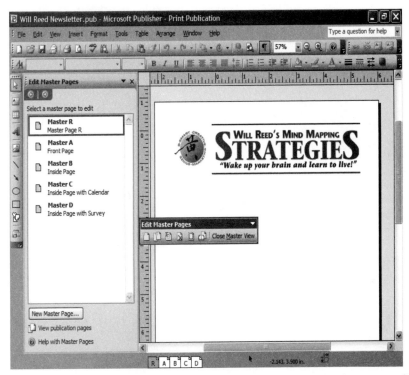

Figure 5-11   You can use the Edit Master Pages task pane to apply, create, edit, rename, and ignore left and right master pages.

Adding Guides to Master Pages

One of the big differences between Microsoft Publisher and word processing programs like Microsoft Word is that you can add *guides* to your pages. Guides are horizontal or vertical lines that are visible on screen but will not be printed. You can add as many guides as necessary to align text and graphical elements.

To create horizontal or vertical guides, first make sure that Publisher's rulers are visible. If they're not visible, click View, Rulers. To create a guide, click on one of the rulers and drag the guide onto the page to the desired location.

It's important that you are in the correct view when adding guides. If you want the guides to appear on every page, add them while working in Master Page view. Otherwise, the guides will appear only on the page where you added them.

Moving from Page to Page

Unlike other software programs, such as Microsoft Word, which let you scroll up and down to access different pages, Publisher concentrates on one page at a time. To move from page to page in Publisher, click the desired page number in the Page Sorter at the lower left of the Publisher screen, as shown in Figure 5-12.

Page Sorter

Figure 5-12   Select a desired page using the Page Sorter.

Developing Efficient Working Habits in Publisher

Efficient working habits translate into years of enhanced productivity. If you're new to Publisher, you'll find many helpful Publisher shortcuts that will save you time. Use them whenever possible.

Accessing Commands

Publisher provides multiple ways to access commands. Publisher often offers alternatives to selecting commands by opening menus and scrolling down the list of commands until you locate the desired one. Two effective alternative techniques are using shortcut menus and using keyboard shortcuts.

Shortcut Menus

Instead of constantly searching for commands in menus, get in the habit of using the right mouse button. Right-clicking a text or graphical element reveals a *shortcut menu* containing the available commands associated with that element. Figure 5-13 shows an example of a shortcut menu.

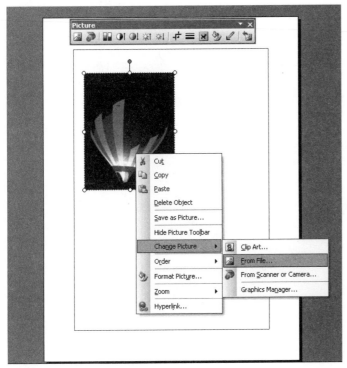

Figure 5-13   Right-clicking a text or graphical element reveals a shortcut menu containing commands associated with that element.

Properly used, these shortcut menus can be a great timesaver. Chances are, the command you're looking for will be there. You can also use a shortcut menu to zoom in on a particular text box or graphic.

Keyboard Shortcuts

Keyboard shortcuts offer one of the best ways to work in Publisher efficiently. Every time you remove your hand from the keyboard and click a mouse button to access a menu or toolbar command, you're going through unnecessary motions.

Keyboard shortcuts consist of holding down the CTRL key, ALT key, or SHIFT key while pressing another keyboard key.

Publisher supports the universal keyboard shortcuts found in many Microsoft Windows–based applications, including the following:

■   Save: CTRL+S

- Copy: CTRL+C
- Cut: CTRL+X
- Paste: CTRL+V
- Print: CTRL+P

These keyboard shortcuts alone can save you a tremendous amount of time, but Publisher includes many additional keyboard shortcuts. As you explore the commands located on Publisher's menus, note the keyboard shortcuts that appear next to many of the commands that you'll use most often.

Using Keyboard Shortcuts to Navigate a Publisher Document   Another way to move from page to page in a Publisher document is to hold down the CTRL key while pressing PAGE UP or PAGE DOWN.

You can also go directly to a desired page by pressing CTRL+G and then typing the number of the page you want to go to. To move between smaller sections of your document:

To move from word to word   Hold down the CTRL key while pressing the LEFT or RIGHT ARROW key.

To move from paragraph to paragraph   Hold down the CTRL key while pressing the UP or DOWN ARROW key.

Using Keyboard Shortcuts to Select Text for Editing or Formatting   Another set of useful keyboard shortcuts involves selecting text by holding down both the CTRL and SHIFT keys while pressing the arrow keys:

To select the next word to the right or left   Hold down the CTRL and SHIFT keys and press the LEFT or RIGHT ARROW key.

To select the previous or next paragraph   Hold down the CTRL and SHIFT keys while pressing the UP or DOWN ARROW key.

Additional keyboard shortcuts will be introduced in later chapters.

Customizing Publisher Default Settings

When you install Publisher, you might find making one or more of the following configuration changes useful:

Turning on full menus   Click Tools, Customize. In the Customize dialog box, click the Options tab, select the Always Show Full Menus check box, and click OK. This eliminates having to click the down arrow to reveal the full menu or wait temporarily until the full menu is revealed.

Setting the default file locations   Click Tools, Options. In the Options dialog box, click the General tab, and then modify the default file locations where Publisher will go to save or retrieve program files as well as graphics files.

Turning on automatic backup   Click Tools, Options. In the Options dialog box, click the Save tab. Make sure that the Allow Background Saves and Save AutoRecover Info Every *XX* Minutes check boxes are selected. Because a lot can happen in a few minutes, you might want to set Publisher to automatically back up your work every few minutes.

Turning off design wizards   Click Tools, Options. Click the User Assistance tab, and then clear the Use A Wizard For Blank Publications check box. Although you might initially find Publisher's wizards helpful, you'll probably soon become comfortable performing frequently repeated tasks without assistance. You can always return to Tools, Options, User Assistance and then recheck the Use A Wizard For Blank Publications check box.

Customizing Toolbars

You can customize the toolbars in Publisher in several ways to provide quick access to your most frequently used commands. To change your toolbar settings, you can click the Toolbar Options down arrow on the right end of each toolbar; click View, Toolbars, Customize; or click Tools, Customize, Toolbars.

Helpful toolbar customizations include the following:

Save As   Adding a Save As button on the Standard toolbar allows you to easily save alternative versions of a publication while trying out different designs or typefaces. To add a Save As button, click Tools, Customize. In the Customize Toolbar dialog box, scroll through the list of commands until you locate the Save As button. Click it, as shown in Figure 5-14, and drag it to a desired toolbar location.

Print dialog box   Clicking the default Print button on the Standard toolbar in Publisher can be responsible for a lot of wasted paper. Click it, and your entire publication will be printed. Consider replacing the Print button with the alternative button labeled *Print....* This Print button opens the Print dialog box, where you can specify which printer you want to use, the desired quality, and—most important— which pages of a multipage document you want to print.

The more buttons you have that lead to just the tools you want, the easier it will be to quickly locate desired commands. However, exercise restraint. Too many buttons can clutter the toolbars and defeat their purpose. Accordingly, consider removing unwanted buttons from your toolbars. To do this, click the down arrow on the right end

of a toolbar, click Add Or Remove Buttons, and then point to the toolbar name. Clear
the check boxes next to the tools you'd like to remove.

Figure 5-14   You can add buttons to any toolbar by dragging them from the Customize
Toolbar dialog box to the desired location on the toolbar.

Summary

Congratulations! You have now familiarized yourself with the basic Publisher
environment. You know where to look for desired tools and commands, and you have
also learned some of the timesaving tricks that Publisher professionals use to work as
efficiently as possible.

In the next chapter, we'll review how to accomplish the most frequently repeated tasks
in Publisher. You'll learn how to use guides to create a structure for your publication,
how to format text, and how to work with color. You'll also learn how to create your
own publication templates.

Test Yourself

Before proceeding further, take a break and visit www.designtosellonline.com
/05chap.html. Here you'll be able to:

- Use a self-scoring assessment and review your comprehension of new terms
  introduced in this chapter.

- Learn about additional keyboard shortcuts and how to create your own shortcuts.

- Review additional customization tips.

Chapter Six

Creating a Foundation for Design Success

What you'll find:

- ❏ Learn how to use a grid to create a flexible structure for your pages.
- ❏ Find out how to add text to text boxes, and master the most important commands involving graphics.
- ❏ Discover how color schemes can help you use color in your publications.

For many, the greatest appeal of Microsoft Office Publisher is its built-in designs. These designs can provide a basis for easily creating attractive flyers, ads, brochures, catalogs, newsletters, and postcards, and make it easy to create a family of publications that project a consistent image.

For other Publisher users, it's more appropriate—and fun—to create publications from scratch by starting with a blank page. This is the recommended approach if you want to create a unique visual identity, based on using layout, color, type, and graphics in a consistent way.

In this chapter, you'll learn the steps needed to create publications from scratch and how to save those publications as templates that you can use again and again. The techniques covered in this chapter are likely to be ones that you repeat over and over as you create various publications.

Creating the Right Framework for Your Pages

After you start Publisher, start a new publication by following these steps:

1. Click **File**, **New**.
2. In the **New Publication** task pane, click **Blank Publications**.
3. In the display of blank publication types, click **Full Page**.

This provides a blank slate for you to begin working.

You can now close the Publication Design task pane, as you'll be creating your own design rather than using one of the designs in Publisher.

As always, it's a good idea to immediately save your work under a file name that describes the type of marketing message you're working on—for example, Promo Postcard, Monthly Newsletter, and so on. If you work with several clients, you might want to create separate folders for each and save your work in the appropriate location.

Selecting Page Size and Orientation

Next click File, Page Setup. On the Layout tab in the Page Setup dialog box, shown in Figure 6-1, you can verify and/or change page size and orientation. When you click an option in the Publication Type list, Publisher will provide default settings for that paper size. If you're working with nonstandard paper sizes, click Custom, and make any desired changes in the Height and Width boxes. You can also choose a different paper orientation, if desired:

Portrait   Refers to vertical pages (that is, tall rather than wide).

Landscape   Refers to horizontal pages (that is, wider than they are tall).

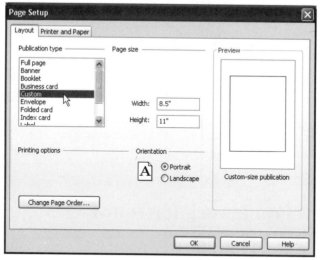

Figure 6-1   The Page Setup dialog box enables you to fine-tune page size and orientation and to specify the target printer and the paper that will be used to print your publication.

At this point, on the Printer And Paper tab in the Page Setup dialog box, you should also identify the final, or *target*, printer that will be used to print your project. This is especially critical if you are going to send your Publisher files to an outside vendor for printing. (After targeting the final printer, you will still be able to print proofs for quality control purposes on your desktop printer.)

As you work on either tab in the Page Setup dialog box, your choices are immediately visible in the Preview pane.

Adding Margins

The next step is to set up the *margins*—that is, the white space separating text and graphics from the *trim*, or edges, of the paper.

Margins play both aesthetic and practical roles. An appropriate amount of white space at the edges of each page not only improves the appearance of your publication, but it also provides space for your readers to physically hold your marketing materials without their fingers obscuring part of the message. Margins in technical and training documents also provide a space for readers to jot down notes and ideas.

To modify Publisher's default margins, click Arrange, Layout Guides. In the Layout Guides dialog box, click the Margin Guides tab, as shown in Figure 6-2. At this point, you'll probably want to enter your own margin settings. Publisher's default 1-inch margins are often wider than desired. Click OK after you've made your choices.

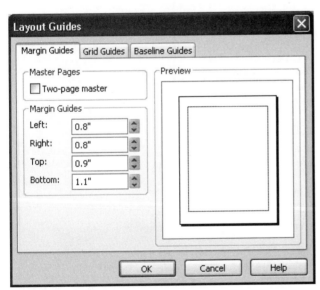

Figure 6-2   Replacing Publisher's default 1-inch margins with custom dimensions in the Layout Guides dialog box.

Notice that you can specify a different margin for each of the four edges of your publication.

Working with Grids

The next step is one of the most important, as it can play a major role in the appearance and readability of your marketing message.

Click Arrange, Layout Guides, and in the Layout Guides dialog box, click the Grid Guides tab, as shown in Figure 6-3. At this point, you can create a series of nonprinting horizontal and–if desired, vertical–guides that you can use to control the placement of text and graphics on the page.

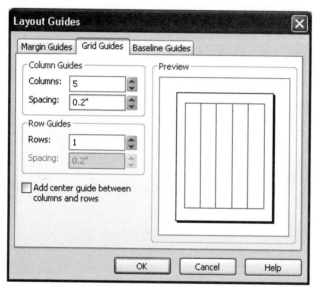

Figure 6-3   One of Publisher's most important features is the grid in the Layout Guides dialog box, which you can use to guide the placement of text and graphics.

Grids vs. Columns

It's important to recognize the distinction between grids and columns:

Grids   Refer to a system of background guides that can be seen on screen but that are not visible in your printed publication. A grid is simply a *system of suggestions*.

Columns   Refer to the physical placement of text boxes on top of a background grid.

The number of text columns on a page is often different from the number of grid columns. Text columns, or—more correctly—text boxes, often span two, or more, grid columns.

For example, a five-column grid provides the spacing necessary to create a page with two "double-wide" columns of text plus white space to the left that can be used for graphics such as photographs or short text elements such as definitions, a table of contents, pull-quotes, or sidebars, as shown in Figure 6-4.

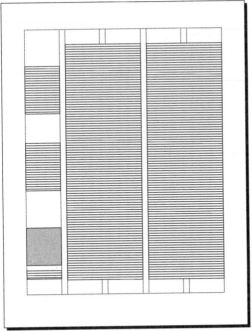

Figure 6-4 A five-column grid provides the ideal spacing for two "double-wide" columns of text plus white space that can be used for short text and graphical elements.

Advantages of Grids

By providing a flexible structure for your publications, grids play a major role in your marketing success.

One of the most important ways that grids influence publication success is by dividing even small spaces into different "selling areas." When creating the front, or *billboard*, side of a postcard, for example, the temptation is to use the space as one large horizontal element, as shown in Figure 6-5.

Yet, if the space on the front of the postcard is based on a grid, you can create two or more selling areas, as shown in Figure 6-6. One selling area might be used for a map to a specific location, while the second area could be used to describe the specific event taking place.

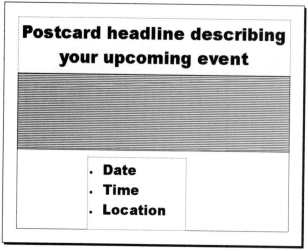

Figure 6-5   Without a grid, there is only one selling area on the front of a postcard.

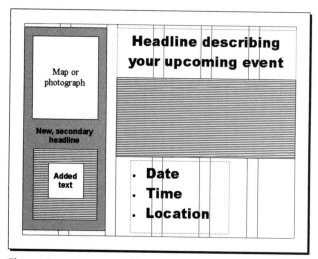

Figure 6-6   Using a grid for even small publications like postcards creates opportunities for adding selling areas.

Taking the idea of grids one step further, you can use colored backgrounds and borders to separate and emphasize the different selling areas on the front of a postcard.

Here's another benefit of grids: as space is subdivided, it is possible to set your messages in a smaller type size without compromising readability. This makes it possible to increase your word count so that you can include more details and benefits.

As you'll see in the next chapter, long lines of type (that is, wide text boxes) generally require larger type sizes and more line spacing than shorter lines of type (that is, narrower text boxes).

Even business cards can benefit from the structure provided by a background grid.

Grid Options

Your choice of underlying grid determines the overall "look" of your publication—in particular, the page balance and the white space that appears on each page.

The use of two-column and three-column grids tends to create "quiet" pages with little white space available to frame the text and graphical elements, as shown in Figures 6-7 and 6-8. Two-column and three-column grids also result in a great deal of left-right symmetry, as shown in Figure 6-9.

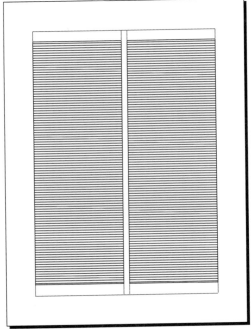

Figure 6-7 Pages with two columns of text often present a symmetrical, "awful lot to read," image without interesting contrast.

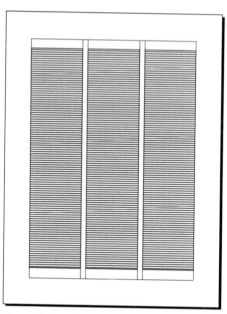

Figure 6-8   Likewise, pages filled with three columns of text often look very "filled" and present a boring left-right symmetry.

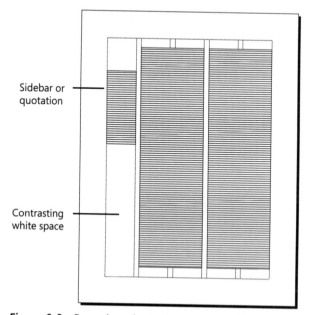

Sidebar or quotation

Contrasting white space

Figure 6-9   Pages based on a five-column grid, however, are characterized by a more interesting asymmetrical layout with contrasting white space that presents an easy-to-read image, plus space for short text elements.

Grids and Graphics

Pages based on five-column grids also add more flexibility for placing graphics like photographs than pages based on two-column or three-column grids.

Pages based on two-column and three-column grids make it difficult to place graphics without either increasing or decreasing the size of the photograph to align with column margins or creating annoying text wraps, as shown in Figure 6-10. Text wraps are to be avoided, as they interfere with your readers' ability to maintain a consistent rhythm as their eyes move across each line of type. This is because the lines of text around the graphic vary in length, disrupting the reader's rhythmic left-to-right eye scans.

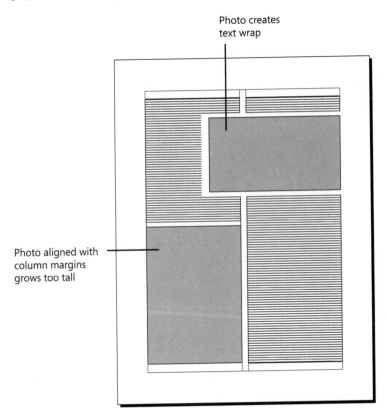

Photo creates
text wrap

Photo aligned with
column margins
grows too tall

Figure 6-10   When resized to an appropriate size, the horizontal photograph at the top creates a text wrap in the next column. The lower photograph, when aligned with the column margins, begins to occupy a disproportionate amount of space on the page.

After reformatting based on a five-column grid, however, you have considerably more flexibility for placing the photographs, as shown in Figure 6-11. Small vertical photographs can be placed in the narrow column, and horizontal photographs can extend into it. More important, readability is enhanced because all lines of text are the same length, permitting optimum left-to-right eye movement.

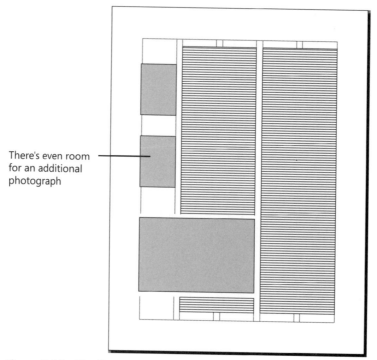

There's even room for an additional photograph

Figure 6-11   The five-column grid offers additional options for placing and resizing photographs. Small vertical photographs can be placed in the narrow column of white space, which will emphasize them. In addition, horizontal photographs can extend into this area.

Grids and Master Pages

Your entire publication can be based on a single grid, or you can create alternative grids for special pages. Here's how to combine "grid power" in Publisher with the power of master pages:

To display the grid in the background of every page   Create the grid in Normal view. When you add new pages, the grid will automatically appear.

To create a grid for special pages   Click View, Master Page (or press CTRL+M). In the Edit Master Page task pane, click the New Master Page button. In the New Master Page dialog box, type a title for the page—for example, **Member Directory**—and then create the grid.

Working with Text and Graphics

In Chapter 5, you learned how to create text boxes, place them in their desired locations, and link them together. In the preceding section, you learned how to align the text boxes with the underlying grid. In this section, we'll build on that knowledge as you learn how to add text and graphics to your text boxes.

Adding Text

You add text in existing text boxes by using either of two techniques:

Type directly in a text box.   You'll probably choose this method for short publications and when you "write to fit" to ensure that you don't prepare too much copy for the space you have available. To learn more about writing to fit, see the next section.

Import previously created Microsoft Office Word files.   Use this method if your coworkers or clients provide copy for you to format and prepare for commercial printers.

To type text in a text box, simply click in the box and begin typing at the blinking insertion point.

To import a previously created Word file:

1. Click to position the insertion point in the desired text box.

2. Click **Insert**, **Text File**.

3. Browse to the folder where you have saved the Word file to be inserted, and then double-click the file.

The file will then flow through all of the text boxes that you've linked.

> The easiest way to work with long files is to create a series of linked text boxes and insert a previously created text file.

Writing to Fit

If you are preparing your own marketing materials—especially ads, newsletters, and postcards—consider the advantages of "writing to fit." Writing to fit involves creating your message directly inside Publisher. Many of my clients swear that this is the most important lesson I've taught them!

Writing to fit offers the following significant advantages.

Providing a Feeling of Progress and Well-Being   Building momentum is the hardest part of any project. Blank pages create a lot of stress. You wonder if you'll ever finish the project. But when you write to fit inside Publisher, you can *see* your message take shape. Each additional word makes your project appear "more real" and more attainable.

> Many of my clients swear that using writing to fit is the most important lesson I've taught them!

Just adding a headline is enough to provide motivation to continue. This is especially true if you start by typing the headlines and subheadings that you're going to be working with. After you type your headlines and subheadings, your daunting writing task is reduced to simply "filling in the blanks," as shown in Figure 6-12.

Figure 6-12 Adding headlines and subheadings provides the structure you need to easily fill in the blanks and complete your project.

Giving Immediate Feedback on Length Equally important, writing to fit helps you avoid writing more than you can comfortably fit in your publication. As you write, you can see how much space you've already filled and how much more text needs to be written.

In many cases, you'll find that writing to fit goes much faster. Editing certainly will go faster if you only need to remove a few words rather than rewrite entire paragraphs.

Improving Writing Quality After preparing hundreds of "write to fit" ads, newsletters, and postcards, I am firmly convinced—and my clients agree—that writing to fit results in better writing. When you can see how your words fit on a page, you gain a greater appreciation for the significant changes in message length that result when you eliminate unnecessary words or replace long words with short words.

Soon you'll enjoy self-editing and look forward to the challenge of making everything fit by including only words that support your message, without any unnecessary "padding."

Adding Graphics

Now that you know how to work with text boxes, you'll find that graphics share many similar characteristics. Publisher enables you to add many types of graphics to your pages, including:

Lines   Added to the top and bottom borders of a page.

Boxes   Surrounding all four sides of a document.

Backgrounds   Placed behind all, or parts, of a page.

Files   Containing charts and graphs, photographs, illustrations, logos, and maps.

Callouts   Created using arrows to emphasize parts of an illustration or a photograph.

AutoShapes   Can contain text; used for creating graphics such as flow charts to illustrate business processes.

WordArt   A simple way to convert text to a graphic by altering letter shapes and adding creative effects.

Tables   Used to organize complex information.

The Objects toolbar, shown in Figure 6-13, is the starting point for adding most graphics. Simply click the desired tool, and add the element—or picture frame—to your page.

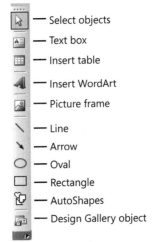

— Select objects
— Text box
— Insert table
— Insert WordArt
— Picture frame
— Line
— Arrow
— Oval
— Rectangle
— AutoShapes
— Design Gallery object

Figure 6-13   Using the Objects toolbar to add additional text and graphical elements to your pages.

Here are some hints for working successfully with graphical objects:

Exercise restraint.   It's easy to get carried away with using these tools to add elements, resulting in unnecessary page clutter. Always ask yourself these questions: Is this element absolutely necessary? Does adding this enhance the transmission of my message?

Never sacrifice readability for impact.   Although you can get away with using a lot of creative effects in your logos and titles, use WordArt's numerous distortions and creative effects with discretion.

Never sacrifice image for impact.   AutoShapes in Publisher include familiar business graphics as well as starbursts and "thought balloons." If you use these elements, make sure that they do not conflict with your overall image goals.

Adding Borders Around Graphical Objects

After positioning a graphic in your publication, you can easily add a border around it. A border around a photograph, for example, helps define the photograph's edges, which is particularly important if the photograph contains large areas of white. To add a border to a photograph or other graphic:

1. Select the photograph by clicking it.

2. Click the **Line/Border Style** tool on the **Formatting** toolbar or the **Picture** toolbar, and choose the desired width.

3. Click the **Line Color** drop-down button on the **Formatting** toolbar, and then click a line color to specify a different color for the border.

Be consistent in your use of borders. If you add a border to one photograph, add the same border to all other photographs in the document.

Working with Photographs

Microsoft Publisher offers a lot of formatting power for photographs, without the need for additional image editing software. In Publisher, you can resize photographs, crop them (eliminate unwanted information along the top, bottom, or side edges of the photograph), and adjust their brightness and contrast.

However, in some instances—for example, when extensive photographic modifications are needed—you might want to manipulate your images using a specialized image editing program before inserting them in your Publisher document.

Before doing so, check with your commercial printer, and ask how they want you to submit the photographic files. Often, they want access to the original files for last-minute fine-tuning.

Arranging Text and Graphical Objects

As you expand your work with objects, you'll want to familiarize yourself with the capabilities of the various commands on the Arrange menu. These commands allow you to align objects and control their "stacking order"—that is, place objects in front of, or behind, other objects, such as when you place text on top of a photograph or background fill, as shown in Figure 6-14.

Figure 6-14   Click Arrange, Order, Bring Forward to move the text box from behind the photograph (above) to in front of the photograph (below).

To align two or more objects   First select the objects, and then click Arrange, Align. You can choose to align the lefts, rights, tops, bottoms, or centers of objects.

To place one object in front of another one   Select one of the objects, and then click Arrange, Order. You can then choose an option to reposition the selected object in front of, or behind, other objects in the stack.

To equally space a series of objects up and down or across your document   Click
Arrange, Order, and then click either Vertically or Horizontally.

Grouping and Ungrouping Objects

Grouping permits you to lock objects together, such as a photograph and its caption or
a logo and its background. After grouping, you can move and resize the objects as one
unit. To group objects, follow these steps:

To temporarily group two or more objects   Hold down the SHIFT or CTRL key and
select the objects one by one. The group will be "disbanded" when you select
another text or graphical object.

To permanently group two or more objects   Hold down the SHIFT or CTRL key and
select the objects, and then click Arrange, Group.

If you later change your mind, you can ungroup a group into its component parts by
selecting the group and then clicking Arrange, Ungroup. After ungrouping—perhaps to
resize one of the elements—you can again select the objects and apply the Arrange,
Regroup command.

To save time when selecting objects for grouping, you can also drag a "marquee box," or
selection box, around the objects to be grouped.

Working with Color

Color is an element of marketing design that either immediately works for you or
against you. Correctly used, color invites readership by appealing to your reader's emotions. Incorrectly used, however, color can immediately undermine your message.

The color schemes in Publisher take the worry out of color. They encourage you to use
a few, carefully chosen colors for your publication. To view the available color schemes,
click Format, Color Schemes. In the Color Schemes task pane, shown in Figure 6-15,
you can select from among dozens of prechosen color palettes.

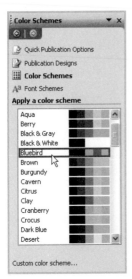

Figure 6-15   Publisher's color schemes resolve the problem of choosing colors that work well with each other.

A palette is a limited selection of colors for foreground and background elements that work well with each other. Each palette communicates a distinct emotional image—for example, royalty, exciting, outdoors, Art Deco, high-tech, and so on.

Color schemes encourage users to limit their color choices to a relatively small number of colors. Color schemes also eliminate the possibility of choosing colors that clash rather than complement each other or that project an inappropriate image.

After you specify a color scheme for your publication, when you select a word or object to change its color, the first options you encounter when you select a text color, line color, or fill color tool will be the options available in that color scheme, as shown in Figure 6-16. This helps avoid an inadvertent "rainbow" effect caused by using too many colors.

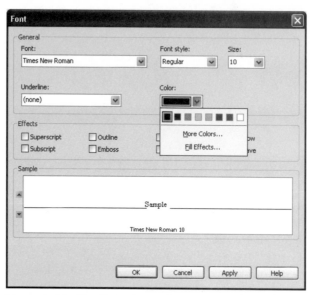

Figure 6-16 The first color options you see when selecting a text color, fill color, or line color tool will be the options available in the currently active color scheme.

Summary

In this chapter, you've learned how to create a strong, custom foundation for your publications. These publications will project a unique and consistent image to your clients and prospects. The time you invest in creating an appropriate structure for each of your publications will pay big dividends throughout the life of your projects.

In the next chapter, you'll learn how to format text to create attractive, easy-to-read marketing messages. You'll also learn how to save you work as reusable templates. By the end of the next chapter, instead of "reinventing the wheel" every time you begin a new advertisement, newsletter, or postcard, you'll be able to get right down to work!

Test Yourself

Before moving on, visit www.designtosellonline.com/06chap.html, where you can:

- Use a self-scoring assessment to test your comprehension of this chapter's topics.

- Review the new terms introduced in this chapter.

- Download and read a bonus chapter, "Advanced Color Techniques," that discusses color models and modifying Publisher color schemes.

You'll also find a list of recommended books and online resources for working with color.

Chapter Seven

Building Design Excellence into Every Page

What you'll find:

- ❏ Create headlines and subheads that attract and maintain your reader's interest.
- ❏ Format attractive, easy-to-read text paragraphs.
- ❏ Create text styles to ensure consistent formatting.
- ❏ Modify styles and share them between publications.

There might not be "rules" guaranteed to produce design excellence, but there *are* tools and techniques that you can use to increase your ability to achieve design excellence on every page. In this chapter, you'll learn secrets of text formatting that will help you create attractive, easy-to-read marketing messages.

In Chapter 6, you learned how to create the overall structure of your project. In this chapter, you'll learn how to:

Improve the communicating power of your marketing messages.　Make your messages easier to read by fine-tuning the elements of page architecture that typically communicate the bulk of your marketing message.

Strengthen the impact of your marketing messages.　Make your messages easier to recognize by building consistency into your marketing messages within and between each of your publications.

Our approach is to examine the building blocks of page architecture in the same order your readers will encounter them: from large to small. Accordingly, we will examine headlines and subheads before we examine body copy.

Later in this chapter, you will learn how to save your text formatting options as styles that can be shared between publications.

Making Sense of Type

A good way to begin your study of type is to separate type into three categories, organized by function. Although these categories blend into each other, organizing by function encourages you to use different standards for choosing typeface designs for each function.

Type for Recognition

The most flexible category of type consists of typefaces intended for use in logos, publication titles, and product packaging. Here, the goal is to project an appropriate and easily recognized image. To achieve this goal, you can break many of the rules concerning typeface readability and get away with it, as shown in Figure 7-1, because logos and titles are intended to be recognized more than to be read.

Figure 7-1 Typefaces for logos and titles can be very stylized, as they are intended to be recognized more than to be read.

Type for Guidance

Type intended for use as headlines, subheads within text, and *pull-quotes* (short phrases usually set in large type to emphasize key points made elsewhere on the page) must be more readable than type intended as image. Headlines and subheads succeed only when they can be easily read.

Type intended for guidance should make a heavier impression on the page than body copy so that readers can easily recognize it. This is why sans serif typefaces, shown in Figure 7-2, are so useful—they form a noticeable contrast with the serif typefaces commonly used for body copy.

Figure 7-2 Sans serif typeface designs are simpler, and often have a stronger presence on the page, making them ideal for attracting your reader's eyes to headlines and subheads.

Serif typeface designs have small strokes added to the edges of each letter, which aid character recognition and help guide your reader's eyes from letter to letter, as shown here:

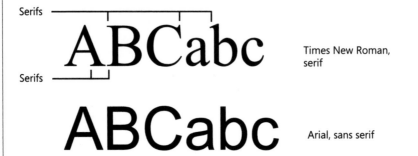

Figure 7-3 shows examples of some popular serif typefaces.

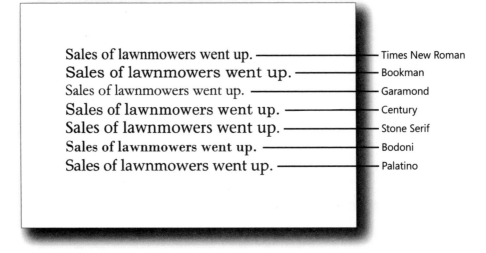

Figure 7-3 Serif typefaces are ideal for extended reading. Many classic designs have been used for hundreds of years.

Type for Extended Reading

Typeface designs intended for extended reading—placed in paragraphs organized in text columns—should be extremely easy to read. Here, *transparency*—the degree to which the type doesn't call attention to itself—is the goal.

Accordingly, body copy typefaces, usually serif typefaces, should not have any characteristics that draw attention to themselves. The ideal body copy typeface is so transparent, and the words it communicates so easily comprehended, that your readers will concentrate on your message, not the typeface used to communicate it.

Nevertheless, there are significant differences between serif typefaces. Some designs appear larger than others, reducing the *word count*—or number of words that can fit in a given amount of space.

Formatting Headlines and Subheads

After publication titles, headlines and subheads are the first text elements your readers are likely to notice. The typeface and formatting choices you make for headlines and subheads will be immediately obvious to your readers and will go a long way toward creating the image your marketing message will project.

Formatting Headlines

Headline formatting is extremely important. In a few fractions of a second, your readers will glance at your headlines and make immediate "read" or "don't read" decisions. Numerous studies going back over seventy-five years have shown that if readers don't read your headlines, it is unlikely that they will read the body copy that follows.

Using Font Schemes to Combine Typefaces

Recent versions of Publisher take the worry out of choosing the right combination of typefaces for headlines, subheads, and body copy. Publisher's Font Schemes offer professionally chosen combinations of the typefaces built into the Microsoft Windows operating system and many of the designs that ship with Publisher.

To put this tool to work, select Format, Font Schemes. When the Font Schemes task pane appears, use the vertical scroll bar to select from among typeface combinations identified by terms like Capital, Casual, Literary, Modern, and Textbook. When you click a desired Font Scheme, your choice will be applied to Publisher's default text styles, such as Heading 1, Heading 2, Normal, etc.

Click Font Scheme Options to modify type sizes or make other changes.

Exploring Headline and Subhead Type Options

Many sans serif typeface designs are available in different *weights* and *widths*. This flexibility offers you the ability to add a distinct look to your publication without sacrificing your reader's ability to quickly scan a page and get an idea of its contents from the headlines and subheads.

Weight options   *Weight* refers to the thickness of the strokes making up each character. Heavy options have strokes that are thicker than bold options. Light options have strokes thinner than the regular, or roman, weight of the typeface, as shown in Figure 7-4.

Width options   Some sans serif typefaces have special condensed versions available, which allow you to fit more words in each line of your headlines and subheads.

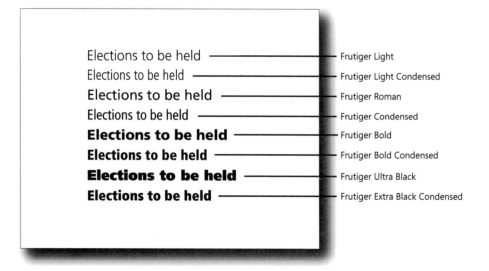

Figure 7-4   The Frutiger typeface, named for its designer, Adrian Frutiger, is a sans serif typeface offering numerous weight and width options.

A different *font* is used for each weight and width option, in addition to formatting options such as bold, italics, and bold-italics. A font is a file containing the information needed to create a specific typeface design in a given weight, width, and style variation (for example, bold). Thus, 8 different fonts were needed to create Figure 7-4; 16 fonts would be needed if the italic versions of each weight and width variation were included.

Making Appropriate Headline Formatting Decisions

Headline formatting in Publisher takes place in three dialog boxes:

Font dialog box   Click Format, Font. In this dialog box, you specify the desired typeface, type size, type style, and case.

Character Spacing dialog box   Click Format, Character Spacing. In this dialog box, you can fine-tune letter spacing to improve your headline's appearance.

Paragraph dialog box   Click Format, Paragraph. In this dialog box, you can specify alignment, line-spacing, space above, and space below. The Space Above and Space Below options are used to add a consistent amount of white space above and below your headlines.

The key to choosing the right typeface and type size is to choose a single headline typeface design—ideally, one with sufficient flexibility, such as weight and width options—and stick with it throughout all of your print marketing materials—including your ads, brochures, newsletters, postcards, and so on.

Not only does this method reduce the investment you need to make in fonts to project a consistent image, but also the use of a consistent headline and subhead typeface will, over time, build familiarity with your readers and differentiate your marketing messages from those of your competition.

Choosing the right headline type size should be influenced by the number of words you (or your boss or client) typically include in your headlines and the amount of space available for the headlines:

- Choose too large a headline type size, and the headline will look "bloated" compared to the width of the column it's placed in, as shown in Figure 7-5.

- Choose too small a type size, however, as shown in Figure 7-6, and the headline will lack the contrast necessary to attract your reader's attention and to make the headline visually distinct from the body copy it introduces.

Choose a single headline typeface and stick with it throughout all of your print marketing materials, including ads, brochures, newsletters, postcards, and so on.

Use subheads to increase message readability

First the bad news: you're likely to be far more interested in the contents of your carefully written brochure, newsletter or proposal than your readers.

Most of your readers are likely to give your publication just a quick glance, *quickly skimming each page* to see if there's anything worth reading. If nothing catches their eyes, your message is likely to be put aside "until later"—which usually means "never."

Why subheads?
Now the good news: subheads make it easy to convert skimmers into readers. Subheads are "mini-headlines" inserted within newsletter articles or sections of your report. Subheads make your newsletters and reports easier to read by breaking them into chunks.

Subheads "advertise" the contents of the paragraphs that follow. They attract the skimmer's interest and tease him into reading on. Each subhead provides an entry point into your message, giving skimmers reasons to begin reading.

Subheads also add visual interest to your message by adding white space and typographic interest.

Formatting tips
To succeed, subheads must be easy to locate and easy to read. Here are some of the best ways to add impact to your subheads:

Typographic contrast. Subheads must appear

noticeably different from adjacent text. One easy technique is to combine subheads set in a bold sans serif typeface (like Arial, Helvetica or Frutiger) with body copy set in a serif typeface (like Garamond, Minion or Times Roman).

White space. Space above subheads makes them easy to locate. There should be more space above a subhead (i.e., between a subhead and the proceeding paragraph) than between the subhead and the text it introduces.

Subhead alignment
Subhead alignment depends on text alignment.

Choose *flush-left subhead alignment* if you are using flush-left/ragged-right text. (You're reading flush-left/ragged-right text right now.)

Center subheads when they appear in columns of justified text. Justified text is characterized by lines of equal length.

How many?
Insert a subhead every time you introduce a new idea or topic. In general, newsletters

look best when articles are broken up with subheads every three or four paragraphs.

Common mistakes
The following are some frequently encountered problems.

Underlining. Never underline subheads. Underlining makes words harder to read instead of easier to read. Underlining bscures the word shapes that readers depend on for easy reading.

Ambiguous relations. Avoid subheads that "float" between the previous paragraph and the text they introduce. Subheads should appear closely related to the paragraphs they introduce.

To learn more
Colored text. Colored type often looks better on screen than it does when printed. Subheads printed in color are often harder to read than the same subheads printed in black.

Figure 7-5   When a headline is set in too large a type size, it looks disproportionately large for its environment and lacks sufficient white space to draw attention to it.

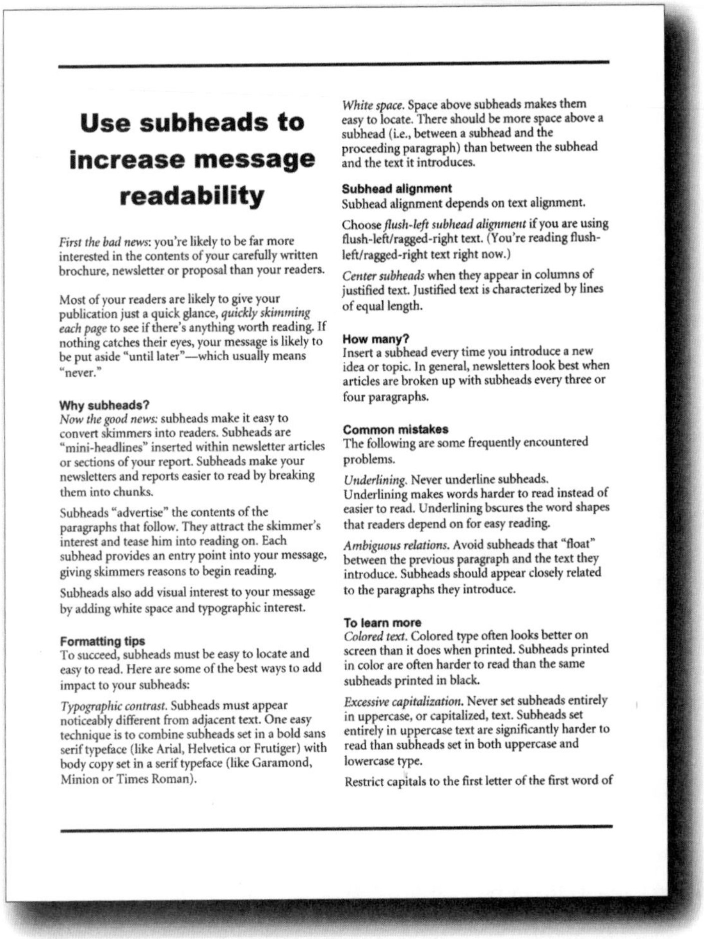

Use subheads to increase message readability

First the bad news: you're likely to be far more interested in the contents of your carefully written brochure, newsletter or proposal than your readers.

Most of your readers are likely to give your publication just a quick glance, *quickly skimming each page* to see if there's anything worth reading. If nothing catches their eyes, your message is likely to be put aside "until later"—which usually means "never."

Why subheads?
Now the good news: subheads make it easy to convert skimmers into readers. Subheads are "mini-headlines" inserted within newsletter articles or sections of your report. Subheads make your newsletters and reports easier to read by breaking them into chunks.

Subheads "advertise" the contents of the paragraphs that follow. They attract the skimmer's interest and tease him into reading on. Each subhead provides an entry point into your message, giving skimmers reasons to begin reading.

Subheads also add visual interest to your message by adding white space and typographic interest.

Formatting tips
To succeed, subheads must be easy to locate and easy to read. Here are some of the best ways to add impact to your subheads:

Typographic contrast. Subheads must appear noticeably different from adjacent text. One easy technique is to combine subheads set in a bold sans serif typeface (like Arial, Helvetica or Frutiger) with body copy set in a serif typeface (like Garamond, Minion or Times Roman).

White space. Space above subheads makes them easy to locate. There should be more space above a subhead (i.e., between a subhead and the proceeding paragraph) than between the subhead and the text it introduces.

Subhead alignment
Subhead alignment depends on text alignment.

Choose *flush-left subhead alignment* if you are using flush-left/ragged-right text. (You're reading flush-left/ragged-right text right now.)

Center subheads when they appear in columns of justified text. Justified text is characterized by lines of equal length.

How many?
Insert a subhead every time you introduce a new idea or topic. In general, newsletters look best when articles are broken up with subheads every three or four paragraphs.

Common mistakes
The following are some frequently encountered problems.

Underlining. Never underline subheads. Underlining makes words harder to read instead of easier to read. Underlining bscures the word shapes that readers depend on for easy reading.

Ambiguous relations. Avoid subheads that "float" between the previous paragraph and the text they introduce. Subheads should appear closely related to the paragraphs they introduce.

To learn more
Colored text. Colored type often looks better on screen than it does when printed. Subheads printed in color are often harder to read than the same subheads printed in black.

Excessive capitalization. Never set subheads entirely in uppercase, or capitalized, text. Subheads set entirely in uppercase text are significantly harder to read than subheads set in both uppercase and lowercase type.

Restrict capitals to the first letter of the first word of

Figure 7-6 A slight reduction in type size adds surrounding white space above, below, and to the left and right of the headline, also enhancing contrast with the body copy that follows.

Choosing the Right Case

One of the biggest mistakes you can make is to set your headlines entirely in uppercase—or capital—letters. In most cases, headlines should be set in a combination of uppercase and lowercase type. The reason for this is word recognition. Reading is based on your reader's ability to recognize *word shapes*—not their ability to "sound out" each word. But words set entirely in uppercase letters have no distinctive shapes. There's simply a "box" around each word.

Words set in lowercase characters are far easier to recognize. This is because lowercase characters can have either *ascenders* or *descenders*:

Ascenders   Refers to the parts of characters—like *b, d, f, h, l,* and *t*—that stick up above the *x-height*, or the height of the letter *x*.

Descenders   Refers to the parts of characters—like *g, p, q,* and *y*—that fall below the *baseline*, or invisible line that the characters rest on.

Each word's unique combination of character ascenders and descenders creates the distinct shapes necessary for easy recognition. Figure 7-7 shows how the ascenders and descenders in the bottom example create a unique word shape, one distinctly different from the simple rectangle around the top example.

Figure 7-7   Words set entirely in uppercase characters lack distinctive shapes. Words set in lowercase type have unique shapes, created by ascenders and descenders.

In addition, headlines set entirely in uppercase type can occupy up to 30 percent more space than the same headlines set in a combination of uppercase and lowercase type.

Choosing Headline Alignment

You can specify headline alignment in the Paragraph dialog box. Many headlines are centered out of habit—in other words, because we're used to seeing centered headlines in magazines and newspapers. But there's a lot to be said for setting headlines flush left.

The right choice depends primarily on the image you want to project and the alignment you have chosen for your body copy:

■   Centered headlines project a "serious" or "classic" image that might be appropriate for your publication. Flush-left headlines, however, project a more contemporary image.

- Your choice of flush-left or centered headlines should be influenced by the text alignment you have chosen for your body copy.

In general, flush-left headlines work best with flush-left text. Centered headlines, however, are most appropriate with *justified text*—characterized by lines of equal length. (Publisher increases or decreases line-by-line word spacing to align the last letters in each line.)

Readers tend to prefer flush-left headlines, because each line begins in the same position, and the first words in each line of your headline are in the same position as the first lines of the body copy that follows.

In addition, flush-left headlines can appear to be surrounded by more white space, because the white space is concentrated to the right of the headline. With centered headlines, however, the white space is divided in two: half to the left of each headline, and half to the right.

Thus, after you determine your body copy text alignment, you might want to review your headline alignment. This is because body copy alignment determines headline alignment: left-aligned headlines work best with left-aligned body copy, and centered headlines work best with justified text.

You might want to review your choice of headline alignment after you format your publication's body copy.

Adjusting Headline Length

Headline length is an example of the close relationship between writing, editing, and design. Whenever possible, edit headlines to the bone—rewriting as necessary—so that they will be as short as possible.

Edit headlines to the bone—rewriting as necessary—so that they will occupy as few lines as possible.

Consider three-line headlines the maximum length you will allow, and whenever possible, limit headlines to two lines. Long headlines are readership killers! In some circumstances, three-line headlines might be necessary, but four lines is definitely too many.

Fine-Tuning Headline Character Spacing

One of the best ways to improve your headlines is to slightly reduce character and line spacing. The purpose of these refinements is to replace white space within your headlines with white space *around* your headlines.

Strive for two-line headlines, and avoid four-line headlines.

Tracking refers to uniformly reducing character spacing between every pair of characters in the headline. To adjust the tracking in your headline text, first select the headline, and then click Format, Character Spacing.

In the Tracking section in the Character Spacing dialog box, shown in Figure 7-8, there are two ways you can fine-tune character spacing. One way is to click the drop-down arrow in the list on the left and choose either the Tight or the Very Tight option. In many cases, however, these options might squeeze letters together more than you would like.

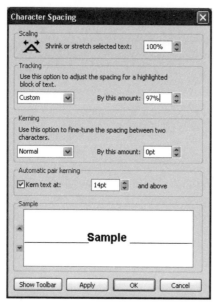

Figure 7-8   Fine-tune the spacing between letters in your headline by entering a specific value in the Tracking section of the Character Spacing dialog box.

A better option is to click in the By This Amount box and then type a more subtle setting. You might start by reducing character spacing in one percent intervals—for example, type **99** for a 1 percent reduction in character spacing, **98** for a 2 percent reduction in character spacing, and so on. You might be surprised to see what a big difference a 1, 2, or 3 percent reduction in character spacing makes. You can preview these changes as you make them.

Use extreme care
when reducing
character spacing.

Use extreme care when reducing character spacing. Remove too much character spacing, and your message becomes very difficult to read.

Fine-Tuning Headline Line Spacing

Default headline line spacing is usually too generous, creating distracting amounts of white space between the lines of a headline. *Leading* refers to the space between subsequent lines of text—a reference to the days when thin strips of lead were added between lines to space the type.

By default, Publisher uses line spaces approximately 20 percent larger than the type size you have chosen. For body text, which is usually 11 or 12 points (there are 72 points to an inch), an additional 20 percent line spacing aids readability. But as type sizes increase to the 18 to 36 points commonly used for headlines, the lines become separated by a distracting amount of white space.

To fine-tune line spacing in headlines, click Format, Paragraph, and then click the Indents And Spacing tab. In the Line Spacing area, select the default value in the Between Lines box, and replace it with either:

- A specific amount of space, proportional to the type size you are using. For example, you might start by typing **32pt** (*pt* is short for points) if you're setting the headline in 36-point type. Figure 7-9 shows how to adjust line spacing in the Paragraph dialog box.

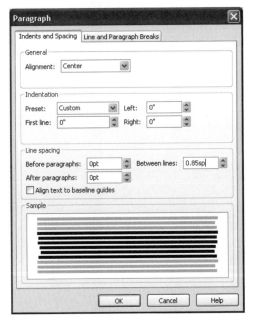

Figure 7-9 Adjusting headline line spacing in the Paragraph dialog box.

- A percentage of a full line *spacing*—for example, **0.85** for a 15 percent reduction in line spacing, or **0.90** for a 10 percent reduction in line spacing. You must enter these percentages in decimal form, so a 120 percent increase in line space would be entered as **1.20sp** (*sp* is short for spaces) or **1.20li** (*li* is short for lines).

Note   Publisher allows you to enter dimensions in points (22pt) or percentages of a line space (either 1.1li or 1.2sp)—whichever you're most comfortable with.

With a little practice, you'll soon be very comfortable making character spacing and line spacing decisions. Although you might be removing only tiny amounts of space, the cumulative effect will be great! Compare Figure 7-6, which shows default line and character spacing, with Figure 7-10, below, which shows the same example with reduced line and character spacing, and you can see the difference these two adjustments can make.

Use subheads to increase message readability

First the bad news: you're likely to be far more interested in the contents of your carefully written brochure, newsletter or proposal than your readers.

Most of your readers are likely to give your publication just a quick glance, *quickly skimming each page* to see if there's anything worth reading. If nothing catches their eyes, your message is likely to be put aside "until later"—which usually means "never."

Why subheads?
Now the good news: subheads make it easy to convert skimmers into readers. Subheads are "mini-headlines" inserted within newsletter articles or sections of your report. Subheads make your newsletters and reports easier to read by breaking them into chunks.

Subheads "advertise" the contents of the paragraphs that follow. They attract the skimmer's interest and tease him into reading on. Each subhead provides an entry point into your message, giving skimmers reasons to begin reading.

Subheads also add visual interest to your message by adding white space and typographic interest.

Formatting tips
To succeed, subheads must be easy to locate and easy to read. Here are some of the best ways to add impact to your subheads:

Typographic contrast. Subheads must appear noticeably different from adjacent text. One easy technique is to combine subheads set in a bold sans serif typeface (like Arial, Helvetica or Frutiger) with body copy set in a serif typeface (like Garamond, Minion or Times Roman).

White space. Space above subheads makes them easy to locate. There should be more space above a subhead (i.e., between a subhead and the proceeding paragraph) than between the subhead and the text it introduces.

Subhead alignment
Subhead alignment depends on text alignment.

Choose *flush-left subhead alignment* if you are using flush-left/ragged-right text. (You're reading flush-left/ragged-right text right now.)

Center subheads when they appear in columns of justified text. Justified text is characterized by lines of equal length.

How many?
Insert a subhead every time you introduce a new idea or topic. In general, newsletters look best when articles are broken up with subheads every three or four paragraphs.

Common mistakes
The following are some frequently encountered problems.

Underlining. Never underline subheads. Underlining makes words harder to read instead of easier to read. Underlining bscures the word shapes that readers depend on for easy reading.

Ambiguous relations. Avoid subheads that "float" between the previous paragraph and the text they introduce. Subheads should appear closely related to the paragraphs they introduce.

To learn more
Colored text. Colored type often looks better on screen than it does when printed. Subheads printed in color are often harder to read than the same subheads printed in black.

Excessive capitalization. Never set subheads entirely in uppercase, or capitalized, text. Subheads set entirely in uppercase text are significantly harder to read than subheads set in both uppercase and lowercase type.

Restrict capitals to the first letter of the first word of

Figure 7-10   After reducing character and line spacing, the headline appears as a distinct visual unit—instead of two separate lines of type—surrounded by plenty of white space.

Setting Hyphenation and Line Breaks

Headlines should never be hyphenated at the end of a line. Hyphenated headlines are an obvious cue that an amateur produced the publication—and this will never do! Your goal is to always project a competent, professional image for yourself, your boss and coworkers, and your clients.

If you are setting your headlines in the same text box used for body copy, you often run into the following problem: if you turn off hyphenation in the headline, you are also turning off hyphenation in your body copy! For reasons you'll see shortly, this is unacceptable.

You can get around this problem by forcing line breaks using Publisher's Line Break command.

Headlines simply work best when certain groups of words—such as first and last names—appear together and when the headlines break at the points where someone reading the headline aloud would normally pause to take a breath.

You can't simply press the ENTER key to break a headline at a desired location. Doing so creates a new paragraph, perhaps with a first-line indent or unwanted spacing between the two lines.

The solution to this problem is to hold down the SHIFT key while pressing ENTER. This forces a line break without adding a first-line indent to the next line or an extra space between the two lines, as shown in Figure 7-11.

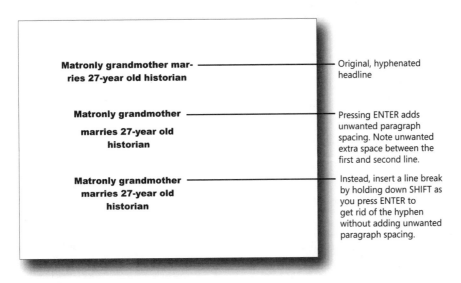

Figure 7-11   Eliminating unwanted hyphenation (top) by pressing the ENTER key (middle) adds unwanted and inconsistent line spacing, which doesn't occur when you press SHIFT+ENTER (bottom).

Formatting Subheads

Subheads represent one of the most effective design tools at your disposal. Subheads break up long text passages into a series of easy-to-read, bite-size chunks. Subheads also add visual interest to your pages.

Best practices for formatting subheads are similar, in many ways, to best practices for formatting headlines. Here are some of the similarities:

Typeface choice   Subheads should form a strong contrast with adjacent body copy. Otherwise, the subheads will blend in with the body copy and fail to receive the attention they deserve.

Length   Shorter is always better. Limit subheads to one line only. Subheads should consist only of keywords, intended to telegraph the importance of the paragraphs that follow.

Hyphenation   Subheads should never be hyphenated.

Case   Subheads set in uppercase and lowercase type are more attractive and easier to read than subheads set entirely in uppercase letters.

Alignment   Subhead alignment should follow headline alignment. Use flush-left subheads in publications with flush-left headlines. Use centered subheads in publications with centered headlines.

White space   There should be more white space above the subhead—separating it from the preceding text—than between the subhead and the text it introduces. The white space above the subhead creates a barrier, visually indicating that a new topic follows.

Style   Avoid underlining subheads. This makes them harder to read instead of easier to read, because underlining interferes with easy recognition of word shapes.

Creating a Subhead Hierarchy

In many cases, you might want to include more than one subhead level. This book, for example, is formatted using three subhead levels:

Level 1 subheads   Are used for major topics, and are indicated by a larger type size and extra white space above them. These subheads are also sometimes *hung*, meaning that they extend to the left of the text column they introduce.

Level 2 subheads   Are a little smaller, and their left margin aligns with the text column.

Level 3 subheads   Are smaller still, although they are significantly more noticeable than body copy.

Two Keys to Subhead Formatting

The keys to effective subhead formatting are found in the Paragraph dialog box (click Format, Paragraph).

The first formatting tool is found on the Indents And Spacing tab. To add extra space above a subhead, type a desired measurement in the Space Above box. Experiment with spacing between one and one and one-half lines of space. (The actual amount will depend on the Space Below text spacing you use for the text paragraph preceding the subhead.)

The second formatting tool is found on the Line And Paragraph Breaks tab. Here you can permanently link a subhead to the paragraph it introduces by selecting the Keep With Next check box.

Choosing the Correct Font File Format

Your choice of font file formats should be determined by both available budget resources and your commercial printer's preferences. Some commercial printers prefer not to work with one format or another. This is just one of the reasons you should consult with your commercial printer as early as possible, to ensure freedom from font file format incompatibilities later on.

Font Formats

There are three commonly used typeface file formats:

TrueType fonts   The so-called *system fonts* included in Microsoft Windows are TrueType fonts; they appear the same on screen and in your printed documents. Additional TrueType fonts are included in Microsoft Publisher to give you more design flexibility. These fonts can be used with other software programs, as well as in Publisher.

Type 1 fonts   These have long been the standard of professional graphic designers. Available from digital typeface vendors such as Adobe, Type 1 fonts sometimes include more artistic variations such as fonts intended for use at large size, or fonts that include special decorative characters. A pair of files is needed for each Type 1 font: one file controls how the font appears on screen, the other file is used for printing. Figure 7-12 shows the swash characters and old-style figures available with several Type 1 fonts.

OpenType fonts   This relatively new format, available from third-party vendors, combines the huge selection of Type 1 font designs and the convenience of the single file design of TrueType fonts. OpenType fonts can be used in either Microsoft Windows or Apple Macintosh operating systems.

Figure 7-12 Swash characters are intended to be used at the beginnings or ends of words. Notice the ascenders and descenders added to the old-style figures, which help the numbers blend in with the adjacent text.

Adding Rules Above and Below Subheads

Another way to add emphasis to subheads is to add rules above or below them. Rules above subheads reinforce the fact that each subhead introduces a new topic. The Rules Below feature is more appropriately used to indicate the end of an article or sidebar.

To add lines to subheads, click the subhead, and then click Format, Horizontal Rules. In the Horizontal Rules dialog box, shown in Figure 7-13, you can specify the location (before or after the paragraph), thickness, color, style, and placement of the horizontal rules.

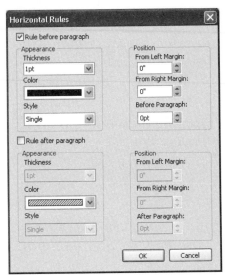

Figure 7-13 Rules above and below subheads are added and formatted in the Horizontal Rules dialog box.

Formatting Body Copy

Your market's ability to easily understand your message depends on your ability to format attractive, easy-to-read body copy. You already possess much of the information you need for successful formatting as you're already familiar with the Font, Character Spacing, and Paragraph dialog boxes.

In this section, we'll concentrate on the criteria you'll be using to make your formatting decisions, as well as some advanced options that can play a major role in visually positioning your marketing message a cut above those of your competition.

How Layout Influences Your Initial Formatting Decisions

You have three initial formatting decisions to make. You'll make the first two—typeface and type size—in the Font dialog box. You'll make the third—line spacing—in the Paragraph dialog box.

To make the right body copy formatting decisions, however, you have to return to the layout decisions you made when setting up the structure of your document, which you did in Chapter 6. This is because typeface, type size, and line spacing decisions must be based on line lengths, which are determined by the number and width of the text columns on each page.

To make the right body copy formatting decisions, you must return to the layout decisions you made when setting up the column structure of your document.

121

Choosing an Appropriate Body Copy Typeface

Remember the differences between serif and sans serif typefaces discussed earlier in this chapter? There has long been disagreement about whether serif or sans serif is easier to read in long text passages. Some claim to like the simpler, more contemporary look of sans serif typefaces like Arial, Helvetica, Frutiger, and Gill Sans.

For significant reasons, however, your readers will probably prefer that you set your body copy in a serif typeface like Garamond, Bookman, or Times New Roman. These reasons include:

Links   The serifs serve as links between characters, helping guide your reader's eyes across each line.

Uniqueness   The size and placement of the serifs helps create a more recognizable shape for each letter. Sans serif typefaces are more uniform.

Contrast   The strokes that make up serif typefaces typically differ in thickness. Some strokes might be heavy, others lighter, helping define each character's shape. Sans serif typefaces rarely exhibit these differences in stroke thickness.

In most cases, you're best off playing it safe and using a tried-and-proven typeface, carefully sized and placed on the page, rather than trying to be "creative" and defy convention. The easier, and more recognizable, your typeface choices are, the easier it will be for your readers to understand your message.

The easier to read and more recogniz-able, your typeface choices are, the easier it will be for your readers to understand your message.

Choosing the Proper Type Size

Setting type too small is as bad as setting type too big. The correct type size is based on the typeface you're using and the width of your columns. Your goal is to create lines of type that contain enough words for your reader to make two left-to-right eye movements on each line.

Undersized type   If you choose a type size too small for the typeface and line length you're using, readers will have to squint. Worse, readers will have to make several left-to-right eye scans on each line. Long lines of small type also contribute to readers getting lost making the transition from the end of one line to the begin-ning of the next line. Equally bad, readers might unintentionally reread the same line (called *doubling*).

Oversized type   Surprisingly, oversized type is as bad as undersized type. When type size is not appropriate for the typeface and line length you're working with, your message appears "bloated." Worse, there are not enough words on each line for readers to maintain a comfortable scanning rhythm.

Figure 7-14 shows how undersized type (left) is as hard to read as oversized type (right).

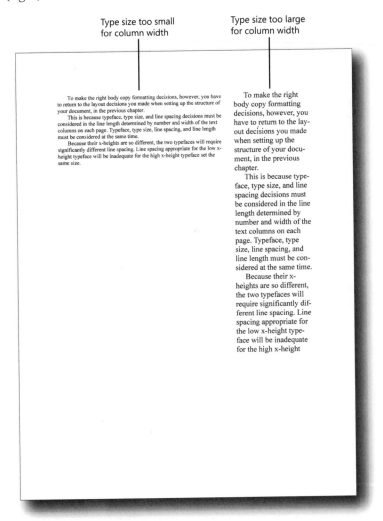

Type size too small
for column width

Type size too large
for column width

To make the right body copy formatting decisions, however, you have to return to the layout decisions you made when setting up the structure of your document, in the previous chapter.

This is because typeface, type size, and line spacing decisions must be considered in the line length determined by number and width of the text columns on each page. Typeface, type size, line spacing, and line length must be considered at the same time.

Because their x-heights are so different, the two typefaces will require significantly different line spacing. Line spacing appropriate for the low x-height typeface will be inadequate for the high x-height typeface set the same size.

To make the right body copy formatting decisions, however, you have to return to the layout decisions you made when setting up the structure of your document, in the previous chapter.

This is because typeface, type size, and line spacing decisions must be considered in the line length determined by number and width of the text columns on each page. Typeface, type size, line spacing, and line length must be considered at the same time.

Because their x-heights are so different, the two typefaces will require significantly different line spacing. Line spacing appropriate for the low x-height typeface will be inadequate for the high x-height

Figure 7-14   Undersized type is as hard to read as oversized type.

When there is *balance* between typeface, type size, and line length, each line will contain between 26 and 40 characters.

Choosing the Right Line Spacing

Pay as much attention to line spacing decisions as you pay to type size decisions. This might not make sense at first, but it will if you remember how typefaces differ from one another. One of the major differences between typeface designs is their x-height. Some typefaces have a high x-height; others have a low x-height.

The reason for this is related to the x-height of the typeface design you are going to use for your body copy. As mentioned earlier, the x-height of a typeface is the height of characters that have neither ascenders nor descenders. These characters include the vowels: *a*, *e*, *i*, *o*, and *u*. X-height is one of the major differences between typefaces and determines the apparent size of a typeface:

- High x-height typefaces appear larger on the page, but their ascenders and descenders are less noticeable.

- Low x-height typefaces appear smaller on the page, but their word shapes are more pronounced, because the ascenders and descenders are more pronounced.

Differing x-heights are the reason that the serif typefaces illustrated earlier in this chapter (see Figure 7-3) appeared so different, even though each example was the same type size. Differing x-heights also influence the number of words that can fit in a given amount of space, as shown in Figure 7-15.

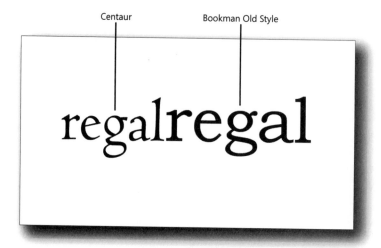

Figure 7-15 When two typefaces with differing x-heights but the same type size are compared side by side, their differences are immediately obvious.

Because their x-heights are so different, the two typefaces will require significantly different line spacing. If the same line spacing is used for both typefaces, the line spacing appropriate for the low x-height typeface will be inadequate for the high x-height typeface set the same size. Figure 7-16 shows Centaur, a low x-height typeface design, and Bookman Old Style, a high x-height typeface design, formatted with the same line spacing. Notice especially how cramped and hard to read the Bookman sample is.

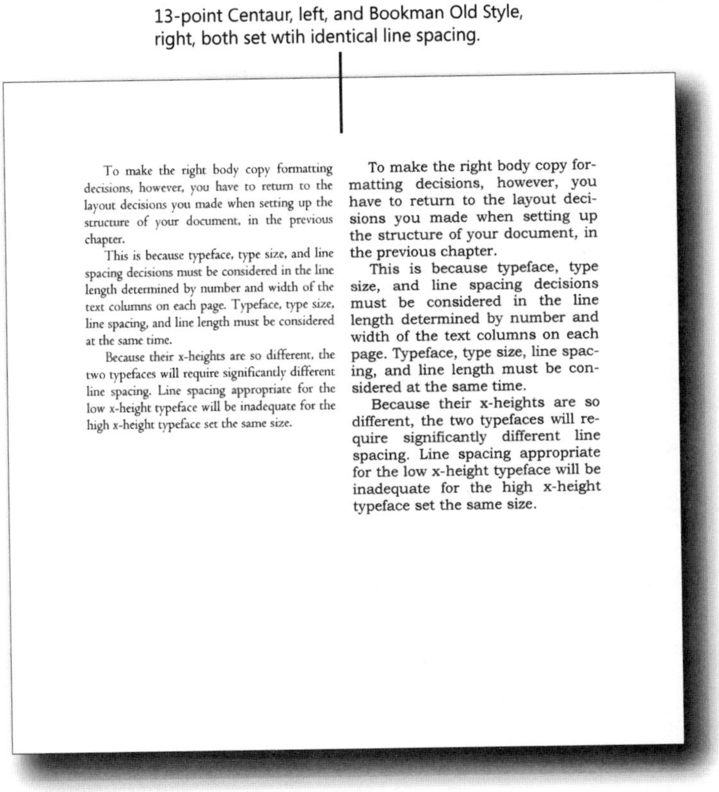

13-point Centaur, left, and Bookman Old Style, right, both set wtih identical line spacing.

To make the right body copy formatting decisions, however, you have to return to the layout decisions you made when setting up the structure of your document, in the previous chapter.

This is because typeface, type size, and line spacing decisions must be considered in the line length determined by number and width of the text columns on each page. Typeface, type size, line spacing, and line length must be considered at the same time.

Because their x-heights are so different, the two typefaces will require significantly different line spacing. Line spacing appropriate for the low x-height typeface will be inadequate for the high x-height typeface set the same size.

To make the right body copy formatting decisions, however, you have to return to the layout decisions you made when setting up the structure of your document, in the previous chapter.

This is because typeface, type size, and line spacing decisions must be considered in the line length determined by number and width of the text columns on each page. Typeface, type size, line spacing, and line length must be considered at the same time.

Because their x-heights are so different, the two typefaces will require significantly different line spacing. Line spacing appropriate for the low x-height typeface will be inadequate for the high x-height typeface set the same size.

Figure 7-16   When set using the same type size and line spacing, on an identical line length, the typeface on the right, with the higher x-height, is significantly harder to read than the typeface on the left.

Readability is greatly enhanced, however, when line spacing is reduced for the Centaur sample and increased for the Bookman sample, as shown in Figure 7-17.

13-point Centaur, left, set wtih 14.5 point line spacing, compared to Bookman Old Style, right, set with 18 point line spacing.

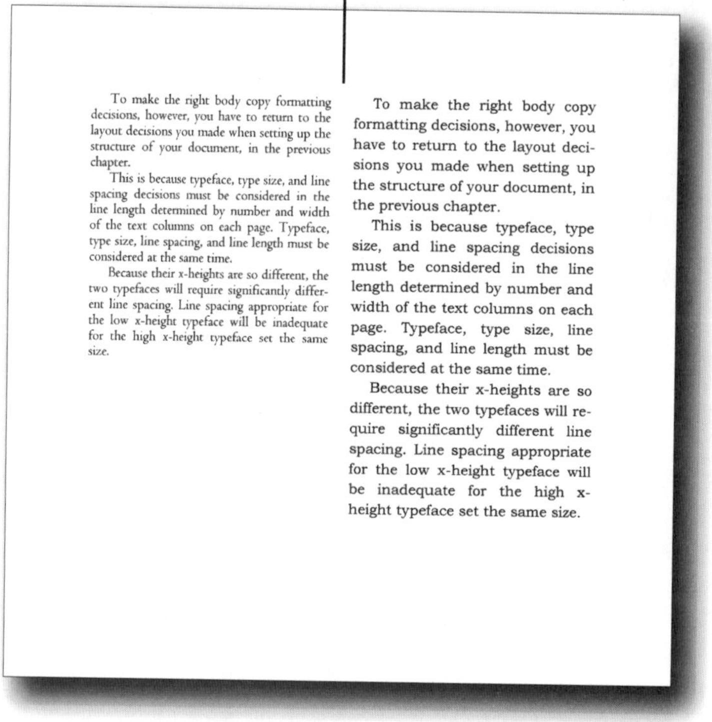

To make the right body copy formatting decisions, however, you have to return to the layout decisions you made when setting up the structure of your document, in the previous chapter.

This is because typeface, type size, and line spacing decisions must be considered in the line length determined by number and width of the text columns on each page. Typeface, type size, line spacing, and line length must be considered at the same time.

Because their x-heights are so different, the two typefaces will require significantly different line spacing. Line spacing appropriate for the low x-height typeface will be inadequate for the high x-height typeface set the same size.

To make the right body copy formatting decisions, however, you have to return to the layout decisions you made when setting up the structure of your document, in the previous chapter.

This is because typeface, type size, and line spacing decisions must be considered in the line length determined by number and width of the text columns on each page. Typeface, type size, line spacing, and line length must be considered at the same time.

Because their x-heights are so different, the two typefaces will require significantly different line spacing. Line spacing appropriate for the low x-height typeface will be inadequate for the high x-height typeface set the same size.

Figure 7-17   By slightly reducing the line spacing in the left column and increasing line spacing in the right column, the appearance and readability of both columns is improved.

As a rule of thumb, add line spacing for high x-height typefaces and reduce line-spacing for low x-height typefaces.

Increasing the line spacing for the typeface with the higher x-height makes it easier to read. There is now more white space surrounding the ascenders and descenders, enhancing the word shapes on each line.

Determining the Appropriate Type Formatting by Trial and Error

The only way you can make the right choice of typeface, type size, and line spacing for the line length (or column width) you will be using in your publication is by creating a test document containing two or three columns (depending on the design of your publication), placing the same typeface and type size in each column, and modifying the line spacing.

Start by experimenting with 1-point and 2-point differences in type size and line spacing. Print your experiments, and keep track of the formatting options used for each sample.

The correct combination of typeface, type size, line spacing, and line length (column width) will soon emerge with startling clarity. The right choice will be obvious at a glance, as you can see in Figure 7-18.

When you print side-by-side comparisons of type size and line spacing differences, the right choices will be immediately obvious.

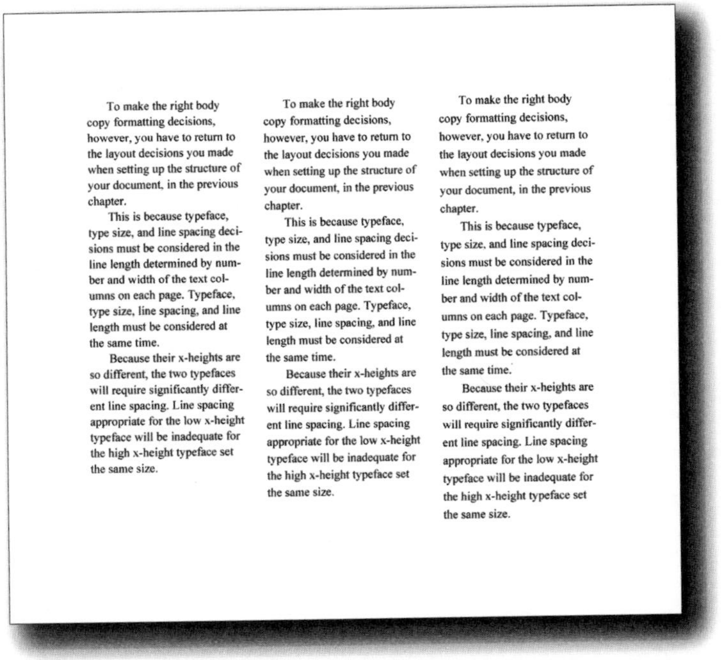

Figure 7-18   Typeface and type size are identical in the three equal-width columns of this sample text document. Line spacing, however, varies from 14 to 15 to 16 points (from left to right). When compared side by side, the right choice—in the center—appears obvious.

Tip   When you work with your comparison, be sure you experiment with half-point differences in type size and line spacing.

Fine-Tuning Body Copy Character Spacing

Like headlines, the appearance and readability of body copy often improves after a slight reduction in body copy character spacing. This is because tighter character spacing aids scanning and makes each word's distinct shape more distinct.

To demonstrate this, copy and paste two identical paragraphs side-by-side. Leave the default character spacing of the left-hand example alone. Select the paragraph on the right, and then click Font, Character Spacing. In the Character Spacing dialog box, locate the Tracking section. Click the By This Amount drop-down arrow, and try different options, printing each version (and immediately noting the character spacing settings).

Notice the subtle improvements that 5 and 10 percent reductions in character spacing make. By analyzing your printed samples, it will soon be obvious which setting is appropriate for the typeface, type size, and line length you're working with, as shown in Figure 7-19. The By This Amount option is superior to the built-in Tight and Very Tight settings, which don't allow as much flexibility.

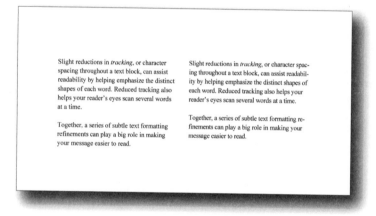

Figure 7-19   Compare the left-hand paragraph, with default character spacing, to the right-hand paragraph, with reduced character pacing.

Formatting Paragraphs

Formatting paragraphs includes deciding how you are going to indicate new paragraphs and choosing the correct alignment.

For most purposes, you have two alignment choices, which you make in the Paragraph dialog box:

Flush-left alignment   Word spacing is consistent from line to line, but the lines themselves are of different lengths. This creates a straight left margin that forms a contrast with the ragged right margin.

Justified alignment   Characterized by lines of equal word length. Publisher varies word spacing on each line so that the last characters of each line align with each other.

The correct choice is primarily based on the image you want to project. Body copy set flush left projects a contemporary and informal image; justified text projects a more "serious" or "classic" image.

There are also two ways to indicate a new paragraph. The appropriate choice depends on the paragraph alignment you have chosen:

Justified text   Insert a first-line indent equal to two *m* characters when formatting justified text. Because each line is the same length, even a modest indent will be enough to indicate the new paragraph.

Flush-left text   With flush-left text, add extra space between paragraphs. Indents are inappropriate for flush-left text, because the line endings differ for each line. A first-line indent will not be as noticeable as extra space between paragraphs.

To apply paragraph formatting, click Format, Paragraph, and then, on the Indents And Spacing tab in the Paragraph dialog box, change settings in the Line Spacing area.

Never press ENTER twice to insert extra space between paragraphs. This introduces too much space. Instead, in the After Paragraphs box in the Line Spacing area, type a value equal to approximately one and one-half lines of text.

Text Alignment and Column Width

Just as type size and line length are tied to typeface and column width, body copy alignment and column width are also closely related.

Avoid setting narrow columns of justified text. Word spacing will vary greatly between adjacent lines, based on word length:

- Large spaces between words will be present in lines containing a few long words. This will be especially apparent in lines containing two long words.

- Word spacing will be very tight in lines containing several short words.

These differences in word spacing will be very distracting and noticeable—especially when lines with widely spaced words and lines containing tightly spaced words appear next to each other.

Adding Emphasis to Body Copy

Never underline to add emphasis to titles or key phrases. Underlining undermines word recognition by interfering with the descenders that help readers scan word shapes. Instead, use italics or bold for emphasis.

Use bold and italics with restraint, however. A single word or short phrase set in bold or italics stands out. But as you add emphasis to more and more words, the emphasis loses strength.

Never press ENTER twice to insert space between paragraphs, because this introduces too much space.

Avoid setting entire paragraphs in bold or italics:

■ Words set in bold are harder to recognize, because as the width of the strokes making up each character is increased, the amount of white space inside the characters decreases. Readers depend on white space inside characters, called *counters*, to recognize the characters.

■ Words set in italics are also harder to recognize. Because characters appear slanted, readers are less familiar with them, which slows readers down, as they have to spend more time decoding the message.

In many ways, type set in bold-italics suffers from the disadvantages of both bold and italics. Although the characters form a strong contrast to adjacent roman, or regular, text, adding both bold and italics often makes your message harder to read.

Run-ins, which refer to the first word or phrase in bulleted list items or a short series of adjacent paragraphs, can be set in either bold or italics and are an alternative to subheads when introducing new ideas.

Tips for Working with Colored Type

Exercise restraint when setting text in color or against a colored background. Colored text, especially body copy text, often looks better on-screen than it will look when printed. This is because on-screen colored text is *projected* to the reader's eyes, whereas printed text is created by color *reflected* from the printed page.

When in doubt, remember that black text against a white background is the easiest type to read, at all sizes.

Here are some suggestions for setting text in color:

Consistency   Limit color choices to your publication's color scheme. Avoid a "rainbow" effect created by using too many different typeface colors. Consider using the same color for headlines and subheads that you used for your publication's title, nameplate, or key graphical accent.

Dark colors   Dark text colors reproduce better than lighter text colors when printed.

Foreground/background contrast   Strive for maximum contrast between the text and its background. Although it might appear attractive, readability inevitably suffers when dark text is set against a lighter background of the same color.

Emphasis   When setting body copy text in color, consider increasing the text size by one-half a point or setting the words in bold, to compensate for the color.

Color works best when it's concentrated in a few key areas, rather than dissipated over a page. That's why headlines and subheads set in color work better than body copy.

Hyphenating Body Copy

Body copy text should always be hyphenated. *Hyphenation*—Publisher's ability to divide words at line endings—is necessary regardless of whether you are using flush-left or justified text:

Hyphenation and flush-left text   Hyphenation avoids an unusually deep *rag*, or zigzag effect of irregular line endings, in flush-left paragraphs. Without hyphenation, lines containing a few long words will be significantly shorter than lines containing several short words. Often, when short lines follow long lines, the effect will be extremely noticeable.

Hyphenation and justified text   Hyphenation is necessary with justified text because it smoothes out word spacing irregularities. Without hyphenation, word spacing in lines containing a few words will be extremely wide, but word spacing in lines containing several words will be very narrow.

To hyphenate text within a text box, click Tools, Language, Hyphenation. In the Hyphenation dialog box, you can modify the *hyphenation zone* at the end of each line. Words that overlap this hyphenation zone will be hyphenated.

- A wide hyphenation zone results in fewer hyphenated words.

- A narrow hyphenation zone results in more hyphenated words.

Using Line Breaks to Control Right Margins

With Publisher, hyphenation within a single text box is an "all or nothing" proposition. However, just as you can use line breaks (press SHIFT+ENTER) to control line spacing in headlines, you can use line breaks in body copy to break lines at desired locations.

However, line breaks should be entered only after you have completely finished editing your project. If you later reedit a paragraph and forget to eliminate the line break, you might end up with an awkward line break in the middle of the paragraph, as shown in Figure 7-20.

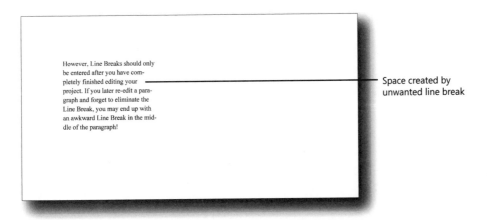

Space created by
unwanted line break

Figure 7-20   Awkward "holes" in text often result from forgotten line breaks used to eliminate a hyphen or force a word break early in a paragraph.

To locate unwanted line breaks, click View, Special Characters to display the unwanted characters, as shown in Figure 7-21.

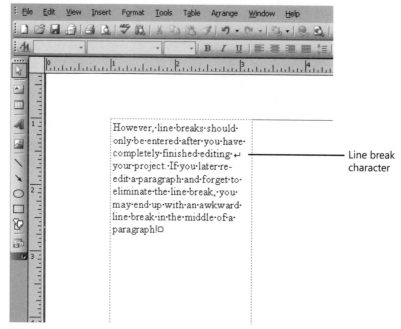

Figure 7-21   Click View, Special Characters to locate unwanted line breaks.

Fine-Tuning Paragraphs

More recent versions of Publisher include commands for enhanced paragraph formatting. To apply enhanced paragraph formatting, click Format, Paragraph, and in the Paragraph dialog box, click the Line And Paragraph Breaks tab.

Here, you'll find two commands of great significance:

Widow/Orphan Control   Select the Widow/Orphan Control check box to make sure that paragraphs at the tops or bottoms of columns (and pages) will contain at least two lines. This prevents single lines that might otherwise be isolated at the top or bottom of a column or page.

Widows and orphans detract from the appearance of your marketing materials and can confuse readers if they forget the context of the paragraph the single line appeared in. Figure 7-22 shows what might occur if you did not take advantage of Widow/Orphan Control, and Figure 7-23 shows the improvement after using this feature.

Keep Lines Together   Select the Keep Lines Together check box (as you should when formatting subheads, as discussed earlier in this chapter) to monitor paragraph placement within text boxes. If an entire paragraph cannot fit at the bottom of a column or page, the entire paragraph is moved to the top of the next column or page. This feature is best utilized if your design allows for *scalloped* columns—that is, columns of different lengths.

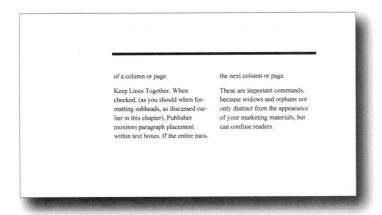

Figure 7-22 Without Widow/Orphan Control, isolated lines might appear at the tops or bottoms of your columns and pages.

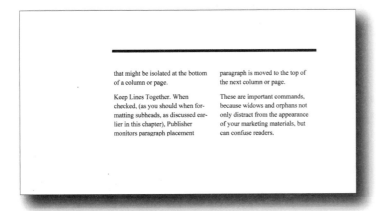

Figure 7-23 After you select Widow/Orphan Control, paragraphs at the tops and bottoms of columns (and pages) will contain at least two lines.

Saving Formatting Decisions as Text Styles

In this chapter, we have explored the numerous text formatting options available to you for formatting headlines, subheads, and body copy. Now it's time to pull everything together and add *accuracy* and *speed* to your Publisher working habits.

Up to now, the missing link has been an easy way to apply the multiple formatting options available for headlines, subheads, and body copy. So next you'll master using text styles to quickly, easily, and consistently apply your formatting decisions.

Text styles contain multiple formatting decisions. The following list shows some of the formatting decisions that you can save and then instantly apply by positioning the insertion point anywhere in a paragraph and choosing a desired text style on the Styles menu at the far left of the Formatting toolbar:

Mastering text styles increases your chances of achieving design and marketing success with Microsoft Publisher.

- Typeface
- Type Size
- Type Style
- All Caps, Small Caps
- Line Spacing
- Baseline Alignment
- Text Color
- Character Spacing
- First-Line Indent
- Space Before
- Space After
- Widow/Orphan Control
- Keep With Next
- Horizontal Rules Above/After
- Bullets And Numbering
- Tabs

Creating Text Styles

To create a custom text style, click Format, Styles And Formatting. In the Styles And Formatting task pane, shown in Figure 7-24, click the Create New Style button near the bottom.

In the New Style dialog box, shown in Figure 7-25, give your new text style a name that will help you remember its purpose—for example, Headline, Body Copy, Caption, and so on—and apply the desired formatting options by clicking the buttons on the right and then clicking options in the dialog box that opens.

Figure 7-24 Clicking the Create New Style button in the Styles And Formatting task pane begins the process of creating and saving a text style.

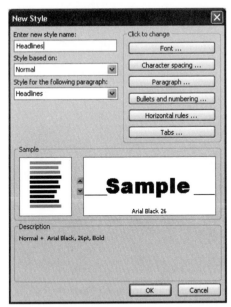

Figure 7-25 Name your new text style, and apply the desired formatting options in the New Style dialog box.

When you close the New Style dialog box, your formatting decisions will be saved with your documents, and the name of your new style will appear in the text styles drop-down menu.

Automating Text Styles

One of the most useful options in the New Style dialog box is Style For The Following Paragraph. By making good use of this command, you can automate your text styles so that, for example, the Body Copy style will always follow the Headline or Subhead style.

Each time you press the ENTER key, the next text style will be automatically applied. If you are formatting paragraphs by indenting the first line, the sequence of text styles might be:

- Subhead
- Body—without first-line indent (for use after a headline or subhead)
- Body—with first-line indent (for all other text paragraphs)

The reason for having two text paragraph styles is that the first paragraph following a headline or subhead is understood to be a new paragraph and thus does not require a first-line indent.

You'll soon come up with other examples where text styles typically follow each other.

Editing Text Styles

You can easily update text styles after they have been created. To edit a text style, click Format, Styles And Formatting. In the Styles And Formatting task pane, click the drop-down arrow next to the style, and then click Modify, as shown in Figure 7-26.

Figure 7-26   A great deal of the power of text styles is based on the ease with which you can modify existing styles.

You can then modify, rename, or delete the style. If you change the formatting of the current text style, the Update To Match Selection option will also be available. Notice that each time you position the mouse pointer over a text style, its current formatting attributes appear.

Text Styles vs. Format Painter

The Format Painter makes it easy to share formatting options among text elements. Simply click the Format Painter tool on the Standard toolbar to "pick up" a formatting option from one text element, and then click another text element. Instantly, the second element will be formatted the same as the first.

The Format Painter is not a substitute for creating text styles, however. Text styles are permanently saved with a publication, whereas Format Painter attributes last only until you select another command.

Sharing Text Styles Among Documents

The ability to share text styles among documents is one of the most important options available in Publisher. Once you have fine-tuned your text formatting decisions for the major elements of page architecture and saved your decisions as text styles, you can reuse the text styles in other publications.

To add a previously created text style to a new publication, follow these steps:

1. Click **Format**, **Styles And Formatting**, and then click the **Import Styles** button.

2. In the **Import Styles** dialog box, shown in Figure 7-27, browse to the Publisher file that contains the desired text styles.

The ability to share text styles from publication to publication makes it easy to project a consistent image throughout all of your firm's, or your client's, marketing materials.

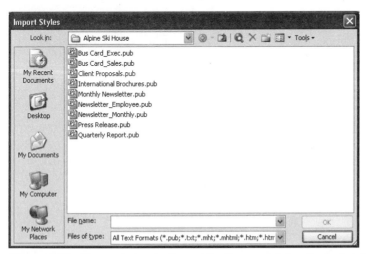

Figure 7-27 Browse to locate the publication containing the text styles you want to add to a new publication.

3. Click the file name, and the text styles associated with that publication will be added to your new publication.

Before adding identically named text styles, however, a Publisher prompt will appear asking whether you want to update the existing text style with the new formatting information or rename the text style you are importing.

Summary

You've now been introduced to the most important commands needed to put Microsoft Publisher to work as a marketing companion. Your search for design excellence is nearly complete.

You now know how to be guided by design as you format the smallest details of the major elements of page architecture: headlines, subheads, and body copy. You have been exposed to the formatting nuances that experienced graphic designers have been profiting from for years.

More important, you know how to save your formatting decisions as text styles, which can apply multiple formatting options with a single click. You also know how to modify existing text styles and share them between documents.

All that remains is to fine-tune your work, which you'll learn to do in Chapter 8, and output your work, which you'll learn to do in Chapter 9.

Test Yourself

Before moving on, take a few minutes to visit this book's companion Web site, at www.designtosellonline.com/07chap.html, and explore some of the resources there. There you can:

- Locate additional resources, including examples and tips not included in this chapter.

- Use a self-scoring assessment to test your understanding of the new terms introduced in this chapter.

- Find online sources for additional quality typeface designs, including Web sites where you can try out different typeface designs before you buy them.

Additional information about the newest version of Publisher will also be available on the Web site.

Chapter Eight

Taking Your Design Success to the Next Level

What you'll find:

- ❑ Turbocharge your messages with additional design enhancements.
- ❑ Add baseline alignment to multicolumn pages.
- ❑ Use punctuation and special characters to clarify your messages.
- ❑ Use templates to maintain consistency throughout your documents.
- ❑ Use Design Gallery objects to create calendars and reply coupons.

Taking your design success to the next level involves building on previously learned design and layout techniques. Other ideas in this chapter might be new to you, such as the importance of using templates to save time and ensure formatting consistency.

In this chapter, once again, we see that design success is based on careful craftsmanship, taking the time to fine-tune even the smallest elements of your publication.

Design success is based on paying careful attention to the smallest formatting details of your publication.

Advanced Type Tools

In the preceding two chapters, you learned how to create effective pages for your publications and fill them with attractive, easy-to-read text. In this chapter, you'll learn how to use several additional Publisher capabilities to add even more design excellence to your words.

Symbols and Special Characters

One of the refinements you can add to your message is to format your body copy by inserting symbols and special characters. These symbols and special characters are accessed by clicking Insert, Symbol and then clicking either the Symbols tab or the Special Characters tab, as shown in Figure 8-1.

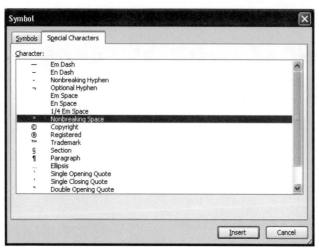

Figure 8-1   The Special Characters tab in the Symbol dialog box lists a range of important symbols and punctuation marks.

In addition to commonly accepted symbols used to replace words like *Trademark* and *Copyright*, you can add refinements such as:

Em dash and en dash   By default, Publisher's AutoCorrect feature will automatically replace two hyphens in a row with an em dash—a single, significantly longer dash used to begin and close parenthetical statements. En dashes are similar, but shorter dashes are typically used to indicate a range—for example, June–September. Unlike em dashes, you must manually insert en dashes where appropriate.

Nonbreaking space   You can insert nonbreaking spaces to prevent first and last names, dates, and cities and states from being split over two lines.

Optional hyphen   Optional hyphens let you specify in advance where a word should be split if it appears at the end of a line.

Nonbreaking hyphen   You can insert nonbreaking hyphens to prevent words, like proper names or groups of hyphenated words, from being split over two lines.

Special characters can make a significant improvement in the appearance of your marketing materials.

When combined with the line break commands in the Paragraph dialog box—Widow/Orphan Control, Keep With Next, and Keep Lines Together—these special characters can make a significant improvement in the appearance of your marketing materials.

Baseline Alignment

Baseline alignment is a relatively new feature in Publisher. Baseline alignment can significantly improve the appearance of multicolumn documents. Here's how.

Baseline refers to the invisible line that text is placed on. Two-column documents look best when the baseline of the text in the first column aligns with the baseline of the text in the second column. (In three-column documents, baseline alignment is even more critical.) Without baseline alignment, the page looks haphazardly thrown together, as shown in Figure 8-2, where the lines of the text in the different columns do not align. Figure 8-3 shows the same page, but with the baselines aligned.

Multicolumn documents look best when the baselines of the text in each column are aligned with each other.

Figure 8-2   Without baseline alignment, multicolumn documents can project an amateurish image. Notice how the lines of type in the two columns float relative to each other.

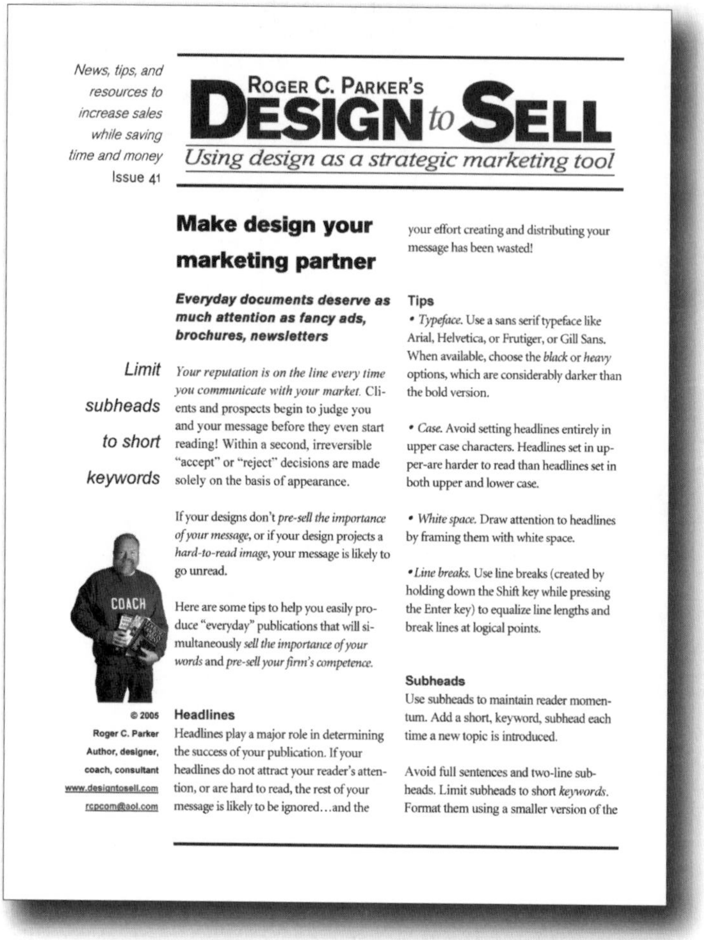

News, tips, and resources to increase sales while saving time and money

Issue 41

ROGER C. PARKER'S

DESIGN to SELL

Using design as a strategic marketing tool

Make design your marketing partner

Everyday documents deserve as much attention as fancy ads, brochures, newsletters

Your reputation is on the line every time you communicate with your market. Clients and prospects begin to judge you and your message before they even start reading! Within a second, irreversible "accept" or "reject" decisions are made solely on the basis of appearance.

If your designs don't *pre-sell the importance of your message*, or if your design projects a *hard-to-read image*, your message is likely to go unread.

Here are some tips to help you easily produce "everyday" publications that will simultaneously *sell the importance of your words* and *pre-sell your firm's competence.*

Limit subheads to short keywords

© 2005
Roger C. Parker
Author, designer, coach, consultant
www.designtosell.com
rcpcom@aol.com

Headlines

Headlines play a major role in determining the success of your publication. If your headlines do not attract your reader's attention, or are hard to read, the rest of your message is likely to be ignored…and the your effort creating and distributing your message has been wasted!

Tips

• *Typeface.* Use a sans serif typeface like Arial, Helvetica, or Frutiger, or Gill Sans. When available, choose the *black* or *heavy* options, which are considerably darker than the bold version.

• *Case.* Avoid setting headlines entirely in upper case characters. Headlines set in upper-are harder to read than headlines set in both upper and lower case.

• *White space.* Draw attention to headlines by framing them with white space.

• *Line breaks.* Use line breaks (created by holding down the Shift key while pressing the Enter key) to equalize line lengths and break lines at logical points.

Subheads

Use subheads to maintain reader momentum. Add a short, keyword, subhead each time a new topic is introduced.

Avoid full sentences and two-line subheads. Limit subheads to short *keywords*. Format them using a smaller version of the

Figure 8-3 When the baselines of the text in each column are aligned, the same publication projects a far more professional image.

To apply baseline alignment to your publication:

1. Refer back to the line spacing that you have chosen for body copy.
2. Click **Arrange**, **Layout Guides**, and then click the **Baseline Guides** tab. In the **Horizontal Baseline** section, in the **Spacing** box, type the line spacing value in points, as shown in Figure 8-4. (You can also specify an offset amount to control the distance between the first line of text and the page margin.) Click OK.

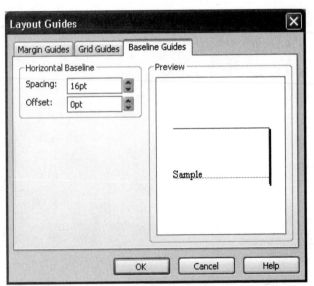

Figure 8-4 Type the line spacing you have chosen for your body copy in the Spacing box on the Baseline Guides tab.

3. Select the paragraphs you want to align, and then click **Format**, **Paragraph**. On the **Indents And Spacing** tab, in the **Line Spacing** section, select the **Align text to baseline guides** check box, as shown in Figure 8-5, on the next page.

Baseline alignment can make a major difference in the appearance of your publications, eliminating the disorganized look caused by unaligned text.

Working with Drop Caps

One way to add impact to long, text-filled publications is to add drop caps. *Drop caps* are oversized initial characters used to emphasize the beginning of the first paragraph of a story. Drop caps can be formatted using the same typeface as the rest of the article, or you can choose a different typeface design.

To draw your reader's eye to the first letter in a story, click in the first paragraph, and then click Format, Drop Cap. On the Drop Cap tab in the Drop Cap dialog box, you can click a drop cap style to format the first letter to rise above, or drop below, the level of the following text, as shown in Figure 8-6.

Drop caps are oversized initial characters used to emphasize the beginning of the first paragraph of a story.

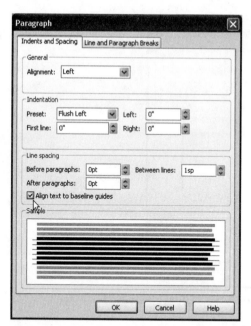

Figure 8-5   Align text to the baseline grid on the Indents And Spacing tab in the Paragraph dialog box.

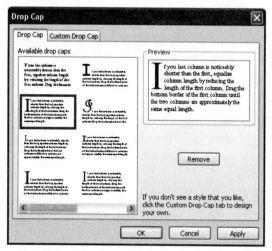

Figure 8-6   Selecting and previewing desired formatting options in the Drop Cap dialog box.

If you don't see an option you like, you can easily format your own drop cap by clicking the Custom Drop Cap tab. On the Custom Drop Cap tab, you can specify the desired typeface design and the placement of the character above or below the baseline of the first line of type.

Clarifying and Reinforcing Your Message

There are virtually no limits to the ways you can add design excellence to your publication. Here are a few additional ways to make your message as visual as possible.

Using Sidebars

Sidebars make it easy to orchestrate the hierarchy and sequence of the way your readers approach your message. Sidebars consist of short "mini-articles" extracted from longer stories. A sidebar can be used to:

- Draw attention to ideas that would otherwise be lost within a longer story.

- Present information on a topic that might otherwise distract the reader from the ongoing narrative by introducing details not critical for understanding the "big picture."

Sidebars should appear next to the longer story but be visually distinct. Often, sidebars appear within a border. If you choose to place a border around sidebar content, make sure that there is a buffer of white space between the border and the sidebar content.

Placing the sidebar against a shaded or lightly colored background can add visual interest to your pages while signaling "something is different." Make sure, however, that the shaded or colored background extends far enough beyond the text area of the sidebar to be noticeable.

Multiple formatting options usually represent overkill: don't add both a border and a background unless you are certain that doing so will not clutter your pages.

Often the best way to emphasize a sidebar is to set it in a contrasting typeface, like a small, bold, sans serif typeface that forms a strong contrast with the serif type used in the longer story.

Avoid redundant formatting: don't emphasize a sidebar with a border, a background, and a contrasting typeface.

Including Pull-Quotes

One of the best reasons to use a grid that builds white space into each page is to create space for pull-quotes. Remember, a *pull-quote* is a short sentence that repeats information found elsewhere on a page.

After headlines and subheads, pull-quotes are likely to be the most-read parts of a page. Pull-quotes represent an ideal way not only to attract the attention of a reader rapidly glancing at each page, but also to drive home the most important idea on the page.

Pull-quotes are often read both before and after the rest of the text on the page.

Using Lists and Tables

Using bulleted and numbered lists is an easy way to highlight and clarify the relation-ship between items in a series. Lists build white space into your message and can also be used to provide a summary of information to be discussed in the paragraphs that follow the list. Information that might be easily overlooked at the end of a sentence takes on new meaning when placed in list form.

Be guided by logic and purpose when choosing the type of list:

■ Use bulleted lists when hierarchy and sequence are not important.

■ Use numbered lists to emphasize order, importance, or sequence.

Figure 8-7 compares information located within a paragraph (top), placed in a bulleted list (middle), and displayed in a numbered list (bottom).

Tables add even more options for clarifying messages, particularly detailed messages, by organizing information and making comparisons easier. Tables make it easy to compare the attributes of several items—presenting the information in *cells*, which are organized in rows and columns.

To insert a table, click Table, Insert, Table, and then in the Create Table dialog box, select the desired number of rows and columns for the table and choose an appropriate table format.

Here are some tips for working with tables:

Use a contrasting typeface.　A contrasting typeface in row and column headers will clearly separate the identifying text from the contents of each cell.

Save typeface formatting.　Save your formatting decisions as text styles, for future use.

Eliminate unnecessary borders and lines.　White space is as good at separating information as are lines indicating row and column borders.

Add selective emphasis to key information.　Emphasize key information by using bold text, colored text, and cell background colors.

Popular fruits grown in the Northeast include apples, cherries, peaches, and strawberries.

Popular fruits grown in the Northeast include:

- Apples
- Cherries
- Peaches
- Strawberries

Fruits from the Northeast, *in order of popularity*, are:

1. Apples
2. Strawberries
3. Peaches
4. Cherries

Figure 8-7 Compare the added impact and storytelling power of information taken out of a sentence and presented first in a bulleted list and then in a numbered list.

Adding Captions

Always add captions explaining the significance of visuals such as photographs, illustrations, charts, graphs, and tables. Captions command high readership. When possible, use the caption to restate the major point you're trying to make in the visual as well as draw attention to important parts of the visual.

Here are some considerations for working with captions:

Typeface   Captions are often formatted using the same typeface as is used for body copy, but set in italics, and often slightly smaller than the body copy. Sometimes, however, the most attractive and easily read captions are set in a bold, contrasting typeface, with generous line spacing.

Location   Although captions are typically placed below visuals, they can also be placed above or alongside.

Alignment   Avoid justified alignment, as awkward word spacing often results.

Writing to fit   Whenever possible, rewrite captions as needed to avoid word breaks and hyphenation.

Inserting Design Gallery Objects

Publisher's Design Gallery includes many timesaving design elements. Creating these elements yourself, from scratch, would take several hours of tedious work. The two most powerful and flexible examples are calendars and reply forms.

Calendars help your readers relate dates to the specific days and weeks of a month. It's one thing to present a date, such as July 17, 2007. It's another thing to show that July 1, 2007, occurs on the third Monday of the month. After you insert a calendar, you can use color and text formatting to highlight important dates.

Publisher's reply forms take the work out of adding an order form, response form, or sign-up form to your publications. A variety of horizontal and vertical options are available, complete with text, check boxes, and lines. After you insert a reply form, you can customize the form by adding or deleting form contents. To preview what's available, click Insert, Design Gallery Object. In the Design Gallery dialog box, shown in Figure 8-8, scroll down to select a desired category of objects.

After you insert a Design Gallery object into your publication, you can resize and format the object to suit your specific needs.

Publisher's
Design Gallery
includes
timesaving
elements that
would take several
hours of tedious
work to create from
scratch.

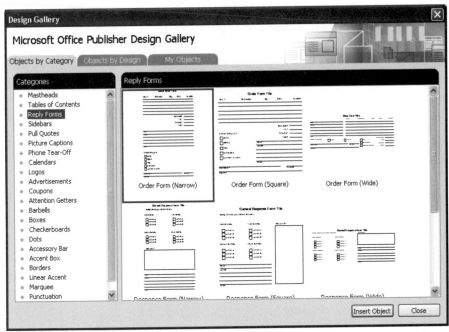

Figure 8-8 Select an object type in the Design Gallery to review the options available for insertion into your publication.

For example, if you choose a Calendar object, you can easily change the date range for the calendar to suit your publication's requirements. To change the date range of a calendar after inserting it into your publication, click the Click To Edit Options For This Calendar button below the calendar, and then in the Calendar Designs task pane, click the Change Date Range button. You can now specify a desired month and year in the Change Calendar Dates dialog box, shown in Figure 8-9.

You can easily change the date range of calendars to suit your publication's requirements.

Figure 8-9 Changing the date range of a calendar added to your publication.

Using Templates to Ensure Design Success

The ability to save your work as a template is one of Publisher's most important features. Templates are read-only files that you can open and use as a basis for a new publication, but they must be saved using a new file name and extension so that they're not overwritten.

Importance of Templates

Templates avoid "creeping standards," which frequently occur when publications build on each other—for example, when the March issue of a newsletter is based on the February issue, which was based on the January issue, which was in turn based on the December issue, and so on. When publication designs are recycled, text and graphical elements are often inadvertently moved, and subtle changes in text formatting become "grandfathered" into the issues that follow.

Because you cannot accidentally overwrite a template, the integrity of the original design remains untouched. In our example scenario, each month's issue would be based *not* on the previous month's issue, but on the original design, safely stored as a template.

Creating Custom Publisher Templates

Creating a template in Publisher is easy. When you're satisfied with your design for a category of publication—e-book, newsletter, postcard, and so on—click File, Save As. In the Save As dialog box, type the desired file name, click the Save As Type drop-down arrow, and select Publisher Template (*.pub).

Publisher will then save the template as a read-only file in the appropriate folder so that the template can be easily accessed when you, or a coworker, start a new project.

Working with Templates Designed by Others

You don't have to both design and produce your marketing messages with Publisher— it's entirely feasible to produce documents based on custom templates created specifically for you.

Although design success is based on having a strong appreciation for the elements of good design, this doesn't mean that you have to do all of the work yourself—including creating your design templates.

Indeed, from the point of view of time management and efficiency, the best use of your time might be in supervising the creation of custom templates for your firm—delegating the initial design to a professional designer, who can take the time to create a series of customized templates for you to work with in the years to come.

Having learned what you have already learned in this book—especially about the importance of using text styles to format your publications—you are now able to make the most of templates, efficiently producing your documents on a consistent basis.

Saving Templates in Categories

You can easily create categories of publication templates, organized by client, department, or document type. Organizing templates by category will save time, and eliminate confusion, when you begin a new project.

To create a category within the folder where Publisher stores templates:

1. On the **File** menu, click **Properties**.

2. On the **Summary** tab of the **Publication Name Properties** dialog box, enter a category name in the **Category** box

3. Click **OK**.

The next time you click File, New, and then click New From A Design, your newly created category will appear.

Basing New Publications on Templates

To base a new publication on an existing template, click File, New. In the New Publication task pane, locate the New From A Design box, select Templates, and then click the template you want to use.

Immediately save your new project based on a template with an appropriate file name in an appropriate folder. Remember that your project must have a different file name from the original template.

Editing Existing Templates

Occasionally, you might have to modify an existing template. An address, phone number, or Web address might have changed, for example.

Immediately save projects based on templates in an appropriate folder with an appropriate file name.

To edit an existing template:

1. Click **File**, **New**, and in the **New from a Design** list in the **New Publication** task pane, click **My Templates**. In the **Preview** pane, click the template you want to revise.

2. Make any desired changes to the layout, text styles, or graphics placeholders.

3. Click **File**, **Save As**. In the **Save As** dialog box, change the **File Type** to **Publisher Template**, and then double-click the file name that the template was originally stored under.

4. A Publisher prompt will appear, asking you to confirm that you want to overwrite the existing file. Click **Yes**, and your template will be updated.

Summary

In this chapter, you learned how to expand on the structure and formatting built into your Publisher projects so far, permitting you to take your designs to the next level. You also learned how to improve your publication's appearance by aligning baselines and inserting symbols. And you learned how to clarify your message using lists and Publisher Design Objects like calendars and reply forms.

Most important, you learned how to use templates to simplify text formatting and ensure consistent formatting *throughout* and *between* your documents. Instead of reinventing the wheel each time, templates make it easy to get a running start on your project.

In Chapter 9—the last chapter in Part Two—you'll learn how to proofread your work to avoid costly and embarrassing errors. You'll also learn how to prepare files for quantity printing and online distribution.

Test Yourself

Before you move on to the next chapter, take a break and visit the book's companion Web site, www.designtosellonline.com. There you can review bonus content, as well as test your understanding of the materials introduced in this chapter. At www.designtosellonline.com/08chap.html, you'll find:

- Bonus resources, including worksheets to help identify custom template needs.
- A self-scoring assessment to help you review new terms introduced in this chapter.
- Bonus content, including, before-and-after examples of Design Gallery objects.

Chapter Nine

Distributing Error-Free Messages in Print and Online

What you'll find:

- ❏ Preview your publication from your reader's point of view.
- ❏ Prepare files for error-free printing.
- ❏ Prepare files for sharing via the Internet.

In this chapter, we take a look at some of the Microsoft Office Publisher features that can help you reap all of the benefits of the design excellence you've achieved using the techniques described in the previous chapters.

The success of your publications depends on the care you take proofreading and printing them. In this chapter, you'll learn how to avoid embarrassing problems by making the most of Publisher's built in design "safety net." You'll also learn how to prepare Publisher files for commercial printing and electronic distribution as e-mail attachments and Web site downloads.

> The success of your publications depends on the care you take proofreading and printing them.

Getting Ready to Print the Perfect Publication

The perfect marketing message arrives error free. Publisher offers several features to help you attain this lofty goal while you work and before printing—including checking your spelling and design and previewing your message from the recipient's point of view.

Avoiding Mistakes While You Work

Some Publisher features, such as AutoCorrect, can be adapted to eliminate mistakes as they happen. Other features can help you identify existing problem areas in your publications.

Making Good Use of AutoCorrect

Here's an easy way to speed your writing and reduce the chances for error. Simply use Publisher's AutoCorrect feature to insert frequently used and easily misspelled words and phrases. This feature is especially handy if you are going to frequently include long and complex strings of words like *Department of Redundancy and TerraTerresterial Affairs.*

Use AutoCorrect to
speed your writing
and reduce the
chances for mis-
spelled technical
terms and proper
nouns.

To have Publisher instantly spell out proper nouns or technical terms while you type in Publisher, click Tools, AutoCorrect Options, and type the term in the With box in the AutoCorrect dialog box. Type an easily remembered abbreviation, such as **dta** in the Replace box. Now, when you type the abbreviation and then either a space or a period, the full term will automatically appear correctly spelled out.

Proofing Your Layout While You Work

Here are some of the options you can use to get a reader's perspective on your project while you work on it:

Hide Borders And Guides   While working on your publication, click View, Boundaries And Guides. The only thing visible on the screen will be the text and graphics you have added. Click View, Boundaries And Guides again to see the guides again.

Two-Page Spreads   Although you'll normally work on individual pages zoomed in at a comfortable degree of magnification, you should get in the habit of checking two-page spreads. *Spreads* permit you to view both left-hand and right-hand pages at one time, to make sure that the content and design of the left-hand page doesn't fight the content on the right-hand page. To view both pages at once, click View, Two-Page Spread. You can view other spreads by clicking the desired page numbers in the Page Sorter area.

Print Preview   To gain an even better view of your publication from your reader's perspective, click File, Print Preview, and then click Multiple Pages. You can now view four or six pages of your publication at one time, to gauge the overall "flow" of your text and visuals. Clicking on a page zooms in on it to review details.

Using Two-Page Spreads and Print Preview to review several pages at a time makes it easy for you to note problems with margins and layout decisions that would be masked when looking at just one page at a time. Problems like slight deviations from the norm, or a series of pages that appear overly similar, become very obvious when you can review several pages at a glance.

Avoiding Spelling Checker Disappointment

Always work with Publisher's Spelling Checker feature activated. Although you might sometimes get tired of the red and green "squiggly" underlines, which flag spelling and grammar mistakes, respectively, it's easier to fix errors as they occur—rather than later, when they might be inadvertently overlooked.

To verify that Publisher's Spelling Checker is activated, click Tools, Spelling. Make sure that the Hide Spelling Errors option is visible, indicating that it is presently active.

Exercise caution when adding new words to Publisher's Spelling Checker dictionary. Be sure you spell the words correctly, or they'll be consistently misspelled! Take the time to enter proper nouns—such as client or employee names—as well as technical terms likely to show up in your writing.

Always run Spelling Checker one last time. Even if you have changed only one word in a headline or caption at the last minute, it's possible that you made a tiny spelling error and overlooked it in your haste. For speed, select only the text you've edited and press F7. To check just a single word, right-click it, click Proofing Tools, and click Spelling.

Adding Entries to the Spelling Checker Dictionary

While using the Spelling Checker to check your document, you can add proper nouns and technical terms unique to your field to Publisher's dictionary so that they will not be identified as errors each time you type them or the Spelling Checker encounters them.

When the Spelling Checker thinks a correct word is misspelled because the word is not in its dictionary, click Add in the Check Spelling dialog box. The word will be added to the dictionary and ignored in future spelling checks.

Always proofread your work. Never depend solely on the Spelling Checker. There are simply too many opportunities for error. Spelling Checker cannot detect missing words or homophones (words that sound the same but are spelled differently), such as *to*, *two*, and *too*.

Always run Spelling Checker one last time, even if you have changed only one word in a headline or caption.

Last-Minute Checks Before Printing and Distribution

Most problems can be solved before printing by using Publisher's Design Checker and printing and distributing proofs of your publication before distributing and duplicating files.

Putting the Design Checker to Work

Use Publisher's Design Checker to identify hard-to-locate potential problems before it's too late. Click Tools, Design Checker, and Design Checker will go through your pages and master pages, looking for problems like:

- Stories with overflow text.
- Pictures that have not been proportionately resized.
- Low-resolution graphics.
- Objects placed too close to the edges of the page.

Another useful way to check your work is to use Publisher's Find And Replace feature to locate unwanted spaces inside your text document. To begin checking for unwanted spaces between words and sentences, click Edit, Replace. In the Find And Replace task pane, type two spaces in the Find box, and then type one space in the Replace box. Click OK, and Publisher will locate every instance of a double space and replace it with a single space.

Next type two paragraph breaks (press ENTER twice) in the Find box and a single paragraph break (press ENTER once) in the Replace box. Publisher will search for and remove unwanted empty lines between paragraphs.

Printing Proofs

Because spelling errors are difficult to detect onscreen, always print your publication before distributing it or preparing final files for commercial printing.

Always print your publication before distributing it or preparing final files for commercial printing. Spelling errors are extremely difficult to detect on-screen. It's especially easy to overlook your own mistakes, because your brain "knows" what you meant and automatically overlooks repeated words and inserts missing words.

Accordingly, print frequent proof versions. In fact, it's a good idea to print your work at the close of every day so that you have a permanent copy for your records in case problems strike.

Distribute your proofs to coworkers, and invite them to circle errors. Whenever possible, invite your client and/or boss to "sign off" on each project before you print and distribute it or send your files to the printer.

You can reduce printing costs when printing interim proofs by not printing graphics at those stages where you're primarily interested in the text of your publications—that is, when you're searching for formatting and spelling errors. To print a set of proofs without graphics, click File, Print and then click Advanced Print Settings. In the Advanced Print Settings dialog box, click the Graphics And Fonts tab, and then click Do Not Print Any Graphics, as shown in Figure 9-1.

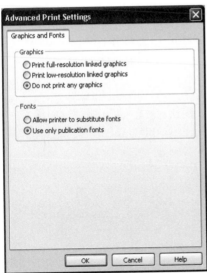

Figure 9-1 Reduce printing costs by instructing Publisher not to include graphics when you print proofs for reviewing text accuracy and formatting.

Another option you can specify in the Print dialog box is to print proofs in black and white. Use this option when you want to focus on your publication's message instead of its color.

Be sure you turn off this option when you print proofs of the final version of your document, of course!

Preparing Files for Error-Free Commercial Printing

Error-free printing involves communicating with your commercial printer as early as possible in the design process. Each printer will likely have their own preferences for file formats. Find out what they want, and follow their instructions to the letter.

There are two primary ways you can deliver your project files to your commercial printer:

Find out your commercial printer's file requirements as early as possible.

- If you have installed a copy of Adobe Acrobat Distiller, you can save your publication as an Adobe Acrobat PDF (Portable Document Format) file. (See *www.adobe.com* for more information.)

- Provide a copy of the Publisher file, along with all graphics files and font files.

Providing Acrobat PDF Files to Commercial Printers

With Adobe Acrobat Distiller or a third-party printer driver, creating an Acrobat PDF file is as easy as specifying the Acrobat PDF format in your Print dialog box.

What isn't as easy, is selecting the proper *resolution*—or file quality.

When creating files for digital duplication, make sure that you select the highest possible resolution. After you click File, Print and specify the Acrobat PDF format, click the Properties button. In the Acrobat PDF Conversion Properties dialog box, click PrePress. This will save your file at the highest resolution setting, permitting the best reproduction of text and graphics.

Unless you clear the Embed Fonts check box, copies of all of the fonts used in the publication will be added to the resulting PDF file.

Submitting Font, Graphics, and Publisher Files

Always find out as early as possible what files, and what font file formats, your commercial printer wants.

Preparing files for trouble-free offset printing, which can produce large quantities of a publication on quality paper with color graphics, is easy because of a Publisher feature that gathers almost all relevant files together and prepares them for transfer to a commercial printer.

As always, find out as early as possible exactly what files, and what font file formats, your printer wants.

Using the Pack And Go Wizard

To take advantage of the Pack And Go Wizard, open the project you'd like to send to a commercial printer, click File, Pack And Go, and then click Take To A Commercial Printing Service.

The Pack And Go Wizard will automatically embed TrueType fonts, include linked graphics, create links to the graphics files, and compress the files and place them in the file and folder of your choice. If you have used Type 1 or OpenType fonts in your publication rather than, or in addition to, TrueType fonts, see the next section, "Gathering Font Files for Commercial Printing."

Letting the Publisher wizard gather the files for the graphics included in your publication makes it possible for your commercial printer to make any last-minute adjustments necessary to ensure the best possible photographic reproduction.

The Pack And Go Wizard also prints copies of color separations, which many printers want to receive along with the files. These help a printer to quickly preview your project to make sure that color has been used properly.

Gathering Font Files for Commercial Printing

You don't have to be concerned with gathering TrueType fonts, because Publisher embeds them in the file. However, you do have to gather all Type 1 and OpenType font files used in your publication. Unless you are providing Acrobat PDF files, your printer must have copies of the same files you used to create your publication.

To identify the fonts used in your publication, click Tools, Commercial Printing Tools, Fonts. The Fonts dialog box, shown in Figure 9-2, displays the status of all the fonts used in your publication—but not the specific file names for the fonts! It is up to you to identify the file names and locate the files.

Unless you are
providing Acrobat
PDF files, your
commercial printer
must have the font
files you used to
create your
publication.

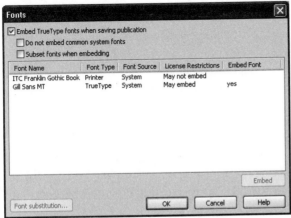

Figure 9-2 The Fonts dialog box displays the status of all of the fonts used in your publication.

If you are using the Adobe Type Manager, you can easily identify the necessary Type 1 and OpenType font file names. Simply right-click the name of a desired font, and select Show Specimen. The file names associated with the font will appear at the top of the specimen page. If you are using Microsoft Windows XP without Adobe Type Manager, click Start, Control Panel, Fonts, and then right-click the font and click Properties on the shortcut menu to find the file name of the font.

When working with Type 1 fonts, you should include both the .pfm and .pfb file for each font.

Packing Files for Another Computer

A similar wizard is available if you want to work on your project on another computer—perhaps a home computer. Click File, Pack And Go, Take To Another Computer. If your project includes Type 1 fonts, you'll also have to make sure that the same fonts used on your office computer are available on your home computer.

Commands You Don't Need to Know About

Publisher includes many specialized commands primarily intended for use by your commercial printer. These include advanced commands for fine-tuning the color separations and controlling the angle and placement of colors—especially where colors appear next to each other.

Unless instructed otherwise, you're best off leaving these advanced commands alone and letting your printer use them, if necessary.

Preparing Files for Internet Distribution

More and more marketing messages are delivered electronically, over the Internet, each year. This includes Publisher-created documents that are:

- Sent as e-mail attachments.
- Downloaded from Web sites.
- Presented for viewing on Web sites.

Microsoft Office Publisher 2007 offers integration with the two leading forms of electronic distribution.

Although there are version-to-version differences, all versions of Publisher can be used to prepare publications for Internet delivery and display. The next version of Publisher, Microsoft Office Publisher 2007, in fact, offers integration with the two leading forms of electronic distribution: Microsoft XPS (XML Paper Specification) and Adobe Acrobat PDF (Portable Document Format).

Sharing Publisher Files with Microsoft Office 2007 and XPS

Microsoft XPS—or XML Paper Specification—is a file interchange format to be introduced in Office 2007 that permits sharing formatted Publisher files with readers who might not have Publisher installed.

The free XPS Reader permits users to access documents created using Microsoft Publisher 2007, as well as any other program included in the Microsoft Office 2007 suite, including Word, Excel, PowerPoint, and so on.

The Microsoft XPS format goes beyond existing file transfer protocols in that it automatically includes working hyperlinks, text searching, and better reproduction of graphics containing transparency and gradient effects. (*Transparency effects* permit readers to see what's behind an object; *gradients* occur when a fill makes a smooth transition from light to dark or from one color to another.)

To save a Publisher file as an XPS file, click File, Save As, XPS Format.

Creating Acrobat PDF Files

For several years, marketing professionals who have invested in Adobe Acrobat Distiller have been distributing their Publisher-prepared messages as Acrobat PDF documents, as e-mail attachments and Web site downloads.

Creating a PDF file with Acrobat Distiller is as easy as specifying the Acrobat PDF driver in the Print dialog box.

But there are a few additional steps you should take, especially if you're using an earlier version of Publisher. One is to specify the appropriate resolution, or quality level, in the Properties dialog box.

In most cases, Standard resolution is sufficient as the ideal compromise between file size and image quality. If you think your readers might print your publication after downloading it as an e-mail attachment or from your Web site, you might want to increase the resolution to High Quality—especially if your publication is relatively short and contains numerous detailed color graphics.

Adding Active Links in Acrobat

An often overlooked step is to add e-mail and Web site hyperlinks in your Acrobat PDF file. This is a two-step process. First you must format the hyperlink, underlining the text and changing the text color to blue. Then you must manually add hyperlinks to the PDF file.

To add links to a Publisher file that has been converted to an Acrobat PDF file using Acrobat Distiller:

1. Click the **Link** tool on the **Advanced Editing** toolbar.

2. Drag a selection box around the hyperlink in the document.

3. In the Acrobat **Create A Link** dialog box, type the desired Web address. To add a link to an e-mail address, insert **mailto** before the e-mail address.

4. Resave your Acrobat publication.

You must re-create links added to a PDF file after returning to the Publisher file to make changes and resave as a new PDF file.

Note that if you return to the original Publisher file and re-create the PDF file, you must re-create all of your links. This is a trap that catches many an unwary marketer.

Summary

In this chapter, you learned about several Publisher features that you can use to simplify proofing and working with commercial printers. You also learned how to create files for electronic distribution.

In Part Three, you'll apply the techniques you've mastered to the preparation of specific categories of marketing publications. In Chapters 10 and 11, we'll explore the worlds of postcards and newsletters.

Test Yourself

Before starting Part Three, take a break and visit www.designtosellonline.com /09chap.html. At this book's companion Web site, you can review bonus content as well as test your understanding of the materials introduced in this chapter.

At www.designtosellonline.com/09chap.html, you'll find:

- A self-scoring assessment to help you review new terms introduced in this chapter.

- A 72-point Preflight And Proofing Checklist.

- Bonus content, including information about creating FlashPaper files.

Part Three
Publisher at Work

In this part

Chapter Ten

Promoting Your Business with Postcards

What you'll find:

- ❏ Discover the power of postcards.
- ❏ Plan your postcard marketing, create effective postcard messages, and assemble a mailing list.
- ❏ Design and produce your postcards.
- ❏ Become a "postcard pro."
- ❏ Use the Internet to send postcards.

For most businesses, advertising and marketing are "events" that take place when sales are slow or on a "time available" basis.

The most profitable businesses, however, operate from a different perspective. Successful firms view advertising and marketing as an *ongoing process*.

To achieve the goal of consistency, marketing tools must be practical. The tools must be simple enough that they can be used easily, even while you spend the majority of your day selling prospects, servicing clients, and doing the hundred and one other tasks that you're responsible for.

Because of the ease with which they can be designed, produced, and mailed, postcards are the first Publisher-created marketing tool that we'll examine in Part Three.

Successful firms view advertising and marketing as an ongoing process.

Discovering the Power of Postcards

Postcards gain much of their value from a combination of *size* and *visibility*. Their small size makes them quick and easy to produce and relatively inexpensive to print and mail. And postcards attract immediate attention—they can be read at a glance when they show up in your prospect or customer's morning mail.

Postcard Advantages

Postcards offer numerous compelling advantages. They are:

Impossible to ignore.   Postcards are like billboards that you can send through the mail. When they arrive, they dominate your prospects' attention and can be read at a glance. Because there are no envelopes to open, your message is immediately visible.

Surprisingly flexible.   In a limited space, postcards offer several distinct areas: the front—or "billboard"—side of the postcard; the area to the left of the address on the back of the card; and depending on how you're printing your cards, an area between the return address and the address panel.

Easy to create.   Because space is limited, you don't have to write much text.

Easy to address.   If you're printing your postcards on your desktop printer, you can address them while you print them.

Easy to track.   You can easily track the results of postcard promotions by color-coding or adding special codes to postcards that must be presented to gain admission to special events.

Because you
control who
receives your
postcard, there's no
"waste" circulation.

Although postal rates will no doubt continue to increase, postcards still cost less to print and mail than inserts and envelopes. More important, postcards are efficient because they are a targeted medium.

Whether you're mailing to your own compiled mailing list or you're renting a list from a list broker, there will be no "waste" circulation; you control who receives your postcard, so you don't pay for exposure to prospects who might never need or want your product or service.

Twelve Ways to Profit from Postcards

Here are just some of the ways you can put postcards to work:

Increased Web site traffic   Postcards permit you to bypass overstuffed e-mail inboxes, spam filters, and changed e-mail addresses. Use postcards to announce new Web site content. Include links to *landing pages*—or unlinked pages accessible only to those responding to postcard or other offers—where recipients can learn more about the subject described in the postcard.

Thank yous   Postcards make it easy to say "thanks" for purchases, visits to your place of business, or referrals. An attractive, brightly colored postcard you can hold in your hand is far more memorable than one more e-mail message.

Announcements   Because they can be quickly and easily prepared, postcards are a great way to announce new product introductions, special demonstrations, teleseminars, or address/staff changes.

Confirmations   After meeting someone at a networking event, sending a postcard confirmation projects a professional image and reduces the chance that the recipient forgets about the meeting. Confirmations can remind new acquaintances to visit your Web site.

Special events   Postcards help you get the word out fast about events like special demonstrations, workshops, or training opportunities.

Reminders   Reminders immediately before important events and previously scheduled meetings can greatly increase attendance.

Tips   Use postcards to remind customers about routine maintenance, seasonal tips, or upcoming holidays or events. Reminders are especially useful when sent just before the customer's supplies are due to run out.

New product introductions   Postcards describing "new and better" products and services help maintain your clients' enthusiasm, making it easier to sell them a new product that might provide greater satisfaction.

Enhancements   Many products can be enhanced by additional purchases. Postcards can show examples of accessories—or complementary products—that will help your customers make better use of their original purchase. After buying an outdoor barbecue grill, for example, buyers will soon realize that they need gloves to protect their hands, better cooking utensils, and covered platters.

Supplies   Many products consume supplies. Outdoor grills, for example, require charcoal or propane. Customers are likely to appreciate timely reminders to check supplies before important holidays or events, such as the Fourth of July or Memorial Day, to avoid the possibility of running out of fuel just when guests are expecting to be fed!

Lead generation   Use postcards to "test the waters" by offering a free incentive—such as a white paper or special report. Outdoor grill buyers might enjoy a collection of "Exciting Recipes for Your New Grill." This is an easy way to identify prospects who might be interested in learning more about your product or service.

Trade show traffic   One of the best ways to guarantee a successful exhibit at a convention or trade show is to announce the location of your booth and a reason for clients and prospects to visit your booth.

Planning Your Postcard Promotions

Planning your postcard promotions involves committing to sending postcards that satisfy both short-term and long-term goals, identifying appropriate opportunities to send postcards, crafting your message as concisely as possible, and building your mailing list resources.

Single-Purpose vs. Multipurpose Postcards

A well-planned postcard satisfies both short-term and long-term goals.

Many postcards fulfill a single purpose—for example, announcing a specific upcoming promotion or event. But a better alternative is to plan your postcards so that they satisfy long-term as well as short-term purposes:

Specific promotional goal   The majority of the postcard should be devoted to a specific task, such as thanking a customer for a purchase or promoting a specific upcoming event.

Long-term reinforcement   In addition, part of each postcard should reinforce your firm's position, by reminding recipients about the reasons to do business with you. These reminders will enhance your firm's visibility, so your firm will be the first one your customers think of when it's time to buy, rebuy, or refer.

Later in this chapter, you'll learn how to divide the space on the front of your postcard into two distinct message areas. This helps create a distinctive format for your postcards as well as organizing content so that each postcard satisfies both long-term and short-term goals.

Each postcard should not only communicate timely news but also reinforce your firm's visibility, resulting in more referrals and higher sales.

Identifying Appropriate Opportunities

Start by identifying occasions when you want to send postcards. Begin by identifying opportunities for preparing and mailing a few postcards a day, and work toward larger mailings, typically in advance of special events and promotions.

Use the following list to identify the types of postcards you should prepare and have ready for mailing:

- Anniversary of purchase
- Client's birthday
- Demonstrations

- Holiday greetings

- Invitations to subscribe to a free newsletter

- Networking —"I enjoyed meeting you last night"

- New products and services

- New staff members

- New Web site content

- Presentations

- Reminders of upcoming meetings

- Sales and promotions

- Seasonal tips

- Teleseminars and demonstrations

- Thank you for your purchase

- Thank you for your referral

- Trade show exhibits

- Updates—new addresses, Web addresses, phone numbers

- Welcome to new arrivals in your area

- We've moved

On this book's companion Web site, at www.designtosellonline.com/10chap.html, you'll find a Postcard Opportunity Worksheet that you can use to keep track of the postcard categories you should prepare artwork for so that you can quickly prepare and mail postcards by inserting relevant information.

You'll find that reducing your choices to a few key categories, as shown in Figure 10-1, makes it easy to identify your most important postcard marketing opportunities and create the necessary postcard templates. Identifying the types of postcards you intend to mail and their frequency will also help you set up a realistic budget for your postcard marketing.

Identify your
most important
postcard marketing
opportunities and
create postcard
templates for them.

Postcard Opportunity Worksheet

Postcard typ e	Frequency	Estimated quantity
Customer thank you	2 to 6 a week	8 to 24 per month
Referral thank you	2 to 3 a week	8 per month
New Web site content	Monthly	800 per month plus latest names
Prospecting "cold calls"	Monthly	250 new prospects per month
Special report	Quarterly	800+ per quarter
Customer Appreciation Day	Once a year	800+ per quarter

Figure 10-1   Example of a filled-in Postcard Opportunity Worksheet. The first column lists the postcard type, the second column lists the frequency of mailings, and the third column lists estimated print quantities.

Planning Your Messages and Your Offers

Use a simple problem-solution-action formula to plan the message you create for each of your postcards.

Use a simple problem-solution-action formula to plan the message you create for each of your postcards. As a starting point, review your product and services and list the reasons that customers purchase each product or service from you.

Start by downloading and filling out the Customer Benefits Worksheet, available at www.designtosellonline.com/10chap.html. Use it to identify your most important products and services and the reasons that customers buy them from you, as shown in Figure 10-2.

After you have identified the products and services that you want to promote, download and fill out the Postcard Message Planner, which is available at www.designtosellonline.com/10chap.html, and shown in Figure 10-3. Fill out a separate Postcard Message Planner for each of the categories of products or services you want to promote.

Customer Benefits Worksheet

Product or service	Benefits buyers enjoy
Gutter repairs	Eliminates source of damaging leaks Protects landscaping Enhances home appeal
Adding sunrooms	Provides space for more family activities Protects adjacent rooms Increases resale value
Siding	Insulates home Offers freedom from future maintenance
Window replacement	Adds comfort—eliminates drafts Cuts heating costs Makes it easier to open and close windows Enhances home's appeal

Figure 10-2   The Customer Benefits Worksheet helps you review your most popular products and services and the reasons that customers buy them.

Focus on the following issues as you complete your Postcard Message Planner:

Problem   Identify the problem that you want to help your client or prospect resolve. Target a problem shared by a large proportion of your clients or prospects. What is the goal you want to help them achieve? What are the symptoms of the problem?

Solution   Describe how the product or service you're offering can help the recipients resolve their problem or satisfy their goal. Specify exactly how recipients will benefit from taking the action you recommend.

Action   Describe the next step recipients should take. Should they call you, visit you, schedule an appointment, visit your Web site, or send an e-mail message? Specify exactly how you want them to respond.

Benefit   Show how taking the recommended action will benefit the prospect. List several benefits in order of importance.

Proof   Provide evidence that supports these benefits, such as case studies and customer testimonials. Be as specific as possible.

Offer   Explain your offer. Emphasize how it is better than the alternatives, such as doing nothing.

Incentive   Encourage immediate action by providing a compelling reason to act now.

Emphasize how your offer is better than doing nothing.

Postcard Message Planner

Problem	Gutter repairs
Symptom	Ice-dams on roof in winter
	Wet spots on ceiling
	Water drips on visitors entering or leaving home
	Damp basement when it rains
	Damage to landscaping and patio
	Unsightly sagging gutters
Solution	Survey condition of existing gutters, determine whether to repair or replace
Benefit	Generates facts needed to make an informed decision, avoid costly problems down the road
Proof	27 years in business
	Locally owned
	Bonded
	Testimonials available
Offer	Call for no-obligation estimate
Incentive	Free tipsheet

Figure 10-3   Filling out the Postcard Message Planner helps you identify the appropriate postcard message.

Always provide an *incentive*, encouraging postcard recipients to take immediate action. Procrastination is the enemy of response. Your prospects' interest is highest while the postcard is in their hands. If they postpone responding, your chances of success are considerably diminished.

Procrastination is the enemy of response. Give prospects a reason to act right now!

Print your finished Postcard Message Planner, and keep it handy as you complete your postcard. Your Postcard Message Planner will guide you as you choose the right words and appropriate design for your postcard.

Simplicity is one of your most powerful tools. Avoid the temptation to send postcards that offer "something for everyone." Instead, focus each postcard on a single problem-solution-action, and then send a sequence of postcards addressing different problems, as described in the accompanying case study.

Assembling Names and Addresses for Mailing

There are two sources for names and addresses: your "house list"—which consists of the names and addresses of past customers and previous prospects—and purchased lists. Both have a place in any successful postcard promotion plan.

Building Your Own Mailing List

Your own mailing list should consist of the names and addresses of all of your prior and current contacts in a single, up-to-date database that you can access.

This list should contain the names and addresses of everyone you've worked with, as well as prospects that you talked to but didn't sell the first time around. Once completed, this exercise will pay you dividends for years to come.

In many cases, customer and prospect names and addresses are stored in different locations, in different media. You might need to compile your list from names and addresses on invoices, proposals, and business cards that you've accumulated.

If you don't already have a customer and prospect mailing list, here's how to create one by using the Microsoft Publisher built-in database feature.

1. Click **Tools**, **Mail and Catalog Merge**, and then click **Create Address List**.

2. In the **New Address List** dialog box, shown in Figure 10-4, scroll down in the **Enter Address Information** area to examine the available fields, including **First Name**, **Last Name**, **Company Name**, and so on.

Case Study: Home Renovation Firm

As an example, let's consider the postcard planning process for a firm specializing in home remodeling:

1. The firm identifies its four most important sales opportunities: installing more gutters, siding, sunroofs, and windows.

2. The firm commits to creating a different postcard for each opportunity.

3. The firm creates a message for each postcard, based on the problem-solution-action structure.

For example, the owner of the firm might come up with the following message for the first postcard:

Problem   Are old and leaky windows wasting your heating dollars?

Solution   New weather-resistant windows cut drafts, reduce heating costs, and enhance the value of your home!

Action   Call today for a no-obligation estimate!

The *incentive* could be a free tip sheet describing 10 things homeowners should look for when evaluating the condition of the windows in their home.

By repeating the message-generating step for each postcard, the owner would soon have a series of four postcards that could be sent to residents in different areas of the city at monthly intervals.

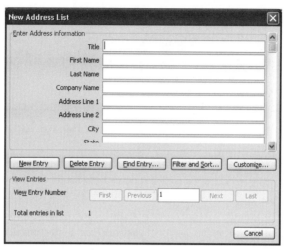

Figure 10-4   Microsoft Publisher's built-in database makes it easy to create a centralized source of prospect names and addresses.

3. To add a new field, perhaps to separate previous clients from prospects so that you can mail separate cards to each group, click the **Customize** button. In the **Customize Address List** dialog box, shown in Figure 10-5, click the **Add** button. In the **Add Field** dialog box, type the word you want to use to identify the field, such as **Status** (to indicate a customer, prospect, or referral), as shown in Figure 10-6, and then click **OK** to return to the **New Address List** dialog box. (You can also delete unnecessary fields.)

Figure 10-5   You can modify Publisher's default database structure by adding or removing fields.

Figure 10-6 Many users add a Status field so that they can indicate, with a
C or P, whether the record refers to a client or prospect.

4. You can now begin to enter customer and prospect names and addresses. Press
TAB to advance through the fields. (Press SHIFT+TAB to return to a previous
field.) Click the **New Entry** button to save the current address and start the next.

5. When you have finished, click **Close**. Publisher will prompt you in the **Save
Address List** dialog box to name the file and save your database. Specify a name
that clearly indicates the database's purpose, such as Customers and Prospects.

In addition to prospects and clients, be sure to add potential sources of referrals to your
database. If you are a home contractor, for example, real estate agents in your area are
probably a very strong source of referrals. People considering selling their homes might
want to increase their home's "street appeal" with strategic upgrades to enhance their
home's value. Recent buyers might want to make changes to customize their new
homes with their own renovations.

Note   It's not necessary to create a new database if you're already maintaining your
customer and prospect mailing list in databases such as Microsoft Office Access or Excel.
Publisher can directly important names and addresses from these file formats, as well as
from contact managers such as Microsoft Office Outlook.

Working with Purchased Lists

After you have assembled your own client, prospect, and referral list, you can explore purchasing mailing lists of qualified prospects. You can easily obtain lists containing the names and addresses of individuals based on criteria like:

- Age
- Car registration
- Home value
- Income
- Occupation or profession
- Position
- Reading habits (for example, magazine subscriptions)
- Trade show and convention attendance
- Vacation habits

An entire industry of *list brokers* is available to help you identify and reach qualified prospects. Consult your local phone book for list brokers in your area or who specialize in your field, or search for **list brokers** or **mailing list rentals** in your Web browser.

People are very tolerant of postcards from strangers in their postal mail, whereas sending unsolicited e-mail messages is both unwanted and illegal.

Sending postcards to new prospects is more cost effective and safer than sending unexpected e-mail messages to prospects you haven't previously dealt with. People are very tolerant of postcards from strangers in their postal mail, whereas unsolicited e-mail messages can get you in very hot water. Unsolicited e-mail is both unwanted and illegal. Penalties can include state and federal indictments as well as Internet service providers blocking your e-mail.

A sequence of mailings always generates more response than a single mailing.

Be sure you understand your rights when purchasing a postal mailing list. Find out whether you are restricted to a single mailing or you can reuse the list within a reasonable amount of time. Remember, a sequence of mailings is always better than a single postcard! Find out what format the list is in. Make sure that this is a format you can use—for example, preprinted address labels or comma-delimited files that you can access with Publisher.

Designing and Producing Postcards

After you've identified the messages you want to communicate and the names and addresses you're going to mail to, it's time to design and produce your postcard. This involves *working backward* from how you're going to print and address your postcards.

Postcards come in a variety of sizes. In addition, numerous alternatives are available from commercial printers and firms that produce blank postcards you can print on your desktop printer.

Choosing Postcard Size and Orientation

Postcard sizes range from approximately 4 by 6 inches to 6 by 9 inches—and occasionally larger. Be sure to check current postal rates for various postcard sizes.

Before producing your cards, familiarize yourself with the current postal regulations—especially if you are using a nonstandard size. Your mailing has to conform to a specified length-to-width ratio and must be printed on a material stiff enough to pass through the postal service's automated mail processing machinery. In addition, return and recipient addresses have to be placed in the proper locations, and you must leave space for postal bar codes, which must appear against a white background.

Another printer variable you have to know before you begin work is whether you have to leave a blank border around the edges of each postcard. Some printing processes permit you to include text and graphics right to the trim edge of each postcard; other vendors require a border.

You also must decide whether you want the front of your postcard to appear in either *landscape* (horizontal) or *portrait* (vertical) orientation.

A final variable involves the number of postcards you want to print at one time. Depending on postcard size, you can print 1, 2, or 4 postcards on each sheet of postcard material loaded into the printer attached to your computer.

The color options you will have available to work with will depend on the printing option you choose. If you have a color laser or ink-jet printer, you have the freedom to include any colors on either the front or back.

If your postcards are going to be printed by a commercial printer, you can choose between the following options for either, or both, sides of your postcards:

- Black and white
- Spot color—that is, black plus an accent color, like blue or green
- Process color, which allows you to include color photographs and any mixture of colors

Before printing postcards, always familiarize yourself with the current postal regulations, especially if you are using a nonstandard size.

Creating a Postcard with Publisher

To create a postcard from scratch, follow these steps:

1. Click **File**, **New**.

2. In the **New Publication** task pane, in the **New From A Design** section, click **Blank Publications**, and then click the **Postcard** option.

3. Click **File**, **Page Setup**, and in the **Page Setup** dialog box, confirm that the height and width settings are appropriate for the method you will use to print your postcards, and then confirm that the postcard orientation is correct. Click the **Change Copies Per Sheet** button if the default setting is not appropriate for the type of printing you will be using. Click **OK**.

4. Click **Arrange**, **Layout Guides**.

5. In the **Layout Guides** dialog box, you can now adjust the margins—or white border—to suit the requirements of the printing technology you will be using.

    You are now ready to start designing your postcard.

Designing an Effective Postcard

Postcards should be thought of in terms of two distinct areas: the front, or "billboard" side of the postcard; and the message area and address panel on the back, which contains your return address plus space for inserting the recipient's name and address (or applying an address label).

Postcard Front

The front of a postcard can contain several text and graphical elements, including:

Visual   A graphical element that sets the mood.

Headline   A brief statement that "telegraphs" your offer to the reader.

Eyebrow   A short phrase *above* the headline that introduces it.

Kicker   A short phrase *under* the headline elaborating on the offer.

Text   The details of your offer, often in bulleted list form.

Proof   Support for your message, often in the form of client testimonials.

Call to action   Description of the action you want recipients to take.

Graphical accents   Design elements such as lines, fills, or borders.

Each of these elements should be formatted as distinctly as possible, avoiding clutter that might confuse the reader. Simpler postcard designs are possible, but you should consider including at least some of these elements.

Postcard Back

The message area of your postcard can contain either text or graphics. The message area can also be personalized by addressing the recipient by name. The address panel should contain your return address plus space for the recipient's name and address, or space for applying address labels.

Before finalizing your postcard design, double-check to make sure it complies with current postal service regulations. It's a good idea to bring a sample postcard, plus a sample of the paper you will be using to print it, to your local post office for them to approve its layout, size, and thickness.

Using Graphical Elements to Organize the Front of Your Postcard

As mentioned earlier, most postcards fail to satisfy both long-term and short-term goals. As a result, the recipient sees only the short-term message and fails to appreciate the broad range of benefits your firm offers.

One of the easiest ways to avoid this problem is to use fills, borders, and colors to organize the space on the front of the postcard.

With careful layout and formatting, you can trade some of the area announcing your short-term message for space to provide a little information about your firm and how you benefit your market.

Compare the two postcards shown here. Notice that the postcard shown in Figure 10-7 includes a boxed area on the left that describes the firm's mission, background, and services. The other version, shown in Figure 10-8, does not include the boxed area, but does contain the same main text, in slightly larger type.

Notice that eliminating the firm's background information didn't really make the short-term offer significantly more compelling or easier to read. Indeed, many might feel that the postcard without the background information is less interesting than the postcard with the background information.

Consider dividing the front of your postcard into two selling areas. Use a smaller area to deliver a message of long-term importance about your firm, and use the remainder to promote a specific event or product. With this format, you will save time creating your postcards, create more interesting postcards, and better serve both short-term and long-term goals.

Bring a proof of your postcard, plus a paper sample, to your post office for approval before printing.

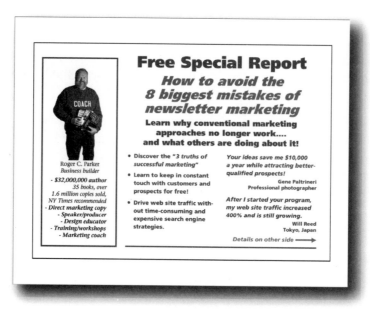

Figure 10-7 Postcard using color and graphical accents to describe the firm's mission, background, and services as well as a current offer.

Figure 10-8 Postcard without background information about the firm. This version contains the same main text set larger but does not include a separate boxed area describing the benefits of buying from the firm.

Streamlining Postcard Production

Publisher's master pages and templates, covered in Chapters 5 and 6, make it easy to speed postcard production. Simply create a template containing a background grid and your firm's long-term positioning message set as a graphic on the postcard's master page, as shown in Figure 10-9. This adds visual interest and allows you to focus on choosing the right words to promote your upcoming event.

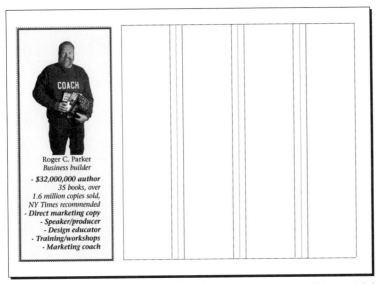

Figure 10-9 To simplify postcard production, create a template containing a grid and a graphical element describing your firm on the postcard's master page.

Here's how to do it:

1. Start by creating a graphic containing your logo or a photograph that symbolizes your business. This graphic can include a mission statement, awards, client testimonials, or any other information that will help recipients understand why they should pay attention to the adjacent message.

2. Create space for the graphic by clicking **Arrange, Layout Guides**. On the **Margin Guides** tab, increase the left-hand margin until there is space for the graphic you have selected, and then click **OK**.

3. Click **Arrange, Layout Guides** again, and then on the **Grid Guides** tab, type **4** in the **Columns** box.

    The four-column grid will allow you to create an attention-getting headline for the specific event or promotion the postcard is announcing. You can also include two columns of text describing why the recipients should attend the event or take advantage of the promotion.

The arrow at the bottom of the postcard front encourages readers to turn the postcard over, to learn more from the message area to the left of the address panel.

4. Save your work as a Blank Postcard template.

You can use this template to create individualized templates—as described in Chapter 8—for the specific categories of postcards you identified on the Postcard Message Planner earlier in this chapter.

The thank you postcard shown in Figure 10-10 was based on the template shown in Figure 10-9. The postcard front contains a description of the firm and its purpose on the left, which remains constant from postcard to postcard. The message on the right supports the postcard's specific purpose.

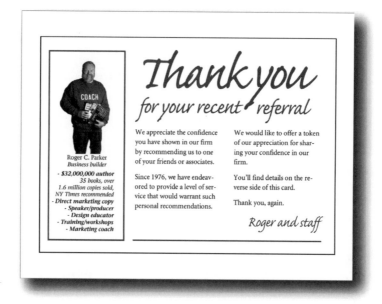

Figure 10-10   Example of a thank you postcard based on the template shown in Figure 10-9.

Becoming a Postcard Pro

Postcards offer far more flexibility than is apparent at first glance. "Postcard pros" take consistent advantage of the numerous options available.

Formatting Publisher Text Boxes

When positioning large text elements on a page, it is often easier to create the text in several overlapping text boxes rather than a single text box, as shown in Figure 10-11. This technique is often necessary to properly align your text, such as when formatting closely spaced text or placing text over a photograph or background fill.

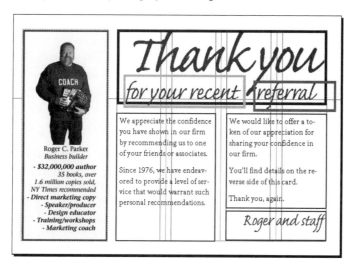

Figure 10-11 Notice the borders of the three overlapping text boxes at the top of the postcard and the horizontal guide used to correctly align the text in the two text boxes under the headline.

By default, Publisher does not allow you to place one text box on top of another. To enable overlapping:

1. Select the text box that you want to overlap another.

2. Click **Format**, **Text Box**.

3. In the **Format Text Box** dialog box, click the **Layout** tab.

4. Click **Wrapping Style**, **None**.

You can now place the text box on top of another.

Multiple Mailing and Addressing Options

The first step to becoming a postcard pro is to set up a postcard marketing process that uses different methods to print and address postcards. Even though all of your postcards should share a common look—based on layout, color, and type—some postcards should be printed and addressed in small quantities on your desktop printer, while others will be printed in larger quantities and addressed with address labels.

Some postcards should be printed and addressed in small quantities on your desktop printer, others printed in larger quantities and addressed with address labels.

You need to know when to use each option, and where to go for the best combination of quality, speed, and price.

As a result, you will simultaneously print and address a few postcards each week, thanking new customers for their purchases and thanking referral sources. Using Publisher's Mail And Catalog Merge Wizard, you can choose postcard recipients on the basis of their status as a customer or prospect, the date they made their purchases, or their postal codes.

In addition, larger mailings will go out once a month, some to clients and some to prospects, informing them of new products and services, important new Web site content, and helpful seasonal hints. Monthly mailings will also be sent to purchased mailing lists, introducing the firm to names and addresses of qualified prospects chosen with the help of a list broker, on the basis of income, interests, or previous purchases.

Finally, on a less frequent basis, you can send promotional postcards to clients and prospects offering special limited-time buying incentives.

A steady diet of any one of these mailings would soon wear out the people on your lists. But by sending an ongoing stream of different postcards for different purposes, you can ensure the success of your marketing effort.

Tracking Postcard Results

Carefully track the results of your postcard promotions.

The next step to becoming a postcard pro is to carefully track the results of your postcard promotions. Promotions can be tracked in a variety of ways:

You can track postcard promotions of special events by sending postcards printed in different colors, or including a response code keyed to the list source, and requiring attendees to bring their postcard with them.

You can track postcards announcing new Web site content by using different Web site landing pages to indicate which lists are producing the best response. Use a Web address in the form *www.yoururl.com/landingpage1* for recipients whose names and addresses are on list 1, and use *www.yoururl.com/landingpage2* for individuals responding from list 2. By adding page visits, downloads, or purchases, it will soon be obvious which list source generates the best response.

Using the Internet to Send Postcards

You can also use Publisher to prepare postcard artwork that can be uploaded to the Internet, for next-day, "hands-free," full-color digital printing, addressing, and mailing. Firms such as AmazingMail, at www.amazingmail.com, permit you to upload and store your customer and prospect mailing list along with your frequently used postcard artwork.

After uploading postcard artwork, you can access your mailing list and postcard artwork from any computer with Internet access, sending one card or a thousand cards at a time. Messages can be personalized with the recipient's name as the cards are printed.

Creating postcard artwork for digital print on demand requires a single additional step. After using Publisher to create artwork files for the front and back of your postcard, click File, Save As, and then save the artwork as a JPG file. Click the Change button, select Commercial Printing (300 DPI) in the Change Resolution dialog box, and then click OK.

Summary

By now, you probably have an entirely new idea of what's possible with postcards.

Postcards can be used to reinforce relationships with existing clients and prospects. You can also use postcards to reach out to new markets that might not be aware you're in business.

In this chapter, you've learned how to make the most of postcards by identifying when to send a postcard, and how to use graphical elements and master pages to create a "look" for your postcards—one that satisfies both short-term and long-term goals.

In the next chapter, you'll learn how to use newsletters and tip sheets to create a *platform* for yourself, one that will permit you to consistently and efficiently promote your ability to provide products and services that benefit your customers and prospects.

Test Yourself

Before moving on to the next chapter, take a few moments to visit www.designtosellonline.com/10chap.html. On this book's companion Web site, you'll find additional resources, including:

- Downloadable and printable copies of the three postcard planning worksheets included in this chapter.

- A self-scoring assessment to help you review your mastery of new terms introduced in this chapter.

- Additional examples of postcards created around a common framework.

- Sample Publisher template files.

- Online sources providing additional print on demand postcard marketing information.

Chapter Eleven

Using Newsletters and Tip Sheets to Promote Your Expertise

What you'll find:

- ❑ Define a platform.
- ❑ Plan your newsletter.
- ❑ Produce a one-page newsletter.
- ❑ Create an effective newsletter template.
- ❑ Produce each issue of your newsletter as quickly as possible.
- ❑ Create tip sheets to promote your newsletter and build its mailing list.

The purpose of this chapter is to teach you how to use Microsoft Office Publisher to create a platform based on newsletters and tip sheets. Newsletters are powerful platform builders because they make it possible for you to *educate your market* without buying expensive media advertising. Newsletters put you in control of your destiny, instead of waiting for things to happen.

Tip sheets are even easier to produce. Tip sheets can be as simple as 8 or 10 numbered recommendations that distill your knowledge and years of experience down to one side of a single sheet of paper.

In this chapter, you'll learn how to apply many of the Publisher-specific techniques described in Part Two. While you read this chapter and create your platform, you'll probably want to refer back to the information in previous chapters.

What Is a Platform?

A platform is your version of a local newspaper or radio station. Just as the owner of a small-town department store or grocery store gains a competitive advantage by owning a local newspaper or radio station, helping the owner to keep in touch with customers, your platform provides a similar way to inform your clients and prospects about the value of buying from you.

Types of Platforms

There are numerous types of platforms. The worlds of business and politics provide many examples. For instance, the name recognition from a background in the entertainment industry can be enough to establish a career in politics—in Ronald Reagan's case, leading to the White House.

Television shows have not only propelled Martha Stewart and Oprah Winfrey to great influence, but their popularity has also enhanced the careers of others, like Dr. Phil.

Television appearances, of course, are just one example of a platform. Other more practical options include using articles and columns, blogs, e-books, audio interviews, podcasts, and Web sites. Jack Canfield and Mark Victor Hansen used their *Chicken Soup* book series to create an international platform

Creating newsletters and tip sheets with Publisher lets you too enjoy the benefits of a platform—but with far less investment of time and money.

Benefits of Successful Platforms

Those who develop successful platforms enjoy numerous advantages, including:

A "stage" to present from   Each of the platform types offers a way to promote your expertise by educating your market and communicating your point of view.

Repeatable   With the exception of trade books sold through local and online bookstores, each of the platform types represents a process that is repeated over and over, maintaining your constant visibility.

Control   The best platforms are totally under your control, so you can choose the topics you want to address and choose the content you want to include.

Efficiency   In contrast to conventional advertising, platforms cost little to set up and maintain. As platforms expand, they can even turn into profit centers. You might ultimately turn your newsletter into a subscription version that people pay to receive or into articles that you are paid to write.

Equity   The ideas and information promoted in your platform rarely go out of date. This permits you to recycle content in different ways. Information that starts as a newsletter or tip sheet, for example, can be recycled as an article, a presentation, an e-book—or even a trade book.

Self-improvement   The effort you put into creating each issue of your newsletter pays off in enhanced confidence and skills. By constantly refining your ideas and improving your ability to express them, you continually improve your message and learn to communicate it more effectively.

Perhaps most important, each of the advantages offered by a platform expands your network of those who know and respect you. This includes those who listen to you and recommend you to others.

Prerequisites for Creating a Successful Platform

The three prerequisites for creating a successful platform are: a *core message*, a *vehicle* (or way of packaging and delivering your message), and a *promotional Web site* that you can easily update yourself.

Message

The starting point for developing a platform is to create a core message that states your value proposition (that is, how your market benefits) and helps differentiate you from your competition. Your core message should be constantly repeated through every one of your marketing communications.

Your core message provides the starting point for choosing the topics and information for each newsletter or tip sheet installment. Your core message should not only reflect your key strengths, but also identify the market you serve and the unique benefits you offer. In addition, your message should reflect your values, style, and enthusiasm. In short, your message should reflect your firm's *mission*—or reason for being:

- My message is that I help firms and individuals use design as a strategic tool. Thus, each newsletter or tip sheet I produce focuses on profiting from a specific aspect of design.

- The platform of someone with a background in radio could be that she helps individuals sound their best when being interviewed on radio or television. Newsletters and tip sheets could describe ways to organize messages, avoid nervousness, and speak with clarity and enthusiasm.

Vehicle

Platforms also require a way of making your knowledge tangible—a *vehicle* for communicating your message—so that you're not just claiming, "I know what I'm talking about," but you're proving it in a way that customers and prospects can immediately appreciate.

For many businesses, newsletters represent an effective option. Newsletters offer an easy way to package your information in a tangible way that can be quickly and easily shared with others to prove your expertise.

More important, once you create a newsletter, you have a reusable module of information that you can recycle into various forms to further promote your platform in:

- ■ Articles for syndication, interviews, books, and e-books.

- ■ Presentations, speeches, teleconferences, podcasts, and training seminars.

- ■ Web site incentives, such as special reports offering in-depth treatment of a timely topic or compilations of previous issues, that you can use to encourage opt-in registrations for your online newsletter. (Tip sheets, described later in this chapter, are ideal for building newsletter circulation!)

Web Site

After you create your platform, you must be able to promote it by using a Web site that you can easily and consistently update yourself.

"Hostage" Web sites—that is, elaborately designed sites that cannot be quickly and easily updated without the delays and costs involved in hiring others—are rarely efficient and responsive enough to effectively promote your platform. Each time a new newsletter or tip sheet appears, you must be able to make it immediately available to clients and prospects.

Planning Your Newsletter

Individuals and firms have long embraced newsletter marketing because it makes sense. Instead of dissipating your time and budget resources on advertisements that inevitably contain a lot of waste circulation—that is, they reach many individuals who might never need your product or service—newsletters permit you to focus on just those most likely to buy.

In contrast to advertising in newspapers or on broadcast media like radio or television, newsletters also provide the space needed to explain the benefits of buying—and rebuying—from you.

Why Conventional Newsletters Usually Fail

The problem is, conventional newsletter publishing rarely works. This is because conventional newsletters typically contain 4, 8, or 16 pages and appear at quarterly or bimonthly intervals.

Because conventional multipage newsletters are printed and mailed, costs and delays are frequent. In addition, because each issue contains so much space, producing each issue takes too much time because there are too many content decisions to be made, and it always takes more time to write and lay out each issue than available.

Because of the time it takes to prepare, print, address, and mail conventional multipage newsletters, topics often go out of date before they appear, and too much time elapses between issues.

Remember our oscilloscope example. Each spike of the trace is similar to the arrival of a newsletter. Although the oscilloscope trace is visible at its peak, it soon disappears into a trough, until the next beep. When too much time goes by between newsletters, firms lose their visibility, and customers who are ready to buy go elsewhere. Little wonder that most conventional, multipage newsletter marketing programs rarely last.

Rethinking Newsletter Goals

The "perfect" newsletter would have several characteristics:

Efficiency   The ideal newsletter would be easy to produce so that any business owner or departmental manager could do it in less than two hours per month. It would also be inexpensive enough to produce every month—often enough to maintain a firm's constant visibility among prospects and clients.

Relevance   The ideal newsletter would be welcomed and anticipated by its readers, rather than glanced at and discarded. Readers would give it top ratings in the "What's In It For Me?" Sweepstakes. The newsletter would be written from the customer or client's point of view, rather than the point of view of the individual or firm producing it.

Consistent image   In contrast to conventional advertisements emphasizing one product or service, each issue would—through its content—create a "halo" effect that would promote every product and service the individual or firm offered.

Multiple points of contact   The ideal newsletter would be created in a format that could be printed, for distribution to key clients and at networking effects, as well as distributed for free online, as a Web site download or an e-mail attachment.

Quick and easy to read   Your customers and prospects are as busy as you are. They too don't have as much time as they used to. Customers appreciate concise, succinct, useful information that doesn't take much time to read.

The One-Page Newsletter Solution

Numerous firms and individuals around the world have discovered the advantages of a monthly one-page newsletter. The defining characteristics of one-page newsletters are:

Short   Each issue consists of a single sheet of paper, printed on both the front and the back.

Formatted   Each issue is carefully formatted to project a friendly and professional image, even before it is read. The newsletter's careful formatting also differentiates the firm from its competition.

Useful   Each issue is focused on a single topic, described in about six hundred words. Illustrations can be included, if they're useful.

Multiple distribution channels   Each issue can be distributed online, offline, and in person. Because many copies are distributed electronically or printed as needed on desktop printers, there are no expensive minimum quantities to print.

One-Page Newsletter Advantages

The one-page newsletter format offers these compelling advantages:

Easy to produce   Because the single-page format focuses each issue on a single topic, planning and writing are simple.

Consistent   Each issue projects a consistent "look" based on a template and grid created using Microsoft Publisher's master pages.

Relevant   Prospects and customers look forward to each issue because each issue contains useful information that helps them make better buying decisions or make the most of an earlier purchase.

Long shelf life   Because they focus on educational topics, issues rarely go out of date, allowing you to archive them on your Web site, where they will attract search engine traffic.

Printed as needed   Rather than printing hundreds or thousands of copies, most copies can be distributed as Web site downloads or e-mail attachments. Copies can be printed as needed for networking events or distribution to key clients.

Producing a One-Page Newsletter

The five steps involved in setting up a marketing program based on a monthly one-page newsletter are:

1. Familiarize yourself with the text and graphical elements used to create a one-page newsletter

2. Plan your newsletter program by selecting an appropriate title and creating an editorial calendar of topic ideas for the first 12 issues.

3. Create a template that you can quickly complete each month.

4. Complete, proof, and distribute each issue.

5. Promote your newsletters online and offline.

Elements of One-Page Newsletter Architecture

Let's start by examining the various building blocks found on the front and back of a one-page newsletter.

Front Page

Figure 11-1 shows a typical one-page newsletter. The numbers in the figure correspond to the list numbers below.

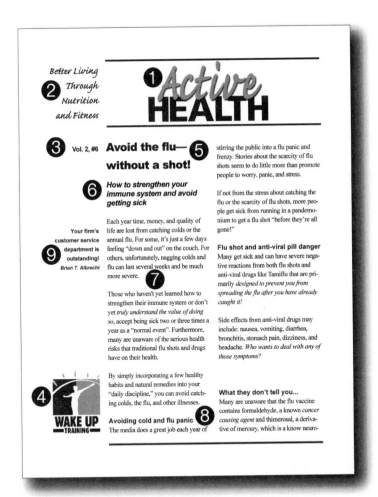

Figure 11-1 The front page of a typical one-page newsletter contains nine building blocks, or distinct type elements.

1. Nameplate   The nameplate at the top of the front page contains the title of your newsletter, set in a large and stylized typeface.

Tips for Using Color in Nameplates

Avoid using too much color in your newsletter nameplate.

A solid colored background might be very attractive, but it will significantly increase the cost of printing your newsletter.

Because you will be printing some copies yourself and you want to encourage your customers and prospects to print each issue that arrives as an electronic file, you should design for the most efficient and economical color printing possible.

And remember, less color is usually more effective than more color!

The best titles are those that communicate a benefit or identify the newsletter's intended market. Titles work best when they consist of words of approximately equal length. Sometimes titles contain active verbs—for example, "Healthy Living" or "Profitable Investing."

The best nameplates often contain two contrasting typefaces—in this case, a script (or handwritten) typeface and a sans serif typeface set in all caps. Interest is added by slightly overlapping the two words.

2. Tagline   Place an explanatory tagline, or motto, below or next to the title of your publication. The tagline should elaborate on the promise offered in the title, helping prospects and clients better understand the benefits of reading the information that follows.

Notice that the tagline in our example is set in the same typeface as the first word in the title, for consistency.

3. Folio   Although the folio can indicate the date your newsletter appears, this has the unfortunate effect of making previous issues look out of date, even if the information is still valid.

A much better alternative is to number your issues. That way, when you send someone a back issue of your newsletter or they download it from your Web site, it will still appear timely and relevant.

4. Logo   Place your firm's logo in the lower left-hand corner of the front page. Avoid the temptation to include contact information such as addresses and phone numbers here, as these can clutter the front page. There's room on the back page for full contact information.

5. Headline   Keep headlines as short as possible—preferably a maximum of two lines. Be as concise as possible, and use the shortest possible words. Rewrite your headlines until they fit the available space, and do not inadvertently separate words that should

be next to each other. Use line breaks (press SHIFT + ENTER) to break words where desired. Never hyphenate headlines.

6. Elaboration   Next provide a segue, or transition, between the headline and the text that follows. Elaborate on the headline's relevance on the three lines that follow it. Describe the benefits that your customers and prospects will enjoy when they read this issue of your newsletter. Never leave anything to chance. Explain the specific benefits they will gain.

Again, rewrite as necessary to fit on three lines and to avoid hyphenation and awkward line breaks. When appropriate, the elaboration can be set in one of the colors used in the newsletter's nameplate.

7. Body copy   Body copy should be as easy to read as possible. Notice the relatively large line spacing and open space between paragraphs in our example—this not only projects an open, easy-to-read image, but also actually contributes to easy reading. The extra white space between lines helps emphasize each word's shape, making the text easier to scan.

Espresso Dave Names a Newsletter

Espresso Dave was one of my clients. Espresso Dave's business provides a portable cappuccino and espresso service at events like conventions and trade shows. When it came time to create his one-page newsletter, the first idea was to emphasize the "coffee" aspect of his business, with a title such as "Coffee Time" or "The Perfect Cup."

On reflection, it became clear that large corporations hired him *not* because of the excellence of his coffee but because his presence at their trade show exhibit boosted foot traffic and encouraged visitors to spend more time at the booth.

Thus, Espresso Dave's newsletter was named "Trade Show Marketing," because *that* was the reason his clients hired him.

When naming your newsletter, go beyond the obvious and choose a title that reflects the benefits you offer your customers and prospects.

Notice too that baseline alignment is used, so that the baselines of the text in each column align with each other, presenting a far more professional image.

8. Subheads   Notice that the subheads in our example newsletter are set in a typeface and color that forms a strong contrast with the adjacent body copy. Notice too that the subhead color is the same as one of the colors in the newsletter nameplate. (You can view the newsletter in color at www.designtosellonline.com/11chap.html.)

For easiest reading, limit capital letters in subheads to the first letter of the first word and any proper nouns. Limit subheads to one line. Most important, add extra white space above the subheads, to emphasize the break with the preceding topic.

9. Testimonial   Place testimonials in the white space to the left of the text. Align the testimonials flush right. Notice that style contrast is employed to separate the

testimonial from the name of the individual who submitted it—in this case, the byline is set in italics.

Notice the horizontal lines, or *rules*, that frame the nameplate and the two text columns. These rules do not extend the full width of the page, further adding to the white space created by the narrow left-hand column.

Back Page

The back page of the newsletter contains several additional elements, as shown in Figure 11-2.

Figure 11-2   The back page of a one-page newsletter includes additional elements such as a photograph, a pull-quote, and full contact information.

1. **Title**   The title of the newsletter appears at the top of the back page, set in the same typeface used for subheads.

2. **Folio**   The volume and number of the current issue is set in the same typeface and type size as the newsletter's title on the same line. Use a horizontal guideline to accurately align the two text elements.

3. **Pull-quote**   A pull-quote set in a larger type size is used to draw attention to the key phrase found on the back page. Although it's not necessary to use the exact same wording, the wording you use should communicate the same idea.

The pull-quote is set flush-right, with extra line spacing, and can be set in an italicized version of the typeface used for the subheads.

4. **Photograph**   A large photograph is used on the back page to personalize the newsletter. Notice that the bottom of the photograph aligns with the baseline of the text, another detail that reinforces the newsletter's professional image.

5. **Contact information**   Copyright and contact information appear below the photo.

6. **Call to action**   The firm's phone number and primary e-mail address are repeated in the last paragraph of text, even though the same information appears in the contact information to the left. This information is repeated to avoid the possibility that someone who wanted to respond might not immediately locate the information under the photograph.

Designing to sell is all about your customers and prospects, not about you—and not about making readers search for contact information. When in doubt, choose the option that eliminates any possibility of losing a sale.

> Designing to sell is all about your customers and prospects, not about you—and not about making your readers search for contact information.

Planning Your One-Page Newsletter Program

A successful one-page newsletter program is based on two key tasks that must be completed before you begin working on the first issue: you have to create the right title, and you have to develop an editorial calendar that identifies the topics for the first 12 issues of your newsletter.

Creating a Title for Your One-Page Newsletter

Creating the right title for your newsletter involves three steps:

1. Identify the benefits that your one-page newsletter offers.

2. Focus on a niche for your newsletter.

3. Fine-tune your title choice.

Identifying newsletter benefits   The starting point for creating a successful title is to recognize that your firm or association's name usually does not constitute a strong title. Your name does not offer a benefit. Your name coupled with the word *newsletter* simply restates the obvious when it arrives in your customer's mailbox (or inbox).

Consider two possible titles:

- The Roger C. Parker Newsletter
- Desktop Publishing and Design Tips

Which title does the best job of promising a benefit or describing the newsletter's contents? There's obviously no benefit described by "The Roger C. Parker Newsletter." It's a "brag and boast" title that elicits a "so what?" reaction.

A glance at the second title, however, is enough to give you an idea of the information to be found in the newsletter. The *Desktop Publishing and Design* part of the title emphasizes that the newsletter will cover both technology and design issues, while *Tips* communicates that the contents will contain short, useful ideas.

Instead of including your name in the title, consider placing your name either before your newsletter's title or in a "published by" statement that follows the title.

You can use the Newsletter Title Planning Worksheet, shown in Figure 11-3, to brainstorm ideas for your newsletter. In the first column, enter some of the topics you're going to include in your newsletter. After you've entered your topics, in the second column, describe how readers will benefit from your ideas. Last, in the third column, jot down some possible words to describe these benefits.

Focusing on a niche for your newsletter   Specialists are always more successful than generalists. The same is true of newsletters. Strengthen the title of your one-page newsletter by emphasizing your firm's particular target market or the particular approach you're going to develop in your newsletter.

Let's reconsider the title "Desktop Publishing and Design Tips." It's strong in that it identifies the contents of the newsletter, but it's weak in terms of describing the particular benefits readers will enjoy. It fails to identify a target market or editorial approach.

Newsletter Title Planning Worksheet

Topic ideas	Reader benefits	Possible words
Keyboard shortcuts	Save time and effort More time to sell	Efficiency
Recent trends and new developments	Keep informed Save reading other publications	Update
Basic techniques	Review forgotten lessons Maintain a fresh perspective	Skill builders Design refresher
Billing suggestions	Don't forget it's a business!	Successful Practical
Marketing ideas	Maintain competitive stance	Growing
Software reviews	Avoid expensive mistakes Keep up to date	Informed
Digital printing info	Keep informed	Trends

Figure 11-3 Brainstorm ideas for your newsletter using the Newsletter Title Planning Worksheet, which can be downloaded from www.designtosellonline/11chap.html.

Accordingly, the next step is to experiment with titles that focus on specific markets or approaches. Here are several options for the title that are more specific:

High-Impact Design   Appropriate if you want to focus on design techniques for professional designers.

Corporate Design   Appropriate if you want to target prospects located in corporate environments or design firms serving corporate clients.

Penny-Pinching Design   Ideal for a newsletter targeting designers who serve the small business market, or "entrepreneurs turned designers."

Profitable Design   Good choice for a newsletter published by a consultant whose clients are design firms interested in higher revenues.

Carrying the idea of identifying a niche even further, here are some additional options:

Four-Color Design   Appropriate if your newsletter is going to focus on the technical and design issues involved in four-color printing.

Corporate Branding   An ideal choice for a designer interested in using design as a tool to visually differentiate firms from their competition.

Each time you focus your newsletter, you become more valuable to a specific market segment. In addition, the increased focus makes it increasingly easy to write and produce each issue.

Fine-tuning your title   Whenever possible, incorporate "action" words into your title. Action words are verbs ending in *ing*. These action words give your title momentum. They imply action and movement. Compare these two titles:

- The Successful Consultant's News
- Successful Consulting

The first title does a good job of identifying its market, but it doesn't communicate action. It projects a static image. It implies a third-person, after-the-fact "analysis" rather than a first-person "process." It lacks immediacy.

The second title is not only considerably shorter, but it implies an ongoing process. It does a better job of communicating that readers will discover steps they can take to become more successful consultants.

To make your title more memorable, try to incorporate repeated starting consonants in your title. This literary technique is known as *alliteration*.

Consider the following two titles for a one-page newsletter for a presentation consultant:

- Presentation Tips
- Persuasive Presentations

Which title is stronger? Which is more unique and memorable?

Chances are, you selected the second title. "Presentation Tips" does a good job of identifying the contents of this newsletter, but the title just sits there on the page. There's nothing memorable about it.

"Persuasive Presentations," however, is different. The repeated parallelism of the "puh!" sound at the beginning of each word projects strength. The alliteration of the repeated *P*s makes it more likely that readers will remember the title.

Newsletter titles succeed to the extent that they are short and to the point. There are two reasons for this:

Short equals big.   The shorter the title, the larger the type size you can use when formatting the nameplate.

Short leads to memorable.   The fewer words you use in your title, the easier it will be for readers to glance at your title and understand it. Short titles are also easier to say and easier to remember.

Plan to invest at least a few days in choosing the right title for your newsletter. The right title will serve you well for years to come.

Developing an Editorial Calendar

The second planning step involves preparing a list of the topics of your first 12 newsletters. Choosing your monthly newsletter topics ahead of time makes them easier to write. Knowing the topics you're going to cover, you can easily jot down ideas for each issue well in advance of the time the issue is scheduled to appear. If you jot down ideas as they occur to you, when it's time to begin preparing each issue, you'll be pleasantly surprised to see that a lot of the work has already been done.

In addition, by frequently referring to your editorial calendar, your subconscious mind will be thinking about upcoming topics while you're sleeping or doing other tasks. Again, the benefit is that you'll find it easier than you thought to prepare each issue.

Referring to your editorial calendar helps avoid "deadline madness," when you don't start work on your newsletter until the last minute. Identifying the topics of each issue in advance helps you avoid being unpleasantly surprised.

You can use the Editorial Calendar Worksheet, shown in Figure 11-4, to create an editorial calendar. The worksheet consists of a simple four-column table, with separate columns for the month each issue will appear, the deadline for preparing it, the topic—or headline title—of the issue, and a growing list of content ideas that occur to you each time you review the list.

Editorial Calendar Worksheet

Issue	Due date	Title	Ideas
January	12/15	Networking for profits	Advantages Locating opportunities Recommended books
February	1/15	Building a typeface library	Advantages Resources "Core" fonts Luxury options
March	2/15	Preparing client proposals	Standard terms Services Benefits
April	3/15	Postcard marketing	Benefits Resources Reasons to send
May	4/15	Identifying problem clients	Importance Warning signs Extrication tips
June	5/15	Training opportunities	Online Workshops Trade-out for speaking
July	6/15	Software upgrades	Better sooner or later? Printers suggestions
August	7/15	Buying a digital camera for the business?	Buy or lease? Rentals Insurance Accessories

Figure 11-4   Use the Editorial Calendar Worksheet, which you can download from www.designtosellonline.com/11chap.html, to jot down ideas to be included in future issues.

Creating a One-Page Newsletter Template

Creating a one-page newsletter template saves you time and ensures that each issue will project a consistent image. A successful template includes the following elements:

Nameplate created and saved as a graphic.   Creating and saving the nameplate as a graphic, rather than simply setting the title as text in Publisher, protects the nameplate from accidental changes and makes it easier to resize and place. Creating your newsletter nameplate as a graphic also makes it easier to reuse the graphic in other publications, such as business cards, postcards, and advertisements.

Front and back page repeating elements located on master pages. Reduces the possibility that you might inadvertently drag or resize a text or graphical element that should appear in the same location in each issue.

Text styles included in the template. Ensures fast, accurate, text formatting and consistent appearance from issue to issue. In addition, using text styles makes it easier for you to later delegate newsletter formatting to an assistant or to someone else.

Creating a Nameplate Graphic

The graphic containing your newsletter's nameplate can be created using the same image editing software you use to resize and enhance photographs before importing them into Publisher.

You can also experiment with setting the text and associated graphics, such as horizontal rules above and below the title, in Publisher.

To create and save a graphic using Publisher:

1. Click **File**, **New**, and then click **Blank Print Publication**.

2. In your new, blank document click **File**, **Page Setup**. In the **Page Setup** dialog box, select **Custom** in the **Publication Type** list, and then in the **Width** and **Height** boxes, type the size of the graphic you want to create.

3. Create your nameplate graphic as desired.

4. When you've finished creating your graphic, click **File, Save As**. In the **Save As** dialog box, type a descriptive file name, and then specify an appropriate **File Type**—for example, **EPS**, **TIF**, or **JPG**.

5. Select the folder in which you want to save the graphic.

6. Before saving, click the **Change** button, change the resolution to **Commercial Printing (300 dpi)**, or dots per inch for printing, and then click **OK**.

Depending on how much space surrounds the graphic, you might want to crop the graphic after you place it on the master page of the first page of your newsletter.

Creating Template Master Pages

The next step in creating a one-page newsletter template is to place text and graphical elements that will appear in each issue on front and back master pages, as shown in Figure 11-5.

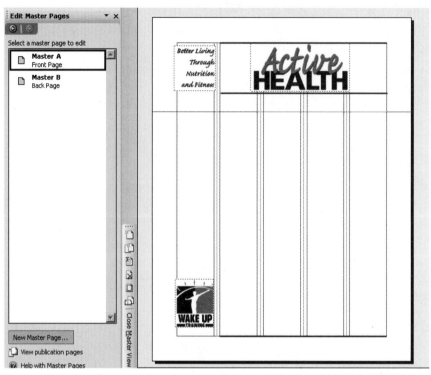

Figure 11-5 Front page text and graphical elements that remain unchanged from issue to issue are placed on a master page, protecting them from unintentional movement or deletion.

Success comes from eliminating problems before they occur. By placing your nameplate graphic, tagline, logo, and graphical accents such as borders on master pages, you can ensure that they're less likely to be inadvertently moved or deleted.

Master pages should be formatted with baseline guides equal to the line spacing of the body copy, to maintain text alignment across the page.

Entering Text Styles

The final step in creating a one-page newsletter template is to create the text styles you'll use. The Styles And Formatting task pane in Figure 11-6 shows text styles used for the "Active Health" newsletter. You might be surprised to learn how many text styles are included in a simple one-page newsletter.

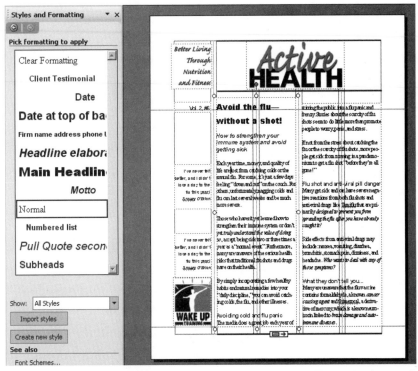

Figure 11-6   A template for a typical one-page newsletter will contain about a dozen text styles.

This careful formatting makes the newsletter's information hierarchy immediately obvious to clients and prospects glancing at the newsletter. The size and weight of each text element should reflect the relative importance of the message it delivers. The headline, for example, should be larger than the elaboration, which should be larger than the body copy, which in turn should be larger than photo captions or client testimonials.

The paragraph formatting of each text style should indicate whether the baseline of text should or should not align with the baseline guides.

Producing Each Issue

Two additional techniques you can use to simplify creating each issue are *list-based writing* and *writing to fit*.

List-Based Writing

The starting point to completing each of your previously identified topics is to build on the ideas you entered on your Editorial Calendar Worksheet.

You'll want to create an expanded plan for each issue. This can be based on the One-Page Newsletter Issue Planner, shown in Figure 11-7.

One-Page Newsletter Issue Planning Worksheet

Text element	Purpose	Content ideas	Length
Headline	Quickly communicate topic benefit	Proposals that get results	2 lines
Elaboration	Engage reader's interest with more information	Four steps to more sales in less time	3 lines
Introduction	Emphasize relevance Describe symptoms Outline solution	Most proposals don't succeed Proposal writing takes a lot of time 3-step structure gets better results	1 to 3 paragraphs
Point 1	First supporting idea	Review client's major concerns Review the costs of not taking action	2 to 3 paragraphs
Point 2	Second supporting idea	Review the benefits you'll help client obtain	2 to 3 paragraphs
Point 3	Third supporting idea	Describe the steps you'll take and the costs	2 to 3 paragraphs
Tips, or Point 4	More information	Present a timeline based on immediate acceptance	Bullet list
Summary	Review topic relevance Emphasize benefits	Review client concerns and benefits of addressing them	1 to 2 paragraphs
Call to action	How to learn more Incentive for action	Offer free consultation Mention proposal writing seminar	1 paragraph

Figure 11-7 The One-Page Newsletter Content Planner, which can be downloaded from www.designtosellonline.com/11chap.html, makes it easy to identify the points to cover in each issue.

Using this worksheet, you can quickly and easily identify the necessary text elements of your newsletter:

Headline   The headline should quickly communicate the topic of each issue and its relevance to your customers and prospects.

Elaboration   The elaboration should contain more information, further engaging the reader's interest.

Introduction   The first paragraph of each newsletter should form a bridge between your reader's special interests and the information you are providing in each issue. If your clients and prospects can't immediately understand the relevance of the topic, they will not read any further. The introduction should also describe the symptoms, or the costs, of the problem and outline a suggested solution.

Point 1   This supporting point can describe the first step toward a solution or describe one aspect of the problem in greater detail.

Point 2   This supporting point introduces another main idea and its principal characteristics.

Point 3   This supporting point introduces a third main idea, and describe its relevance to the topic.

Tips, or Point 4   Either describe a fourth idea in two short paragraphs or create a bulleted list of ideas that point the way for further reading or action.

Summary   Conclude by reviewing the importance of this issue's topic and its relevance to your readers.

Call to action   Describe the next step your customers and prospects should take to learn more, apply the information you have presented to their business, or request your assistance in taking further action. Be as specific as possible and, when appropriate, include an incentive for immediate action, such as registering for an upcoming seminar or teleseminar, downloading a report from your Web site, or ordering a book.

Procrastination is your enemy. Your goal is to encourage clients and prospects to take immediate action.

The sooner your clients and prospects take action, the better.

Writing Each Issue to Fit

Completing each issue of your newsletter involves a simple three-step process:

1. Click **File**, **New**, select **Templates** in the **New From a Design** list, and then double-click the file name of your one-page newsletter template.

2. Click **File**, **Save As**, and then save the file using a name that describes your newsletter's issue number, title, and the topic of the current issue.

3. Copy the headline, elaboration, and main ideas you entered in your One-Page Newsletter Issue Planner into your one-page newsletter template, as shown in Figure 11-8. Each of your main ideas becomes a subhead.

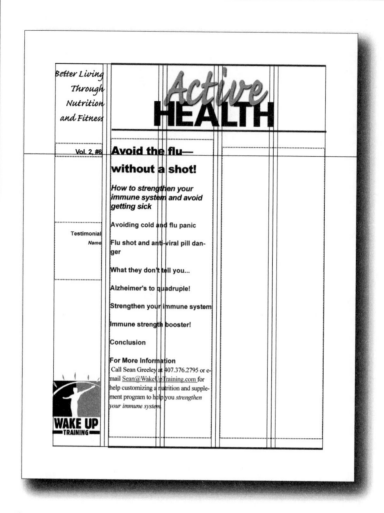

Figure 11-8   Start each issue of your platform-building newsletter by transferring information from your planning sheets to your newsletter template. Enter and format each idea as a subhead.

After you have entered the headline, elaboration, and main ideas as subheads in your newsletter, all that remains is to "fill in the blanks" with the words needed to introduce the topic and describe each point in a paragraph or two, as shown in Figure 11-9.

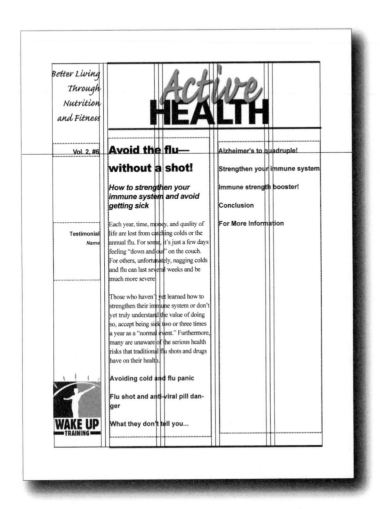

Figure 11-9 After entering your ideas as subheads, write a short introduction that describes the relevance of the topic to your readers.

It's not necessary to complete each subhead in order. If you prefer, select the easiest subhead to complete, then move on to the next easiest subhead, and so on. As you complete the paragraphs needed to support each subhead, you'll find that writing becomes easier and easier. Soon, you've finished!

Conclude by summarizing the relevance and major points of the issue, and add a call to action that describes what readers should do next.

As you write, pay attention to the bottom of the second column on the back page. When the Text In Overflow symbol appears, you know that you have written too much. You will have to review your text, looking out for:

- Unnecessary words.
- Long words that can be replaced by short words.
- Too many supporting points.
- Sentences containing unnecessary detail.
- Paragraphs that can be summarized in bulleted lists.

Finish by updating each issue's volume and issue number on the front and back pages, adding a pull-quote on the back that summarizes the most important idea on the page, and entering client testimonials.

Editing and Distributing

Edit from the perspective that the purpose of your one-page newsletter is to build your platform by positioning you (your firm or your client) as an authority, not to communicate every bit of information you know. Your goal is to promote your expertise, and "tease" customers and prospects into contacting you to learn more.

Proofing

Edit from the perspective that the purpose of your one-page newsletter is to build your platform by positioning you as an expert in your field.

After checking the spelling and grammar in each issue, use Publisher's Design Checker to check for formatting and layout errors. Then print your document and read it out loud.

You'll be surprised how many errors and rough spots you'll notice in your printed newsletter. Many find it easier to locate errors on a printed page than on screen. It's even easier to locate awkward phrasing when you read your newsletter aloud. Word combinations that look good to you might be difficult for your customers and prospects to read.

Deciding How Many Copies to Print

Ideally, the majority of your one-page newsletters will be distributed electronically, through your Web site or as e-mail attachments. Nevertheless, there are still many circumstances in which you will want to be able to distribute printed copies of your newsletter:

Networking   Always carry copies with you to distribute at networking meetings such as Chamber of Commerce events or weekly meetings of your local business networking groups.

Proposals   Include copies of previous issues with your proposals to subtly reinforce your credibility.

Key customers and prospects   Get in the habit of mailing copies of your latest newsletters to your A-list customers and prospects. Attach a personal note asking them what they think of the issue.

Special events   Distribute copies of previous issues at conventions, trade shows, and special promotions.

Point of sale distribution   Have copies of previous issues available in your office or store. You can find numerous wall and countertop display options at local office supply stories or stationery sources on the Web. One good source is PaperDirect (www.paperdirect.com).

Press   Maintain your visibility with business editors and writers in your local media as well as with trade media serving your market. It takes just one favorable mention to greatly enhance your visibility.

Lenders and vendors   Keep your credibility and visibility high among bank loan officers and key vendors by sending them copies, often with a personal note.

Affiliated marketers   Locate noncompeting firms that serve the same markets as you, and explore ways you can work together to promote each other by distributing newsletters and other marketing messages.

As you review this list, estimate the numbers of copies you'll need for each category. The total will help you decide between printing copies as needed on your desktop printer or using a commercial printer.

Online Distribution

Once created, you can save copies of your one-page newsletter in a variety of file formats for electronic distribution, including:

- Adobe PDF for Web site downloads and e-mail attachments.

- Macromedia FlashPaper for immediate Web site display and printing (no need to download).

- Microsoft XPS, the file format for sharing formatted documents online in the upcoming version of Microsoft Office, code-named Office 12.

For more information about creating PDF, FlashPaper, and XPS files, see the Adobe, Macromedia, and Microsoft Web sites, respectively. Be guided by your market's preferences as you choose your online distribution options.

Many find that one of the major indications that their one-page newsletter is a success is the improved Web site traffic they enjoy each month, when customers and prospects visit their site to download each new issue.

In addition, their Web sites benefit from search engine traffic and from attracting repeat visits by making copies of previous issues available online.

Recycling Each Issue

By focusing your one-page newsletters on educational topics, not only will each issue enjoy a long shelf life, but the contents of each issue can also serve as the starting point for additional marketing materials and fee-based products and services.

Marketing opportunities based on newsletter issues include:

- Teleseminars and Web presentations that explore each topic in greater depth.
- Speeches and presentations at networking events.
- Special reports exploring topics in greater detail.
- Articles and columns based on newsletters placed in local, regional, or trade publications.
- Articles syndicated to other publications, and through Web site portals that make your work available to others, as long as you receive proper credit.
- Interviews and referrals based on others seeing copies of your newsletters and wanting to learn more.
- Compilations of previous newsletters used as Web site registration incentives.

Additional Profit Opportunities

Many have found that their one-page newsletters form the basis for future sources of income, including:

- Fee-based seminars, speeches, workshops, or teleseminars.
- Trade books and e-books, created by expanding each newsletter into its own chapter.

Using Tip Sheets to Further Promote Your Expertise

Once you have created a one-page newsletter, you can carry the idea of promoting your competence one step further by using tip sheets.

How Tip Sheets Differ from Newsletters

Tip sheets differ from newsletters in that they are shorter and more focused. Typically, they are simple lists of ideas and techniques that help prospects and customers perform a specific task or achieve a desired goal.

Tip sheets are great partners for one-page newsletters because they do not compete with each other:

- Newsletters are best at introducing new ideas to your market, exploring the "what" and the "why."

- Tip sheets are more action-oriented, and focus on the "how-to" of doing something.

Using Tip Sheets to Build Your Newsletter's Circulation

You can use tip sheets as Web site registration incentives to build your one-page newsletter's circulation. There is a near-universal appeal to offers like:

- Learn How to Buy...

- 10 Questions to Ask When Buying...

- 8 Things to Look for When Buying...

- 12 Ways to Save on Your Next...

- 8 Ways to Cut...

- 6 Ways to Save Time When...

Simple messages like these, describing how to obtain tip sheets, can be placed on the back of your business card or on the home page of your Web site. You can also use offers of tip sheets as the basis of pay-per-click search engine advertising campaigns that can attract qualified prospects to your Web site, where they can subscribe to your monthly one-page newsletter.

Creating Tip Sheets

Once you have created the template for your one-page newsletter, you'll find it easy to create a template for a one-sided tip sheet. You can use the same basic format, based on your original one-page newsletter template, as shown in Figure 11-10.

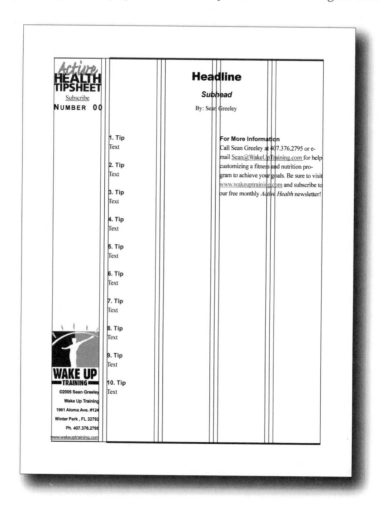

Figure 11-10 After completing your one-page newsletter, you'll find it easy to create your own tip sheet template, which you can use to create your first tip sheet.

In most cases, you won't have to make significant changes to the layout or text styles originally created for your newsletter template. Some of the changes you might want to make include:

■ Replacing the nameplate with a prominent headline and subhead.

- Adding a byline to personalize the tip sheet.

- Creating a title graphic for your tip sheet that visually relates it to your newsletter.

- Numbering the subheads so that each introduces a tip.

Each tip sheet can include the same contact information, or you can customize the call to action to fit each tip sheet's topic. Figure 11-11 shows a finished tip sheet.

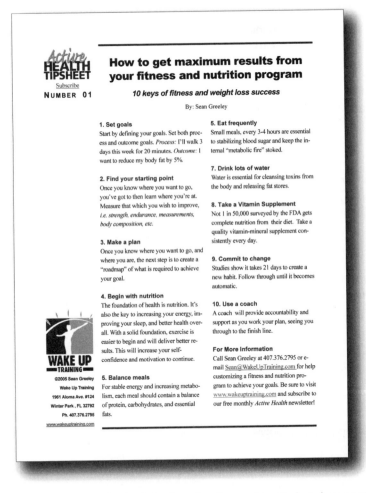

Figure 11-11 The finished tip sheet has its own identity but shares a strong—and desirable—family resemblance with the newsletter.

Saving Money by Preprinting Colored Areas

If your logo or tip sheet graphic contains color, consider printing several months' worth of blank tip sheets, containing just the colored areas of the borders, tip sheet title graphic, and your logo. To do this, create a file containing just the text and graphical elements that remain the same on each tip sheet, such as your tip sheet's logo, contact information, and border elements. Then have your commercial printer print enough sheets to supply you for the next several months.

You can then use the paper printed with colored logos and graphical accents in your desktop printer. You simply print your black-and-white text in whatever quantities you need!

This will cut costs and give you maximum flexibility to duplicate only those tip sheets you need each month at minimum cost.

Summary

In this chapter, you learned how to efficiently create newsletters and tip sheets. These make it possible for you to promote your expertise and distribute proof of it at minimum cost. The ideas presented in this chapter have helped firms and individuals around the world promote their expertise and propel their firms, and their careers, to new heights.

In the next chapter, you'll learn how to create small ads that get results when placed in directories, magazines, and newspapers. You'll also learn how to create ads to promote your newsletters and tip sheets.

Test Yourself

Before proceeding further, visit www.designtosellonline.com/11chap.html, and review the additional resources available there. You'll find:

- A self-scoring assessment to test your understanding of new terms introduced in this chapter.

- Downloadable copies of ready-to-use planning worksheets that you can fill out by hand or download as Word documents.

- Additional examples of nameplates and sample newsletters.

- Recommended online resources.

Chapter Twelve
Profiting from Small Ads

What you'll find:

- ❏ Put the power of small ads to work.
- ❏ Plan a small ad program.
- ❏ Create your small ads.
- ❏ Use small ads to drive traffic to your Web site.

The first chapter in Part Three was devoted to using postcards to focus your marketing resources on those most likely to buy from you. The second chapter in Part Three described how to consistently educate your market by using one-page newsletters and tip sheets.

In this chapter, you'll learn how to promote your newsletters, tip sheets, and if appropriate, your Web site—using an ongoing series of small ads. Small ads are intended for use in directories, magazines, and newspapers. The term *small* typically refers to ads less than two columns wide and 6 inches high. Small ads permit even David-size firms to stand up against their Goliath-size competitors.

Small ads can also refer to banners placed on Web sites that your market might visit. The goal of these ads is to drive traffic to your firm's Web site.

Small ads permit
even David-size
firms to stand up to
their Goliath-size
competitors.

Putting the Power of Small Ads to Work

Small ads possess surprising sales power. This is because small ads:

Are noticed.   Their small size does not diminish their effectiveness. The effectiveness of an advertisement is determined by its relevance to those who are in the market to buy. If a small ad offers relevant content, it will be noticed and acted on.

Permit consistency.   Because the only people who really notice ads are those who are in the process of buying or have recently purchased, the more frequently your message appears, the greater the likelihood it will be acted on. It generally takes seven or eight impressions before an advertisement is noticed and acted on. If your ad appears only once, it will likely be ignored.

Do Small Ads Work?

Visit your favorite newsstand and turn to the back pages of a magazine like *The New Yorker*. How many 1-inch-by-one-column ads do you find? Jot down some typical advertisers. Take your list to your local library, and check back issues of the publication. Notice how many of the advertisers were advertising six months ago, one year ago, or two years ago.

Longevity in an expensive advertising environment provides proof that a consistent program of small ads can pay big dividends.

Build familiarity. Fear of making a mistake is one of the biggest obstacles to making a sale. Fear of the unknown is frequently stronger than fear of making the wrong choice. The more frequently your small ads appear, however, the more familiar prospects are with it, adding to their comfort when they finally act.

Promote every product and service you sell. When you run a price-oriented ad for a specific product or service, only the featured product or service benefits. But every product or service you sell benefits when you run a small ad that promotes your expertise.

Planning a Small Ad Program

Every product or service you sell benefits from small ads that promote your expertise.

Start by analyzing the desired outcome of your small ads. Use the Small Ad Planning Worksheet, shown in Figure 12-1, to develop answers to questions like:

- What is the main idea you want prospects to remember?
- What is the next step you want prospects to take?

Small Ad Planning Worksheet

Question	Answer
What is the main idea you want prospects to remember?	Alpine Ski House is the best place to choose ski bindings and accessories.
What is the next step you want prospects to take?	Visit their store or Web site for informed advice and selection.
What kind of incentive will best encourage an immediate response?	10-point tip sheet to help choose the right bindings and accessories.
What is the best way to deliver the incentive?	Photocopied in-store handout or Web site download.
How can you track responses?	Ask store visitors where they saw offer. Possibly offer an e-mail or Web site survey.

Figure 12-1 Use the Small Ad Planning Worksheet to identify your message.

In many cases, the main idea will be a reflection, or statement, of your mission statement or market position: "We are the best place to buy *XX* because we provide the best *YY*." (Don't forget to include a "reason why" statement.)

After you have identified the main idea and the next step, you're more than halfway home. All that remains is to answer the following questions:

- What kind of incentive can you use to persuade prospects to take the desired step?

- What is the best way to deliver the incentive?

- How can you track ad response?

If you have already created a tip sheet or the first issue of your one-page newsletter, as described in Chapter 11, you already have a compelling and low-cost incentive that you can use to persuade prospects to take the desired step!

All that remains is to determine how the incentive will be delivered. Do you want prospects to schedule an appointment at their place of business, visit your place of business, call you, or download the incentive from your Web site?

Choosing the Right Words

After you have identified the desired outcome of your ads, copywriting becomes a simple matter of stating your offer and call to action as concisely as possible—it's more an "editing" function than a "copywriting" function. Here are some tips:

Use active voice. There's no room to waste in a small ad. Passive constructions, such as "was created," take more space than subject-verb-noun phrases. For example, "Choose from over 125 lines" is both shorter and easier to understand than "Over 125 lines are available for your convenience."

Use imperative verbs. Save more space by using action verbs that omit the subject and imply a "you" in front of them.

Learning from Search Engine Advertising

In addition to analyzing the one-column-by-1-inch ads in a magazine such as *The New Yorker*, consider learning from the advertisements that appear when you use a search engine. The principles are the same: because only a very small amount of space is available, you can be relatively certain that any ads you see are there because they generate a profitable response.

As you survey the ads you encounter, analyze the various functions the ads perform. Even though the number of words is limited, notice how most ads perform one or more of the following functions:

- Target prospects.
- Position each firm.
- Offer an incentive.
- Provide a call to action.

Note the ads that attract your attention and do the best job of persuading you to take the next step. Copy and paste them into an "inspiration" document, and refer to it often.

Or, omit verbs.   You can safely limit items in lists to keywords and benefits.

Be specific.   Instead of offering "plenty of free parking," emphasize "165 parking spaces within two blocks."

Choosing the Right Media

Where should you run your ads? Only you can answer that, by analyzing where your most profitable customers come from. Does your business primarily serve local, regional, national, or international clients?

Perhaps, if your firm has been in business a long time, you could send clients a postcard survey, attempting to identify which local newspapers or business publications they read.

Creating Your Small Ads

Because space is so limited in small ads, you'll want to give yourself plenty of time to edit and refine your ideas to the fewest number of words possible. Indeed, you might find yourself investing more time creating small ads than some issues of your newsletter, because you have to assemble multiple elements into a cohesive whole in a limited amount of space.

Elements of a Small Ad

Small ads include the following elements (although some might be combined to save space):

Border   Small ads must have strong borders to separate them from adjacent editorial material and competing advertisements.

Focal point   Small ads must include a single text or graphical element to attract the prospect's attention and provide a transition to the message and the call to action. The text and graphics of the focal point should reinforce your firm's image or your reader's desired expectations.

Headline   The headline typically appears below the border at the top of the ad. You can sometimes save space by setting the headline in white type against a dark-colored enlarged border at the top of the ad, which becomes the focal point of the ad.

Offer   Depending on available space, the headline can emphasize your most important buyer benefit, or the headline can simply describe the incentive you're offering.

Evidence   A single, well-chosen sentence can be enough to reinforce the headline, or you can include a short bulleted list describing your firm's benefits or how prospects will benefit from obtaining your incentive.

Call to action   The easier you make it for prospects to respond, the better your response will be. This is where e-mail and your Web site can play a big role.

White space   Even though space is limited in a small ad, you still can't cram everything together. White space is necessary to isolate elements and make your ad appear inviting and easy to read.

Contact information   Not everyone is Web-savvy. Always provide a phone number and a mailing address, or reference a local landmark or freeway exit to help visitors locate your physical address.

Because small ads contain relatively few elements, most of your time will be spent fine-tuning each of the elements and refining your choice of words until everything fits.

Getting Started

Visit the Web site of the publication where your ad will run, or call and request a rate card, to learn the exact specifications for a one-column ad.

After you have determined the column width for your small ad, proceed as follows:

1. In Publisher, click **File**, **New** to open a new file, and then click **Blank Document** and **Full Page**.

2. Click **File**, **Page Setup**, and then, on the **Layout** tab in the **Page Setup** dialog box, click **Custom** in the **Publication Type** box. Change the default height and width to the exact height and width specified by your publication. The desired width will probably be approximately two inches, or slightly less, for most one-column ads.

3. Before leaving the **Page Setup** dialog box, click the **Change Copies Per Sheet** button, and in the **Small Publication Print Options** dialog box, select the **Print One Copy Per Sheet** option. Click **OK** twice to close the two dialog boxes.

4. Click **Arrange**, **Layout Guides**, and then click the **Margin Guides** tab. Reduce the **Margin Guides** settings to **0.125"** all around to leave an appropriate margin around your ad, and click **OK**.

5. Click **View**, **Zoom**, and then click **Whole Page**.

Having created the structure for your ad, begin to add contents by creating a text box at the top of the ad:

1. Use the **Text Box** tool to create a text box that covers the top quarter of the page.

2. Click **Format**, **Text Box**, and on the **Text Box** tab, change the default margin settings for this text box to zero, and then click **OK**.

3. Enter the text shown in Figure 12-2, emphasizing the *Free* at the top by clicking **Format**, **Font** and specifying a a larger type size and a heavier weight than are used for the remaining lines. To create reversed-out text, fill the text box with black and select **white** for the text color. When you've finished formatting the text, your ad should resemble Figure 12-2.

Figure 12-2   Begin by creating the text box for the headline at the top of the ad, with a black fill and white text. Describe your offer as concisely as possible.

4. Create a second reversed text box for the information that will appear at the bottom of the ad. Add address and contact information, as shown in Figure 12-3.

Figure 12-3   Create a similar text box at the bottom of the ad, containing the store's tagline, address, and phone number.

5. Create a text box for the middle of the ad, as shown in Figure 12-4. Remove the text box margins, and change its fill color to gray.

Figure 12-4   Create a text box with a contrasting fill for the middle of the ad.

6. Anchor the middle text box with your firm's logo, or set your firm's name in a typeface that resembles the type used on your business cards or the sign in front of your business, as shown in Figure 12-5. Be sure to include your Web address or a call to action.

Figure 12-5   Add your store's logo plus your Web address or a call to action.

Completing Your Ad

Complete the ad by adding your message, as shown in Figure 12-6. Create a bulleted list, and carefully adjust the left margin and the space between the bullet and the text. To adjust bullet and tab spacing, click Format, Bullets And Numbering, and then make the desired changes in the Bullets And Numbering dialog box.

Figure 12-6   The first draft of the final ad shows a lot of information communicated in a small space.

Indent the list to the right so that there is plenty of space surrounding the bullets. To adjust bullet spacing, click Format, Tabs, and then make the desired changes in the Tabs dialog box.

As you add the various text elements to your ad, save each of your formatting decisions as a text style. This will speed revisions and the creation of future ads.

Refining Your Ad

Print your ad and carefully analyze it. You might notice that minor adjustments in line spacing and paragraph spacing could pay big dividends. Try out different combinations of line and paragraph spacing in the bulleted list.

As you can see in Figure 12-7, slightly reducing the line spacing and slightly increasing the Space After paragraph spacing improves the appearance of the bulleted list and permits you to increase the space between the store's logo and Web address. This is the type of artistry that separates "good" design from "great" design. The final text formatting specifications could not be predicted in advance—they are arrived at only by taking the time to try, and refine, alternatives.

Save each of your formatting decisions as a text style, to speed revisions and creating future ads.

The final text formatting specifications could not be predicted in advance—they are arrived at only by trying and refining alternatives.

Figure 12-7   Compare this figure with Figure 12-6. Notice the significant improvement created by subtle changes in line and paragraph spacing.

After you have established the basic structure of your ad, save it as a template. You can use this template to save time when you create additional ads featuring different offers or for different seasons.

Efficient Working Habits

One of the challenges you face when creating small ads is working in tight quarters. By using the File, Page Setup command to create a custom page size and adjusting the zoom to a comfortable level by using View, Zoom, you will soon create a comfortable workspace and become comfortable working at high magnification.

Here are some additional tips and hints for creating an efficient small ad program:

Keep borders simple.   Keep borders as simple as possible. Instead of a box border on all four sides, consider using slightly thicker (for example, 4 to 6 point) rules above and below your ad.

Consolidate elements.   Save space by eliminating the top border and replacing it with a headline reversed out of a box at the top of the ad. Explore the possibility of creating a similar reverse for your Web address, phone number, or tagline at the bottom of the ad.

Replace borders with fills.   Instead of using a border to isolate your ad from its competitors, consider placing part or all of the ad against a shaded (for example, light gray) or light-colored background. Ask your media representative which background levels (for example, 20 percent, 30 percent, 40 percent, and so on) work best for maintaining text readability.

Use clip art sparingly.   Use clip art with discretion. Avoid the temptation to add unnecessary decoration to your ads. Even a small "atmospheric" addition often introduces clutter that detracts from your intended reader response or call to action.

Explore color.   Explore the possibility of adding a color highlight to your ad—perhaps for your logo or for a colored background with a reversed-out word such as *Free*.

Edit, and then reedit.   Begin working on your small ads well in advance of their start day. Because space is at a premium, you should frequently reexamine your work, searching for long words that you can replace with short words and statements that you can safely omit.

Six Tips for Text Formatting

Consider the following issues when formatting your text:

Typeface choice   Pay special attention to typeface choice and text formatting. Use typeface, type size, type style, and other contrast tools to separate headlines from body copy.

Line spacing   Small, bold sans serif type often benefits from extra line spacing.

Tabs and indents   Tighten up spacing between bullets and the text they introduce. Default spacing is usually too generous because it is based on bulleted lists in documents printed on letter-size paper.

Text alignment   Avoid justified text. Flush-left, ragged-right alignment will generally avoid problems caused by awkward word spacing and end-of-line hyphenation.

Logo   Examine how your logo looks after it has been reduced in size. Make sure that it still presents a quality image. If you don't have a logo, set your name in a distinctive typeface and use small caps and extra character spacing to add uniqueness to the name.

Consistency   Format your small ads using the same typefaces and logo placement used on your business card, letterhead, and newsletters, and so on.

Resisting Premature Change

Resist the urge to prematurely change your small ads. Clients typically lose interest in their advertising just when their market is beginning to notice the ads!

Give your ads time to succeed. Remember, not everyone is in the market to buy at one time. New prospects are entering the market every day. Your goal is to *be visible* on the day prospects suddenly decide they're interested in your product or service category.

Think in terms of agriculture. Plants need water to grow. But too much water—in the form of a flood—is as bad as no water at all. To succeed, farmers must drip-irrigate their crops, providing a continuing stream of manageable amounts of water throughout the growing season. But if farmers open the floodgates and flood their fields with too much water, their plants are likely to be washed away!

Plants, like your marketing messages, need to be nurtured throughout the growing season, not washed away during a flash flood.

Using Small Ads to Drive Traffic to Your Web Site

One of the best ways to profit from a series of small ads is to drive traffic to your Web site, where prospects can register for your monthly one-page newsletter and download your tip sheet incentive.

When a prospect encounters your small ad, the ad should describe your business and—most important—your incentive and how to obtain it. Prospects should be instructed to visit your Web site to download your incentive and/or register for your monthly newsletter.

Web site delivery of electronic incentives, like tip sheets and previous issues of newsletters, has many advantages. It is:

Free.   In contrast to the costs involved in printing and mailing, there are *no direct costs* involved when prospects download an electronic file or receive it as an e-mail attachment.

Immediate.   There are no delays. The incentive arrives in your prospect's e-mail inbox within seconds, while interest is at a peak.

Unlimited.   Although the small ads themselves might not have much space to tell a story, you can tell a lot about your firm when you deliver the promised incentive. There's no limit to the information that you can send.

Hands-off.   Fulfillment takes place automatically when you put the Internet to work. Incentives are delivered to new prospects and your newsletter e-mail mailing list is constantly growing while you are selling and serving others. This greatly increases your efficiency, allowing you to invest your time in activities that generate the highest profit.

Summary

In this chapter, you've discovered the surprising power of small ads. Small ads permit you to maintain consistency and generate qualified leads for follow-up. They provide ongoing opportunities to promote your newsletters, tip sheets, and Web site content.

Chapter 13, "Reviewing the 10 Most Common Design Errors," summarizes the most important ideas by describing common design mistakes and how to fix them. In most cases, you can learn how to make major improvements in an unsatisfying document by referring back to earlier chapters in this book.

Test Yourself

Before proceeding further, take a minute to visit www.designtosellonline.com /12chap.html and explore additional resources associated with this chapter, including:

- A downloadable worksheet for planning your small ad campaign.
- A self-scoring assessment to review important ideas introduced in this chapter.
- Additional resources, including small ad templates, more tips, additional copy and layout suggestions, and so on.

Part Four

Wrapping It Up

In this part

Chapter Thirteen

Reviewing the 10 Most Common Design Errors

What you'll find:

❏ Decide between makeovers and incremental changes in your designs.

❏ Identify common layout problems.

❏ Review headlines and subheads.

❏ Fine-tune body copy content and formatting.

❏ Build improvement into every project.

Design success involves more than *knowing* the principles of design and how to use them in Microsoft Office Publisher. Instead, design success is based on consistently *applying* what you know in an orderly and disciplined way.

This chapter describes the design problems I've most frequently encountered during decades of helping clients and graphic design students review their work and refine their design skills.

Details spell the difference between effective and ineffective marketing. Whether your message is read or languishes in obscurity depends on how effectively you consistently review and fine-tune the following issues.

Avoid printing and distributing publications immediately after completion. Instead, review them from a fresh perspective the next day.

Identifying Common Layout Problems

Boredom and clutter are the two most common examples of layout problems. Learn to identify the underlying causes of these problems, and your designs will immediately start to improve.

Problem 1: Boring Pages

Boring pages often result from not taking advantage of Publisher's layout guides. Pages based on a two-column grid with narrow margins often appear static because both the left and right sides of the page balance each other. Restructuring the page with a five-column grid, with two text columns plus a narrow outside column of white space, projects a more dynamic, asymmetrical image.

By using layout guides, you can add a narrow border of white space to the outside of each page, reduce line lengths, and create an asymmetrical or off-center layout that is more interesting to look at and easier to read.

By using contrast, you can add visual interest to your message and make it easier to understand. Contrast refers to the close proximity of opposites: large and small, light and dark, empty and filled.

Without sufficient typographic contrast, there's no obvious beginning point for customers and prospects to scan a page and determine whether it contains relevant information. With contrast, pages are not only more attractive because of the interplay between heavy blocks of text and graphics framed by areas of white space, but selected content on the page can make its case for the reader's attention and guide the reader through the message.

Graphics, too, benefit from contrast. Pages with two or more graphics of equal size are less attractive and they fail to communicate the relative importance of their visual elements. Two photographs sized the same, for example, communicate equal importance. When one photograph is significantly larger, however, readers instantly understand which photograph is the more important.

Of course, you can overdo the use of contrast. Selective emphasis, highlighting one idea on the page over others, is impossible when too much contrast is present. Selective emphasis requires a quiet, relatively consistent, background against which change can be used to communicate importance. A single male voice in a women's choir is far more noticeable than one more male voice in a choir containing both men and women. The key is to design with restraint and to employ contrast with care, achieving a balance between predictability and surprise.

Deciding Between Makeovers and Incremental Improvements

When do makeovers rather than incremental improvements make sense? Knowing when each option is appropriate is important.

Total makeovers are rarely necessary. In most cases, you can significantly improve publication effectiveness by improving one aspect of publication layout and formatting at a time.

Makeovers are called for only when the original design shows a lack of planning, meaningful message, and call to action, or when the publication reflects a lack of appreciation for the fundamentals of design—for example, simplicity, editing, contrast, and so on.

Incremental improvements, however, can be made immediately after a publication is finished, and—ideally—before it is printed and distributed. Often, the best procedure is to avoid the temptation to immediately print and distribute a publication as soon as it's finished. Instead, put it aside for the night, and review it from a fresh perspective the next day. Chances are, you'll notice several new problem areas that you need to address.

Problem 2: Cluttered Pages

Cluttered pages project a disorganized, unprofessional image, and they're hard to read because it's difficult to tell where to begin reading. The two primary causes of clutter are a lack of visible message hierarchy and unnecessary graphical accents.

A lack of an obvious message hierarchy results when too many elements of equal weight compete with each other. Successful pages use text contrast to add visual interest and clarify message meaning. Headlines should be larger and more noticeable than sub-heads, and subheads should be more noticeable than body copy.

Because graphical accents such as borders and fills are so easy to create, designers tend to overuse them. Boxed borders are often added to pages out of habit rather than function. Clutter makes it harder to separate the important from the decorative.

Note To review the tools of contrast, refer to Chapter 3, "Principles of Design Success," and to review the text formatting tools, go to Chapter 7, "Building Design Excellence into Every Page."

Figure 13-1 illustrates the clutter that results from problems like these. Before reading further, stop and take a few moments to visit www.designtosellonline.com/14chap.html and take the self-scoring assessment you'll find there. See how many problems you can identify.

Reducing Clutter with Organization

Organization in page design, the careful alignment of text and graphic elements, communicates competence and professionalism.

Consider headline alignment, for example. Although you'll frequently see centered headlines, flush-left headlines are often preferable. When headlines are centered, each line of each headline begins and ends at a different point on the page. With flush-left headlines, however, the first word of each line of each headline aligns with the left margin of the text.

Similarly, pages containing subheads set flush left project a more orderly appearance than pages with centered subheads.

Graphics, too, work best when there is a purpose to their position on the page. Photographs that align with the margins of adjacent columns project a more organized image than photographs that break into adjacent text columns, creating text wraps. In fact, text wraps are an excellent example of a page layout program feature that can hinder, rather than enhance, the purpose of your marketing communication, which is always to make your message as easy to read as possible.

Figure 13-1   Clutter often results from a lack of visual hierarchy and the use of too many graphic accents.

The same content, arranged differently, can project a more professional image and can be significantly easier to read, as shown in Figure 13-2.

Reviewing Headlines and Subheads

Headlines and subheads attract and maintain your reader's interest. Your message will suffer when the following problems occur.

Figure 13-2 Eliminating unnecessary graphic accents, avoiding unnecessary "creativity," and creating an obvious visual hierarchy of text elements projects an entirely different image.

Problem 3: Hard-to-Locate Headlines and Subheads

Headlines and subheads must be easy to locate and must obviously have more importance than the adjacent text. Headlines and subheads must form a strong contrast with other text on the page. Consider the following suggestions:

Use a contrasting typeface for subheads. Combine serif body copy with sans serif subheads.

Use significantly different type sizes for headlines and subheads. Choose types sizes that form a strong contrast with body copy.

Add white space around headlines and above subheads.   You can adjust spacing in Publisher's Paragraph dialog box, on the Indents And Spacing tab.

Avoid subheads that "float" between adjacent paragraphs.   On the Indents And Spacing tab in the Paragraph dialog box, set subhead Between Lines spacing to **1**, and type a zero in the After Paragraph box.

Avoid inconsistent headline and subhead formatting.   Inconsistency in headings can be avoided by using text styles, as you learned in Chapter 8, "Taking Your Design Success to the Next Level."

Avoid lost subhead formatting.   Subhead formatting can be lost if you inadvertently allow a subhead to pick up the formatting of the previous paragraph, which can occur when you edit the end of the last sentence in the previous paragraph and you accidentally eliminate the hard return at the end of the paragraph. After you replace the hard return, the typeface and type size formatting of the subhead appear the same, but the space before the subhead is deleted and space is added after the subhead, making the subhead inconsistent with other subheads and thus harder to recognize.

Problem 4: Hard-to-Read Headlines and Subheads

Even if readers can locate your headlines and subheads, the headlines and subheads must be formatted for easy reading. Watch out for:

Hyphenated headlines.   Publisher does not allow you to turn hyphenation on or off at the paragraph level. Hyphenation is "all or nothing" for all of the text within a text box. To eliminate headline hyphenation, insert manual line breaks by pressing SHIFT+ENTER. To eliminate subhead hyphenation, limit subheads to one line.

Awkward line and word breaks in headlines.   To break headlines where you want them to break, to equalize line length, or to keep proper nouns and phrases on one line, insert line breaks (press SHIFT+ENTER).

Multiline headlines and subheads.   Shorter is always better. Limit subheads to one line, headlines to three lines (and preferably, just two lines). Each additional line significantly reduces readership.

Isolated subheads.   Click Format, Paragraph, Line And Paragraph Breaks, and then select Keep With Next and Widow/Orphan Control to eliminate subheads isolated at the bottoms of columns or pages.

Note   To review headline and subhead formatting in Publisher, refer to Chapter 7, "Building Design Excellence into Every Page."

Fine-Tuning Body Copy Content and Formatting

The bulk of your marketing message is usually communicated in columns of text. When these columns are hard to read, the effectiveness of your messages dwindles to nothing. Here are the major problems involving text that undermine the credibility and readability of your message.

Problem 5: Planning and Editing Errors

Often, design problems are the result of planning and editing errors, such as:

Lack of clarity and purpose. No amount of "design" can rescue a publication that lacks a purpose, call to action, and obvious message hierarchy. Time spent planning often reduces time spent designing and revising.

Long sentences and paragraphs. Good design cannot compensate for excess length. Beware of long sentences and long paragraphs. Long sentences slow down readers, making it easy for them to lose track of your central message. Use simple subject-verb-noun constructions. Limit paragraphs to three or four concise sentences.

Spelling errors. Always make sure that Publisher's Spelling Checker is turned on so that you can locate errors as they occur. Double-check the spelling of proper nouns and technical terms. Watch out for correctly spelled but improperly used words like *to*, *too*, and *two*.

Problem 6: Inappropriate Typeface and Type Size Choices

Here are some considerations for making the right body copy typeface selections:

Easy scanning. In general, serif typefaces, like Times New Roman, are easier to read than sans serif typefaces like Arial. The serifs on each letter emphasize the shapes of the words and lead your readers' eyes across the page.

Type set too large. When type is set too large for the line length, only a few words can fit on each line. This deprives readers of the speed and ease of reading that serial pattern recognition offers.

Type set too small. Small type sizes force readers to squint. In addition, several left-to-right eye movements must be made on each line, increasing reader fatigue and the possibility that readers will get lost between the end of one line and the beginning of the next.

Problem 7: Insufficient Line Spacing

Line spacing is as critical to easy reading as typeface choice and type size. Correct line spacing should be based on the typeface, the type size, and line length or column width.

Often, the best way to improve a publication is to start by slightly reducing the type size while increasing line spacing. Then, if the original designer pressed the Enter key twice at the end of each paragraph, add paragraph spacing equal to one and one-half lines of type. This two-step approach can do wonders for the readability of your message without changing the number of words that can fit on a page. As a result, you end up with a better-looking, easier to read publication, without needing to delete a lot of text or add pages to your publication. Figure 13-3 shows how there is just a 16-word difference between the column on the left, which is hard to read, and the easier-to-read column on the right.

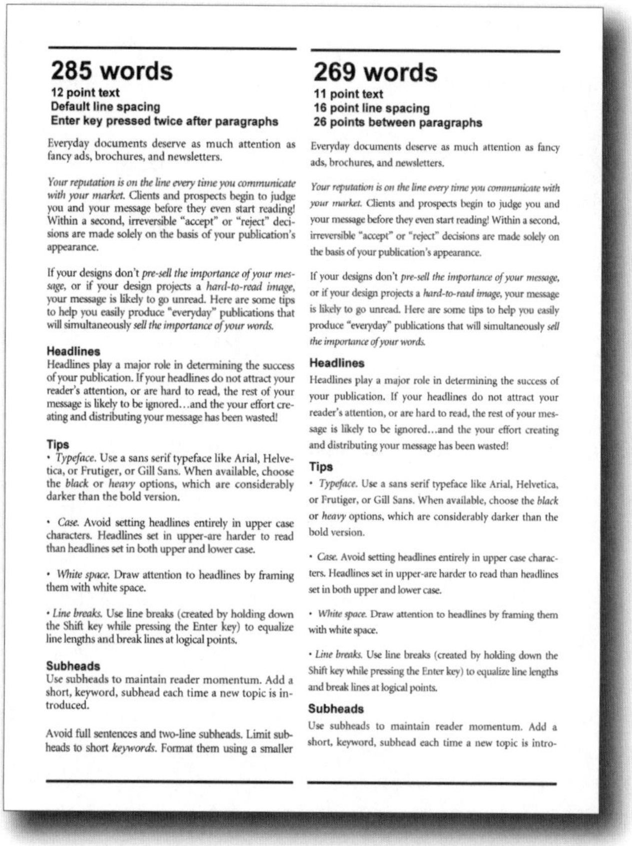

285 words
12 point text
Default line spacing
Enter key pressed twice after paragraphs

Everyday documents deserve as much attention as fancy ads, brochures, and newsletters.

Your reputation is on the line every time you communicate with your market. Clients and prospects begin to judge you and your message before they even start reading! Within a second, irreversible "accept" or "reject" decisions are made solely on the basis of your publication's appearance.

If your designs don't *pre-sell the importance of your message*, or if your design projects a *hard-to-read image*, your message is likely to go unread. Here are some tips to help you easily produce "everyday" publications that will simultaneously *sell the importance of your words.*

Headlines
Headlines play a major role in determining the success of your publication. If your headlines do not attract your reader's attention, or are hard to read, the rest of your message is likely to be ignored…and the your effort creating and distributing your message has been wasted!

Tips
• *Typeface.* Use a sans serif typeface like Arial, Helvetica, or Frutiger, or Gill Sans. When available, choose the *black* or *heavy* options, which are considerably darker than the bold version.

• *Case.* Avoid setting headlines entirely in upper case characters. Headlines set in upper-are harder to read than headlines set in both upper and lower case.

• *White space.* Draw attention to headlines by framing them with white space.

• *Line breaks.* Use line breaks (created by holding down the Shift key while pressing the Enter key) to equalize line lengths and break lines at logical points.

Subheads
Use subheads to maintain reader momentum. Add a short, keyword, subhead each time a new topic is introduced.

Avoid full sentences and two-line subheads. Limit subheads to short *keywords*. Format them using a smaller

269 words
11 point text
16 point line spacing
26 points between paragraphs

Everyday documents deserve as much attention as fancy ads, brochures, and newsletters.

Your reputation is on the line every time you communicate with your market. Clients and prospects begin to judge you and your message before they even start reading! Within a second, irreversible "accept" or "reject" decisions are made solely on the basis of your publication's appearance.

If your designs don't *pre-sell the importance of your message*, or if your design projects a *hard-to-read image*, your message is likely to go unread. Here are some tips to help you easily produce "everyday" publications that will simultaneously *sell the importance of your words.*

Headlines
Headlines play a major role in determining the success of your publication. If your headlines do not attract your reader's attention, or are hard to read, the rest of your message is likely to be ignored…and the your effort creating and distributing your message has been wasted!

Tips
• *Typeface.* Use a sans serif typeface like Arial, Helvetica, or Frutiger, or Gill Sans. When available, choose the *black* or *heavy* options, which are considerably darker than the bold version.

• *Case.* Avoid setting headlines entirely in upper case characters. Headlines set in upper-are harder to read than headlines set in both upper and lower case.

• *White space.* Draw attention to headlines by framing them with white space.

• *Line breaks.* Use line breaks (created by holding down the Shift key while pressing the Enter key) to equalize line lengths and break lines at logical points.

Subheads
Use subheads to maintain reader momentum. Add a short, keyword, subhead each time a new topic is intro-

Figure 13-3 The left column is harder to read than the right column, which is formatted using a type size one point smaller, increased line spacing, and less paragraph spacing.

Problem 8: Missing Text

Sometimes the last few words or the last few lines of a story are missing. Publisher cuts off text when there is too much text to fit in a previously created text box. To avoid this problem, keep an eye out for the Text In Overflow icon, shown in Figure 13-4, and rewrite to fit or—if possible—increase the size of the text box.

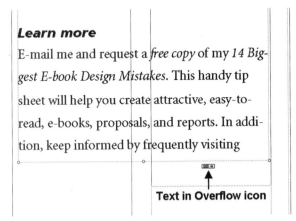

Learn more

E-mail me and request a *free copy* of my *14 Biggest E-book Design Mistakes*. This handy tip sheet will help you create attractive, easy-to-read, e-books, proposals, and reports. In addition, keep informed by frequently visiting

Text in Overflow icon

Figure 13-4 Always check the end of each story in your publication to make sure that overflow text is not missing, indicated by the Text in Overflow icon.

Problem 9: Incorrect or Missing Symbols and Punctuation

Avoid putting too much trust in Publisher's AutoCorrect feature. Sometimes an en dash (used to indicate a range) is more appropriate than the em dash that Publisher automatically uses to replace two hyphens in a row.

Get in the habit of manually inserting the proper symbols for words like *trademark* and *copyright* by clicking Insert, Symbol and selecting the symbol you want on the Special Characters tab in the Symbol dialog box.

Problem 10: Visual Distractions

Visual distractions can undermine your reader's ability to comprehend your message by either attracting their eyes away from your message, or interrupting their consistent, rhythmic, left-to-right eye movements.

One of the most common categories of distraction results from the use of decorative artwork, referred to as clip art. Clip art is often accompanied by exaggerated text effects. In either case, the goal is to entertain your readers. In most cases, however, as Figure 13-5 shows, the added "creativity" distracts from your message and undermines the image you're trying to project.

Figure 13-5 Attempts to use text effects and decorative artwork to embellish, or "decorate,"your message usually backfire, adding cluttering to the page, confusing your message, and undermining your image.

Other categories of distraction are caused by text formatting problems. Efficient reading is based on consistent word spacing and freedom from visual distractions. Distractions like the following interfere with the serial pattern recognition that reading is based on:

Text wraps   Text wraps occur when the edges of a graphic do not align with the edges of a text column. As a result, line length is reduced in adjacent columns, interrupting the reader's rhythmic left-to-right eye movements.

Two spaces after periods   Many typists press the SPACEBAR twice after every period. In typewriter days, this was the only way to emphasize sentence spacing. You can use Publisher's Edit, Replace command to locate every instance of two adjacent spaces and replace them with a single space.

Excess paragraph spacing   Many people unwisely press the ENTER key twice at the end of each paragraph to enter an extra paragraph break. This separates the two paragraphs by the equivalent of two lines of type. To fix this problem, click Edit, Replace and have Publisher replace every instance of two paragraph breaks with a single paragraph break. To replace two paragraph breaks with one, search for ^P^P and replace it with ^P.

Awkward word spacing   A failure to hyphenate justified text can cause awkward word spacing. Without hyphenation, word spacing becomes tight in lines containing several short words and becomes loose in lines containing a few long words. To fix this, click anywhere in a text box, click Tools, Language, Hyphenation, and then select the Automatically Hyphenate This Story check box. Compare the hyphenated and non-hyphenated examples in Figure 13-6.

Distracting right-hand margins   A failure to hyphenate flush-left text results in awkward variations in line lengths, creating distracting shapes along the right-hand column margin. Lines containing several short words become very long, and lines containing several long words become very short. To fix this, click Tools, Language, Hyphenation, and then select Automatically Hyphenate This Story. To better appreciate the importance of hyphenating flush-left text, see Figure 13-7.

Excessive hyphenation   Strive to avoid more than two hyphenated lines in a row. When excessive hyphenation occurs, review your line length and type size decisions. Use nonbreaking hyphens to prevent compound words from splitting over two lines.

Word splits   Sometimes words and phrases that should remain together on one line are split over two lines. Examples include first and last names, city and state names, and months, days, and years. To keep words together, click Insert, Symbol, and then, on the Special Characters tab in the Symbol dialog box, click Nonbreaking Space.

Note   To review the Publisher commands for formatting body copy, refer to Chapter 7, "Building Design Excellence into Every Page." Other formatting details are located in Chapter 8, "Taking Your Design Success to the Next Level."

**Alignment: justified
Hyphenation: off**

Everyday documents deserve as much attention as fancy ads, brochures, and newsletters.

Your reputation is on the line every time you communicate with your market. Clients and prospects begin to judge you and your message before they even start reading! Within a second, your customers and prospects make irreversible "accept" or "reject" decisions are made solely on the basis of your publication's appearance.

If your designs don't *pre-sell the importance of your message,* or if your design projects a *hard-to-read image,* your message is likely to go unread. Here are some tips to help you easily produce "everyday" publications that

**Alignment: justified
Hyphenation: on**

Everyday documents deserve as much attention as fancy ads, brochures, and newsletters.

Your reputation is on the line every time you communicate with your market. Clients and prospects begin to judge you and your message before they even start reading! Within a second, irreversible "accept" or "reject" decisions are made solely on the basis of your publication's appearance.

If your designs don't *pre-sell the importance of your message,* or if your design projects a *hard-to-read image,* your message is likely to go unread. Here are some tips to help you easily produce "everyday" publications that will simultaneously *sell the importance of your words.*

Figure 13-6 Hyphenation, added to the right-hand column of justified text, eliminates the extremes of wide and narrow word spacing found in the left-hand column, which is not hyphenated.

**Alignment: left
Hyphenation: off**

Everyday documents deserve as much attention as fancy ads, brochures, and newsletters.

Your reputation is on the line every time you communicate with your market. Clients and prospects begin to judge you and your message before they even start reading! Within a second, irreversible "accept" or "reject" decisions are made solely on the basis of your publication's appearance.

If your designs don't *pre-sell the importance of your message,* or if your design projects a *hard-to-read image,* your message is likely to go unread. Here are some tips to help you easily produce "everyday" publications that will simultaneously *sell the importance of your words.*

Headlines play a major role in determining the

**Alignment: left
Hyphenation: on**

Everyday documents deserve as much attention as fancy ads, brochures, and newsletters.

Your reputation is on the line every time you communicate with your market. Clients and prospects begin to judge you and your message before they even start reading! Within a second, irreversible "accept" or "reject" decisions are made solely on the basis of your publication's appearance.

If your designs don't *pre-sell the importance of your message,* or if your design projects a *hard-to-read image,* your message is likely to go unread. Here are some tips to help you easily produce "everyday" publications that will simultaneously *sell the importance of your words.*

Headlines play a major role in determining the success of your publication. If your head-

Figure 13-7 Note how hyphenation, in the right-hand column, eliminates the very short, and very long lines, in the non-hyphenated left-hand column.

Building Improvement into Every Project

The easiest way to improve your design skills and mastery of Microsoft Publisher is to take the time to carefully review your publications before printing and distributing them.

The best way to review your publications is to use the Last-Minute Design Worksheet, shown in Figure 13-1. This worksheet focuses entirely on the planning and design problems discussed in this chapter and is intended for easy use. You can download a printable copy from www.designtosellonline.com/13chap.html.

Last-Minute Design Worksheet

	Question	Yes	No	Necessary action
1	Are pages attractive and not boring?			
2	Do pages suffer from clutter?			
3	Can you easily locate headlines and subheads?			
4	Are headlines and subheads easy to read?			
5	Can you identify any planning or editing problems?			
6	Was body copy set in the right typeface and type size?			
7	Is line spacing appropriate to line length?			
8	Is any text missing?			
9	Are punctuation and symbols correct?			
10	Are there any visual distractions?			

Figure 13-8   Get in the habit of using the Last-Minute Design Worksheet to review your planning and formatting decisions.

Get in the habit of completing the Last-Minute Design Worksheet before you print and distribute your marketing messages.

You can also use the Last-Minute Design Worksheet to review previous publications and those of your competitors. Your design abilities will grow to the extent that you train yourself to carefully analyze the details of every publication you encounter.

Summary

In this chapter, you've seen that complete makeovers are often not necessary to create a major difference in publication appearance and effectiveness. Most publications can be saved by applying incremental improvements. Get in the habit of using the Last-Minute Design Checklist to review the potential trouble spots described in this chapter.

Test Yourself

Additional free resources are available at this book's companion Web site, at www.designtosellonline.com/13chap.html, including:

- A self-scoring assessment to test your mastery of the topics covered in this chapter.

- A downloadable Last-Minute Design Worksheet.

- Online resources for further design exploration.

- Recommended books and newsletters.

Chapter Fourteen

Developing a Plan for Your Marketing Publications

What you'll find:

❑ The importance of preparing a marketing plan for using the publications you've created in this book.

❑ Creating a marketing plan that works for you.

You're now ready for action—and great success! In the previous chapters, you've learned more about successful marketing and design than the majority of entrepreneurs, self-employed professionals, and corporate managers around the world.

More important, you now know how to use Microsoft Publisher to format your marketing messages to attract attention, invite readership, and project a unique, appropriate image. Most important, you've learned how to work as efficiently as possible and how to check your work before you print and distribute your publications.

You also know where to turn in this book—and where to find its companion Web site—www.designtosellonline.com—if you have a question or need to brush up on some of the details.

All that remains is to translate ideas and intentions into action, which you'll learn about here. It all boils down to a single sheet of paper—a year-long marketing plan—a document you'll learn to create in this chapter.

Why You Need a Marketing Plan

Marketing plans are powerful tools used by successful firms, individuals, and organizations. When sufficient time and budget resources are available, as they might be in large corporations, marketing plans can be large, formal, and comprehensive. But this doesn't have to be.

An effective marketing plan can be as short as a *single-page document*. A single page marketing plan can be enough to provide the structure you need to make marketing an on-going *process* rather than an isolated *event*. It can do this by helping you:

Avoid deadline madness.   A marketing plan shows you what needs to be done, and by what date. (It's simply impossible to do good work under continuing last-minute deadlines.)

Avoid overspending or underspending.   A marketing plan helps you set a realistic marketing budget.

Delegate tasks to others.   A marketing plan makes it possible for you to analyze what needs to be done each month so you can identify tasks to assign to others.

Track the results of your marketing.   *A marketing plan* provides a framework for evaluating the results generated by your monthly postcards, newsletters, tip sheets, and small ads.

Creating a Marketing Plan

You've already made great progress towards creating a marketing plan by filling in the worksheets you've encountered in various chapters of this book.

You can base a lot of your marketing plan on the worksheets created in previous chapters.

In Chapter 10, the Customer Benefits Worksheet (Figure 10-2), helped you to translate the products and services you offer into benefits that buyers can enjoy. The Postcard Message Planner, (Figure 10-3), carried the idea one step further. These worksheets are good for planning individual projects, but what's needed for success is a yearly plan for each month's marketing.

Now, your primary duty is to transfer the information from the worksheets in Chapters 10 and 11 into a single-page marketing plan.

Note   Just as subheads make long articles easy to read by breaking them into manageable chunks, a step-by-step approach to a marketing plan makes a complicated project much easier to complete.

Step One: Identify Months and Themes

Download a copy of the Marketing Plan Worksheet from www.designtosellonline.com /14chap.html. If you download the Microsoft Word version, you can type directly into it. If you want to work in pencil, download and print the PDF version.

■ In the first column, enter the name or initials of the upcoming month. (If you're reading this in July, for example, you don't want your Marketing Plan to begin with January of next year, it makes more sense to begin with August of the current year.)

■ In the second column, write down a theme, or focus, for each month's marketing. Each theme should correspond to the category of products and services you want to highlight that month.

Marketing Plan Worksheet

Month	Focus	Postcard house list	Postcard rented list	Newsletter title	Deadline / mailing date	Small ads	Total spent/tracking comments
Jan	Inside repairs						
Feb	Windows and doors						
Mar	Kitchen updates						
Apr	Garage clean-up						
May	"Curb appeal"						
Jun	Outdoor living						
July	Tree trimming						
Aug	Heating systems						
Sept	Gutters and drainage systems						
Oct	Winterizing home						
Nov	Landscaping						
Dec	Interior accents						

Figure 14-1 Begin your Marketing Plan Worksheet by listing the next 12 months and identifying the theme of each month's marketing.

Step Two: Focus on Postcards

In the next two columns, enter how you are going to support your monthly marketing theme by sending postcards to two different markets:

Existing customers and prospects. In the third column, labeled "Postcards house list," describe the number of postcards and the cost of sending them to those who have dealt with you.

Outreach to new prospects. In the fourth column, labeled "Postcards rented list," describe the quantity and cost for sending postcards to a purchased, or compiled, mailing list each month.

Marketing Plan Worksheet

Month	Focus	Postcard house list	Postcard rented list	Newsletter title	Deadline / mailing date	Small ads	Total spent/tracking comments
Jan	Inside repairs	100, $85	300, $250				
Feb	Windows and doors	100, $85	300, $250				
Mar	Kitchen updates	100, $85	300, $250				
Apr	Garage clean-up	125, $105	300, $250				
May	"Curb appeal"	125, $105	300, $250				
Jun	Outdoor living	125, $105	300, $250				
July	Tree trimming	150, $125	300, $250				
Aug	Heating systems	150, $125	300, $250				
Sept	Gutters and drainage systems	150, $125	300, $250				
Oct	Winterizing home	175, $150	300, $250				
Nov	Landscaping	170, $150	300, $250				
Dec	Interior accents	200, $165	300, $250				

Figure 14-2 In columns three and four, enter the quantity and costs of the postcards you'll send to previous customers and to new prospects from purchased mailing lists.

Step Three: Describe Your Newsletter Program

Before entering the data in the next two columns, you might want to review the worksheets you filled out in Chapter 11, "Using Newsletters and Tip Sheets to Promote Your Expertise." Pay particular attention to Figure 11-4, which shows the Newsletter Title Planning Worksheet, and Figure 11-5, which shows the Newsletter Yearly Editorial Calendar Planner.

In particular, you'll be referring back to the Newsletter Yearly Editorial Calendar Worksheet for the titles of each newsletter. The Newsletter Title Planning Worksheet will help you fine-tune the title of each month's newsletter.

Enter the title for each month's newsletter in the "Newsletter title" column. In the next column, enter the deadline for completing each issue of your newsletter. In addition, enter the date you plan to distribute your newsletter each month. This date should be a week after you've completed it, giving you time to review and fine-tune your ideas, words, and design. Listing both the completion deadline and distribution date of each month's newsletter will help you keep on track with your program.

As an option, in the column labeled "Deadline/mailing date," you can also enter the costs of printing and mailing each issue, if you're planning to print and mail each issue to key clients and prospects, as well as distributing each issue as an e-mail attachment and Web site download. Or, you might want to include the costs of printing and mailing Tip Sheets to those who request them.

When you have finished Step Three, your Marketing Plan Worksheet should resemble Figure 14-3. When you get to this point, the basic outline of your Marketing Plan Worksheet is almost complete. Already, you can see how the major pieces of your marketing plan fit together.

Showing both the completion deadline and distribution date of each month's newsletter helps you plan your time and keep on schedule.

Marketing Plan Worksheet

Month	Focus	Postcard house list	Postcard rented list	Newsletter title	Deadline / mailing date	Small ads	Total spent/tracking comments
Jan	Inside repairs	100, $85	300, $250	Putting bad weather to good use	Dec 27 **Jan 3**		
Feb	Windows and doors	100, $85	300, $250	Insulation can cut heating costs	Jan 27 **Feb 7**		
Mar	Kitchen updates	100, $85	300, $250	Updating counters and cabinets	Feb 28 **Mar 7**		
Apr	Garage clean-up	125, $105	300, $250	Preparing for summer landscaping	Mar 28 **Apr 7**		
May	"Curb appeal"	125, $105	300, $250	Landscaping to increase home value	Apr 25 **May 2**		
Jun	Outdoor living	125, $105	300, $250	Decks, patios, and outdoor entertaining	May 30 **Jun 6**		
July	Tree trimming	150, $125	300, $250	Preventing fall and winter wind damage	Jun 27 **Jul 5**		
Aug	Heating systems	150, $125	300, $250	Furnace cleaning and new filters	Jul 25 **Aug 1**		
Sept	Gutters and drainage systems	150, $125	300, $250	Preparing for winter snow and rain	Aug 29 **Sep 5**		
Oct	Winterizing home	175, $150	300, $250	Taking an energy conservation audit	Sep 26 **Oct 5**		
Nov	Landscaping	170, $150	300, $250	Covering shrubbery and protecting trees	Oct 31 **Nov 7**		
Dec	Interior accents	200, $165	300, $250	Getting ready for holiday entertaining	Nov 28 **Dec 6**		

Figure 14-3   The title of each month's one-page newsletter should reflect the month's focus.

Step Four: Plan Small Ads

The final step in completing your Marketing Plan Worksheet involves adding a column for Small Ads intended to drive prospects to your Web site, where they can download tip sheets and register to receive the e-mail version of your monthly one-page newsletter. You can also use these small ads for monthly promotions based on the current month's focus. List the number of small ads you plan to run in the first remaining column, along with the estimated monthly cost.

For now, leave the remaining column, Total spent/tracking comments, blank.

You're going to be using the last column throughout the year to track the results of each month's marketing, comparing results with what you spent each month. Use whatever measure you feel most comfortable with, such as:

- Monthly sales

- Percentage sales increase over same month last year

- Margins (how much you actually made each month)

- Growth of mailing list—the number of new names added

- Web-site visits

- Downloaded newsletters and tip sheets

- Favorable mentions in the press

- Favorable customer comments

What's important is not so much the specific measurement tool you use, but that you come up with a consistent way of measuring the results of your marketing from month to month, and compare them to the specific topics you promoted each month and the money you invested in marketing. Figure 14-4 shows how a typical marketing plan looks before it's implemented.

Creating Your Own Marketing Plan

There is nothing "written in stone" about the Marketing Plan Worksheet described here. You might want to use it as is, or you might want to customize it, adding or removing column, or choosing different typefaces and type sizes. You can also reformat the Marketing Plan Worksheet to fit on a larger, legal-sized sheet of paper, permitting additional columns, such as tracking results using more than one criteria, or measures of the profitability of promotions targeting special markets.

Another option is to recreate the Marketing Plan Worksheet as a Microsoft Excel spreadsheet. This would allow you to easily total and update expenditures. As you fill out your Marketing Plan Worksheet, avoid paying too much attention to formatting or, if you're filling your plan out by hand, neatness. You won't be graded on your work. What really matters is that you can view a year's worth of marketing plans on a single sheet of paper—and you'll be able to view the *what*, *when*, and *how much* as you gauge the growing positive results you will soon be enjoying each month.

Marketing Plan Worksheet

Month	Focus	Postcard house list	Postcard rented list	Newsletter title	Deadline / mailing date	Small ads	Total spent/tracking comments
Jan	Inside repairs	100, $85	300, $250	Putting bad weather to good use	Dec 27 Jan 3	1, $150	
Feb	Windows and doors	100, $85	300, $250	Insulation can cut heating costs	Jan 27 Feb 7	1, $150	
Mar	Kitchen updates	100, $85	300, $250	Updating counters and cabinets	Feb 28 Mar 7	1, $150	
Apr	Garage clean-up	125, $105	300, $250	Preparing for summer landscaping	Mar 28 Apr 7	2, $300	
May	"Curb appeal"	125, $105	300, $250	Landscaping to increase home value	Apr 25 May 2	2, $300	
Jun	Outdoor living	125, $105	300, $250	Decks, patios, and outdoor entertaining	May 30 Jun 6	1, $150	
July	Tree trimming	150, $125	300, $250	Preventing fall and winter wind damage	Jun 27 Jul 5	1, $150	
Aug	Heating systems	150, $125	300, $250	Furnace cleaning and new filters	Jul 25 Aug 1	1, $150	
Sept	Gutters and drainage systems	150, $125	300, $250	Preparing for winter snow and rain	Aug 29 Sep 5	2, $300	
Oct	Winterizing home	175, $150	300, $250	Taking an energy conservation audit	Sep 26 Oct 5	2, $300	
Nov	Landscaping	170, $150	300, $250	Covering shrubbery and protecting trees	Oct 31 Nov 7	2, $300	
Dec	Interior accents	200, $165	300, $250	Getting ready for holiday entertaining	Nov 28 Dec 6	1, $150	

Figure 14-4   A completed Marketing Plan Worksheet, ready to be put into action. Notice that the last column is not filled in until each month is completed.

Summary

There's no single right or wrong way to create a Marketing Plan Worksheet. What's important is that it enables you to:

- ■ *View* a year's worth of marketing at a glance.
- ■ *Focus* each month's marketing on a single topic, or theme.
- ■ *Keep track* of upcoming deadlines.
- ■ *Work* within a realistic monthly budget.
- ■ *Track* monthly results.

Get Started Now!

Visit www.designtosellonline.com/14chap.html and download a free copy of the Marketing Plan Worksheet so you can get ready to start planning your way to marketing success.

Appendix

All too often, shortly after I've completed a book and approved the final proofs, I discover several important resources I wish I could have added. Which is why *Design to Sell* has a companion Web site, www.designtosellonline.com. This site will allow me to keep this book alive with new ideas, resources, and tips as I locate them. Accordingly, I can keep you informed about new print and online resources, free teleseminars, and share new ideas with you from readers.

What Else You'll Find

Equally important, the Internet environment permits me to offer some really exciting, free book enhancements, such as:

Self-scoring assessments.   Readers can use these to test their understanding of new words and ideas introduced in each chapter. Teachers and corporate trainers can also use these assessments to test their students' mastery of each chapter.

Downloadable templates.   There are several templates you can download for free if you're in a rush to send a postcard or create a newsletter, tip sheet, or small ad.

Additional content.   This includes new topics, such as more information about color printing, color versions of many of the figures in this book, as well as additional illustrations that couldn't be included because of space limitations.

Advantages of Registering

At www.designtosellonline.com, you can also register to receive my *Design to Sell* newsletter, with advance notification of upcoming special events, like speaking engagements, workshops, and free teleseminars. You'll also receive notification of new Web site resources, tips, templates, articles, reader suggestions, and updated and annotated book reviews. Already, I'm exploring future options, including downloadable audio and video files.

In short, if working with Microsoft Office Publisher is an important part of your marketing activities, you'll want to visit www.designtosellonline.com and register as a reader. And let me know what additional topics you'd like to see me cover in future editions of this book!

Worksheets

At www.designtosellonline.com, you'll also find downloadable examples of the worksheets included in this book. These are available for download without cost. After downloading them, you can either work directly in them using Microsoft Word, or print them and fill them out in pen or pencil.

The next few pages show the worksheets that are available for download.

Chapter 2. Planning Your Way to Design Success

Roger C. Parker's
Design to Sell
Project Planning Worksheet

1. What is the purpose of this project?

2. Who are your readers and what do you know about them?

3. What are the important elements of your message?

4. How do your messages compare to those of your competitors?

5. How will your message be distributed?

6. Are there any resource limitations?

Chapter 9. Distributing Error-Free Messages In Print and Online
72-point Preflight and Proofing Checklist

Chapter 10. Promoting Your Business with Postcards

Postcard Opportunity Worksheet		
Postcard type	Frequency	Estimated quantity

Customer Benefits Worksheet	
Product or service	Benefits buyers enjoy

Postcard Message Planner	
Problem	
Symptom	
Solution	
Benefit	
Proof	
Offer	
Incentive	

Chapter 11. Using Newsletters and Tip Sheets to Promote Your Expertise

Newsletter Title Planning Worksheet		
Topic ideas	Reader benefits	Possible words

Editorial Calendar Worksheet			
Issue	Due date	Title	Ideas

One-Page Newsletter Issue Planning Worksheet

Text element	Purpose	Content ideas	Length

Chapter 12. Profiting from Small Ads

Small Ad Planning Worksheet

Question	Answer

Chapter 13. Reviewing the 10 Most Common Design Errors

	Last-Minute Design Worksheet			
	Question	**Yes**	**No**	**Necessary action**
1	Are pages attractive and not boring?			
2	Do pages suffer from clutter?			
3	Can you easily locate headlines and subheads?			
4	Are headlines and subheads easy to read?			
5	Can you identify any planning or editing problems?			
6	Was body copy set in the right typeface and type size?			
7	Is line spacing appropriate to line length?			
8	Is any text missing?			
9	Are punctuation and symbols correct?			
10	Are there any visual distractions?			

Chapter 14. Developing a Plan for Your Marketing Publications

		Marketing Plan Worksheet					
Month	**Focus**	**Postcard house list**	**Postcard rented list**	**Newsletter title**	**Deadline / mailing date**	**Small ads**	**Total spent/tracking comments**
Jan							
Feb							
Mar							
Apr							
May							
Jun							
July							
Aug							
Sept							
Oct							
Nov							
Dec							

Index

Roger C. Parker

Roger C. Parker is a design evangelist whose goal is to teach everyone to "think like a designer" and use design as a strategic marketing tool.

For over twenty years, Roger C. Parker has been helping others profit from the "Three Truths of Marketing" —targeting, education, and consistency. These truths have transformed the careers of numerous self-employed professionals while helping many start-ups grow and prosper. (One father-son business grew to the point where Best Buy bought it for $87,000,000 cash!)

To clients like Apple Computer, Bang & Olufsen, Bose, Hewlett-Packard, Microsoft, Shearman & Sterling, and Yamaha, Roger has brought fresh perspectives plus content, critiques, direction, templates, and workshops.

Roger's previous books have launched the careers of numerous designers and helped non-designers profit from proven design and marketing techniques. Over a million and a half readers through the world own copies of his books, including his landmark *Looking Good in Print*, praised by The New York Times as "the one book to buy when you're buying one," and now in its 6th Edition. Other books include *Roger C. Parker's One-Minute Designer* and the *Streetwise Guide to Relationship Marketing on the Internet*.

With *Design to Sell*, Roger returns to one of his favorite passions; showing business owners and their assistants how to use Microsoft Publisher to increase sales and reduce costs.

What do you think of this book? We want to hear from you!

Do you have a few minutes to participate in a brief online survey? Microsoft is interested in hearing your feedback about this publication so that we can continually improve our books and learning resources for you.

To participate in our survey, please visit:

www.microsoft.com/learning/booksurvey

And enter this book's ISBN, 0-7356-2260-4. As a thank-you to survey participants in the United States and Canada, each month we'll randomly select five respondents to win one of five $100 gift certificates from a leading online merchant.* At the conclusion of the survey, you can enter the drawing by providing your e-mail address, which will be used for prize notification *only*.

Thanks in advance for your input. Your opinion counts!

Sincerely,

Microsoft Learning

Learn More. Go Further.